U·X·L
ENDANGERED SPECIES

3RD EDITION

U·X·L
ENDANGERED SPECIES

3RD EDITION

VOLUME 3

AMPHIBIANS

CORALS

FISH

PLANTS

REPTILES

Julia Garbus
Noah Berlatsky
Kathleen J. Edgar, Project Editor

U·X·L
A part of Gale, Cengage Learning

GALE
CENGAGE Learning·

Farmington Hills, Mich • San Francisco • New York • Waterville, Maine
Meriden, Conn • Mason, Ohio • Chicago

U•X•L Endangered Species, 3rd Edition

Julia Garbus and Noah Berlatsky

Project Editor: Kathleen J. Edgar

Acquisitions Editor: Christine Slovey

Contributing Editor: Elizabeth Manar

Rights Acquisition and Management: Amanda Kopczynski and Ashley Maynard

Composition: Evi Abou-El-Seoud

Manufacturing: Wendy Blurton

Product Design: Kristine A. Julien

For product information and technology assistance, contact us at **Gale Customer Support, 1-800-877-4253.** For permission to use material from this text or product, submit all requests online at **www.cengage.com/permissions.** Further permissions questions can be emailed to **permissionrequest@cengage.com**

Cover photographs: © Orangutan by Stephen Meese, © Rothschild's Starling by Nagel Photography, and © Grand Cayman Blue Iguana by Frontpage, all Shutterstock.com.

While every effort has been made to ensure the reliability of the information presented in this publication, Gale, a part of Cengage Learning, does not guarantee the accuracy of the data contained herein. Gale accepts no payment for listing; and inclusion in the publication of any organization, agency, institution, publication, service, or individual does not imply endorsement of the editors or publisher. Errors brought to the attention of the publisher and verified to the satisfaction of the publisher will be corrected in future editions.

LIBRARY OF CONGRESS CATALOGING-IN-PUBLICATION DATA

Names: Garbus, Julia, author. | Berlatsky, Noah, author. | Edgar, Kathleen J., editor. | Gale (Firm)
Title: U X L endangered species / Julia Garbus, Noah Berlatsky ; Kathleen J. Edgar, project editor.
Other titles: Endangered species.
Description: 3rd edition. | Farmington Hills, MI : U-X-L, A part of Gale, Cengage Learning, 2016. | Includes bibliographical references and index.
Identifiers: LCCN 2015037374| ISBN 9781410332981 (vol. 1 : alk. paper) | ISBN 9781410332998 (vol. 2 : alk. paper) | ISBN 9781410333001 (vol. 3 : alk. paper) | ISBN 9781410332974 (set : alk. paper)
Subjects: LCSH: Endangered species--Juvenile literature.
Classification: LCC QL83 .G37 2016 | DDC 591.68--dc23
LC record available at http://lccn.loc.gov/2015037374

Gale
27500 Drake Rd.
Farmington Hills, MI 48331-3535

978-1-4103-3297-4 (set)
978-1-4103-3298-1 (vol. 1)
978-1-4103-3299-8 (vol. 2)
978-1-4103-3300-1 (vol. 3)

This title is also available as an e-book.
978-1-4103-3296-7
Contact your Gale sales representative for ordering information.

Printed in China
1 2 3 4 5 6 7 20 19 18 17 16

Table of Contents

U•X•L Endangered Species, 3rd Edition

VOLUME 2: ARACHNIDS, BIRDS, CRUSTACEANS, INSECTS, AND MOLLUSKS

Arachnids

Birds

VOLUME 3: AMPHIBIANS, CORALS, FISH, PLANTS, AND REPTILES

Reader's Guide

U•X•L Endangered Species, 3rd Edition, presents information on endangered and threatened mammals, birds, reptiles, amphibians, fish, corals, mollusks, insects, arachnids, crustaceans, and plants. Its 242 entries were chosen to give a glimpse of the broad range of species currently facing endangerment. While well-publicized examples such as the polar bear, tiger, and giant sequoia are examined, so too are less conspicuous—yet no less threatened—species such as the Ganges River dolphin, Knysna seahorse, and golf ball cactus.

The entries are spread across three volumes and are divided into sections by classes. Within each class, species are arranged alphabetically by common name.

Each entry begins with the species' common and scientific names. A fact box containing classification information—phylum (or division), class, order, and family—for that species follows. The box also lists the current status of the species in the wild according to the International Union for Conservation of Nature and Natural Resources (IUCN) and the U.S. Fish and Wildlife Service (USFWS, which administers the Endangered Species Act). Finally, the box lists the country or countries where the species currently ranges.

Locator maps outlining the range of a particular species are included in each entry to help users find unfamiliar countries or locations. In most entries, a color photo provides a more concrete visualization of the species. Sidebar boxes containing interesting and related information are also included in some entries.

Each entry is broken into three sections:

- The information under the subhead **Description and biology** provides a general description of the species. This includes physical dimensions, eating and reproductive habits, and social behavior.

- The information under the subhead **Habitat and current distribution** describes where the species is found today, its preferred habitat, and, if available, recent estimates of its population size. Research studies are not conducted at regular intervals for some of these species, so 10 or more years may pass before new estimates become available.

- The information under the subhead **History and conservation measures** relates, if possible, the history of the species and the factors currently threatening it. Conservation efforts to save the species, if any are underway, are also described.

Included in each volume of *U•X•L Endangered Species, 3rd Edition,* is an overview of the history and current state of endangerment and its causes. It is followed by an explanation of the fact boxes and classifications used in the set and then a discussion of the International Union for Conservation of Nature and Natural Resources (IUCN) that includes a brief history of the organization, its current focus, and a brief explanation of the status categories in which the IUCN places imperiled species. The next section focuses on the Endangered Species Act (ESA), briefly examining its passage, purpose, implementation, status categories, and current state. A look at the changes in species' status from the 2nd to 3rd edition follows. Each volume also includes a **Words to Know** section that provides definitions of words and terms used in the set.

At the back of each book is a selection of **Critical Thinking Questions** that encourage reflection on the causes of endangerment and human efforts to protect wildlife. A **Classroom Projects and Activities** section follows, offering ideas for discussion and collaborative problem-solving.

A **Where to Learn More** section lists books, periodicals, websites, environmental organizations, and other resources such as movies and apps. The book listing is annotated. The environmental organizations list—a selected catalog of organizations focusing on endangered species—contains contact information and a brief description of each organization.

Finally, the volumes conclude with a cumulative index providing access to all the species discussed throughout *U•X•L Endangered Species, 3rd Edition*.

The scope of this work is neither definitive nor exhaustive. No work on this subject can be. The information presented is as current as possible, but the state of endangered species changes almost daily.

A note about the 3rd Edition

Since the publication of *U•X•L Endangered Species, 2nd Edition*, in 2004, the endangered or threatened status of many of the species included in these volumes has changed. Through the efforts of conservationists (people who work to manage and protect nature) and legislators, some of these species have recovered or have been assigned a less-threatened status (known as downlisting). The bald eagle, for example, listed as threatened under the ESA at the time of the *U•X•L Endangered Species, 2nd Edition*, has been removed from the list entirely and downlisted to "Least Concern" by the IUCN. The bald eagle population had plummeted, in part, because the powerful pesticide DDT weakened the shells of the birds' eggs. Listed as endangered in 1967, the U.S. national bird recovered after DDT was banned, its habitat was protected, and captive breeding programs were instituted. Other successes include the grizzly bear, the American bison, the black-footed ferret, and the Steller sea lion in the United States; the Iberian lynx in Europe; the African elephant; the markhor, a wild goat that is Pakistan's national animal; and three monkey species from Central and South America.

Along with successes, there have been serious setbacks. Other species previously listed have declined to the very brink of extinction. Several are familiar, such as the gorilla, endangered because of hunting and disease, and the northern white rhino, of which only three are known to remain. But less well-known or beloved species suffer equally, especially if their populations have always been small. For example, the mongoose lemur, a monkey-like animal native to several islands near the coast of Africa, has dropped from vulnerable to critically endangered status due to the destruction of its forest habitat for agriculture. Some more developed countries with stable, strong governments, such as the United States and Australia, may have ample resources to devote to conservation, whereas less economically developed and less stable countries and regions often lack such tools. Of the 24 species described in this book that have moved to a more threatened status since 2004, more than half are from such areas, including many from war-torn or impoverished regions of Africa.

U•X•L Endangered Species, 3rd Edition, cannot cover all threatened species worldwide, but 38 new species have been included in this edition to ensure that the situations of animals and plants worldwide—as they stand 12 years after the publication of *U•X•L Endangered Species, 2nd Edition*—are represented. New species described include the most familiar butterfly in the United States, the monarch, which is under consideration as an endangered species by the USFWS. The vibrant black-and-orange insect feeds on milkweed plants, which are becoming rare because of pesticide use. The new species presented reflect the diversity of the world's endangered creatures. There are mammals such as the okapi, birds such as the African penguin, arachnids such as the peacock tarantula, crustaceans such as the vernal pool tadpole shrimp, insects such as the Morrison bumblebee, mollusks such as the freshwater pearl mussel, amphibians such as the axolotl, fish such as the great hammerhead shark, plants such as the whitebark pine, and reptiles such as the bog turtle. Corals are included for the first time. These ocean invertebrates, animals without backbones, are moving toward extinction more rapidly than other animals such as amphibians, mammals, and birds.

Conservationists today face similar concerns to those described in *U•X•L Endangered Species, 2nd Edition*, many with more urgency. Some species described in this book, such as the saiga, the gray and Indiana bats, and the Wyoming frog, have declined in number because of disease. Scientists are working hard to understand the illnesses and develop ways to prevent them. The biggest reason for endangerment, however, continues to be habitat loss. Species as diverse as the Grand Cayman blue iguana, the giant catfish, the peacock tarantula, and Chapman's rhododendron, a flowering plant, have become endangered because people have logged forests, planted crops, grazed animals, built homes, dammed rivers, and engaged in other activities that destroyed these species' habitats. Habitat fragmentation, when development results in animals' living areas being broken up into smaller, separated areas, has threatened species such as the maned wolf, pygmy hippopotamus, and California tiger salamander.

The problem of commercial exploitation has nearly doomed some species included in these volumes. Animals such as the long-tailed pangolin and the great hammerhead shark are captured illegally and are then sold for food or because their bodies are thought to have medicinal properties. In the oceans, overfishing continues to threaten such species as the southern bluefin tuna. Bycatch—being caught by mistake in nets intended for other animals—threatens other species such as sea turtles and sawfish. Laws and treaties protecting species can help preservation efforts, as can educating local communities about the importance of species that share their environment. However, laws and education may not stop people driven by hunger from eating endangered animals, or those driven by poverty from capturing and selling them. Conservationists say that one of the best ways to conserve threatened species is to help local communities find new ways of surviving that do not endanger wildlife.

Since *U•X•L Endangered Species, 2nd Edition*, was published in 2004, scientists, authors, and the media are using new terms to describe the effects of human activity on the environment, although the changes these terms describe have been ongoing for many years. First, scientists have begun referring to our era as that of a sixth great extinction. All species become extinct eventually, at a natural rate of several species per year. Before the era of humans, the planet experienced five periods of mass extinctions, when most living species disappeared. But since 1900, extinctions have increased to more than 100 times the natural rate. This sixth wave, unlike the earlier five, is human-caused. The **Endangerment and Its Causes** section discusses the different ways human actions threaten animal and plant species. Another change in terminology is that since 2004, climate change has become increasingly evident and increasingly discussed. Several animal species described in this book, such as polar bears and corals, have already been harmed by climate change. Scientists predict that if people continue burning fossil fuels (oil, gas, and coal) at the current rate, many more species will be at risk of extinction by the end of the 21st century.

Since 2004, the realities of climate change and the sixth wave of extinction have demonstrated even more strongly than before that the fates of humans and other living species are inextricably interwoven. It is possible to take measures that rescue endangered species from the edge of extinction, prevent others from becoming threatened, and improve people's lives at the same time. These measures, however, require more than intense efforts to save particular animals. They call for people to reflect on how their actions affect not only other humans, but also the species with which we share our planet. And then these reflections must turn into actions that will improve not only the situations of today's people, animals, and other species, but the lives of those that will come in the future.

Acknowledgments

Special thanks are due for the invaluable comments and suggestions provided by the *U•X•L Endangered Species* advisory board:

Ela-Sita Carpenter, Museum Educator, Maryland Science Center, Baltimore, Maryland

Adam J. Eichenwald, Neighborhood Nestwatch Researcher; Atlanta Representative at Smithsonian Migratory Bird Center, Atlanta, Georgia

Martha N. Mather, 6th grade science teacher, Kennewick School District, Kennewick, Washington

Carrie Radcliffe, Restoration Coordinator and Safeguarding Database Manager, Atlanta Botanical Garden, Atlanta, Georgia; Mountain Bog Project Coordinator, Georgia Plant Conservation Alliance, Athens, Georgia; Consulting Botanist, Georgia Department of Natural Resources and U.S. Forest Service Southern Region

The U•X•L staff would also like to offer its profound thanks to Cinqué Hicks, Director, and Jamie Vidich, Operations Manager and Content Development Lead, of Bookbright Media for their invaluable contributions to this set. Their vision, skill, and enthusiasm are much appreciated.

Comments and suggestions

Cengage Learning welcomes your comments on *U•X•L Endangered Species, 3rd Edition*, and suggestions for species to be included in future editions of this work. Please write: Editors, *U•X•L Endangered Species, 3rd Edition*, 27500 Drake Rd., Farmington Hills, MI 48331-3535; call toll-free: 1-800-877-4253; fax: 1-877-363-4253; or send an e-mail via www.gale.com.

Endangerment and Its Causes: An Overview

Living organisms have been disappearing from Earth since the beginning of life on the planet. Most of the species that have ever lived on Earth are now extinct. Extinction and endangerment can occur naturally as a normal process in the course of evolution or as the result of a catastrophic event, such as the collision of an asteroid with Earth. Scientists believe some 65 million years ago, an asteroid struck near Mexico's Yucatán Peninsula, bringing about the extinction of almost 50 percent of plant species and 75 percent of animal species, including the dinosaurs. Scientists have identified five great extinction episodes in Earth's history before humans appeared on the planet. Although these five periods were marked by widespread, rapid extinction, species are continually disappearing; species become extinct at a rate of one to five species a year due to disease, competition among species, or natural climate change.

When humans became the dominant species on the planet, however, the extinction rate of other species began to increase dramatically. Especially since the 17th century, technological advances and an ever-expanding human population have changed the natural world as never before. At present, scientists believe extinctions caused by humans are taking place at 100 to 1,000 times nature's normal rate between great extinction episodes. Species are disappearing faster than they can be created through evolution. Therefore, the planet has entered a sixth wave of mass extinction that scientists believe is caused by human activity.

Because scientists have described and named only a small percentage of Earth's species, it is impossible to measure the total number of species endangered or going extinct. At least 1.9 million animal species and 450,000 plant species have been identified, but scientists say that possibly millions more have not yet been discovered. According to the International Union for Conservation of Nature and Natural Resources (IUCN), amphibians and corals are the animal groups at highest risk of extinction, with about 40 percent of each group threatened. About 25 percent of mammals and 13 percent of birds are at risk. Since 1980, birds and mammals as a whole have become slightly more endangered, the status of amphibians has dropped more sharply, and the outlook for corals has plummeted.

Humans are endangering species and the natural world primarily in three ways: habitat destruction, commercial exploitation of animals and plants, and the introduction of nonnative species into a habitat. Human activity has also accelerated climate change, which already threatens some species. Some experts state that if climate change continues at its current level, 25 percent of all species could be at risk by 2050.

Habitat destruction

The destruction of habitats all over the world is the primary reason species are becoming extinct or endangered. Houses, highways, dams, industrial buildings, and ever-spreading farms now dominate landscapes formerly occupied by forests, prairies, deserts, scrublands, and wetlands. For instance, 46,000 to 58,000 square miles (119,000 to 150,000 square kilometers) of forest each year are destroyed worldwide, the equivalent of 36 football fields each minute. Tropical rain forests, home to 50 percent of all animal and plant species, once occupied 6 million square miles (15.5 million square kilometers) worldwide. Now, only 2.4 million square miles (6.2 million square kilometers) remain.

Habitat destruction can be obvious, or it can be subtle, occurring over a long period of time without being noticed. Pollution, such as sewage from cities and chemical runoff from farms, can change the quality and quantity of water in streams and rivers. To species living in a delicately balanced habitat, this disturbance can be as fatal as the clear-cutting of a rain forest.

When remaining habitats are carved into smaller and smaller areas or fragments, species living in those smaller areas suffer. The fragments become crowded, with increased competition for scarce resources and space. Access to food and water may become limited. In search of such resources, animals may be killed while crossing roads or may venture into areas inhabited by people, causing conflicts with them. And, very importantly, habitat fragmentation limits access to mates. A smaller pool of mates reduces a species' genetic diversity, the number of different genes in a population. Genetic diversity plays a key role in the evolution and survival of living things, allowing a species a greater chance of adapting to changing environments and resisting disease.

Commercial exploitation

Animals have long been hunted by humans, not only for their meat but also for parts of their bodies that are used to create clothing, medicines, love potions, trinkets, and other things. Overhunting has caused the extinction of many species and brought a great many others to the brink. Examples include some species of whales, slaughtered for oil and baleen; the black rhinoceros, which is killed for its horns; and bluefin tuna, which are prized as a delicacy in Asia. Species that people find attractive or interesting, such as certain corals and arachnids, may become threatened in the wild as they are collected or captured for the pet or hobby trade.

Although international treaties outlaw the capture and trade of many endangered or threatened species, these laws are difficult to enforce, especially in countries that lack resources or a stable government. The smuggling of endangered species is a huge international business, estimated to be worth $10 billion to $20 billion a year. One reason people may hunt, capture, and trade endangered species is because they feel they have little economic alternative. So they may eat endangered animals for protein or capture and sell them as a livelihood.

Introduced species

Native species are those that have inhabited a given biological landscape for a long period of time. They have adapted to the environment, climate, and other species in that locale. Introduced or exotic species are those that have been brought into that landscape by humans, either accidentally or intentionally. In some cases, these introduced species may not cause any harm. They may, over time, adapt to their new surroundings and fellow species, becoming "native." Most often, however, introduced species seriously disrupt ecological balances. They compete with native species for food and shelter. Often, they prey on the native species, which may lack natural defenses against the intruders. They may also carry diseases that infect the native species or may take the resources that native species require for survival. When introduced species cause or are likely to cause harm to an environment, they are called invasive species. In the last 500 years, introduced plants and animals, including insects, cats, pigs, and rats, have caused the endangerment or outright extinction of hundreds of native species. In fact, more than 40 percent of threatened or endangered species are at risk because of invasive species.

Climate change

When humans burn fossil fuels, carbon dioxide is released into the air. This gas in the atmosphere creates a layer of insulation that stops Earth's heat from going into space. The more carbon dioxide in the atmosphere, therefore, the warmer Earth becomes. Since the 19th century, when the Western world became industrialized, the levels of carbon dioxide in the atmosphere have increased by 33 percent. Earth became 1.5°F (0.8°C) warmer from 1901 to 2012. Scientists estimate that Earth could warm anywhere from 0.5 to 8.6°F (0.28 to 4.78°C) over the next 100 years. This trend is referred to as global warming. A related term, climate change, refers to all major, long-lasting changes in climate, including global warming but also encompassing longer, more severe heat waves and changes in rainfall that lead to floods or droughts. These heat waves and rainfall changes are linked to increased levels of carbon dioxide and other gases in the atmosphere.

Climate change threatens many species in many ways. Warming temperatures in polar regions threaten animals that live or hunt on ice, such as polar bears. As melting sea ice causes sea levels to rise, these rising waters could engulf areas near the shore where animal and plant species live. Warmer ocean temperatures kill or weaken corals, while warmer temperatures on land can force animals to move to cooler areas or wake animals too early from hibernation. Droughts threaten many animals, especially amphibians, and plants. The effects of climate change on species can be direct; for example, the endangered Australian ant only emerges in cool weather. Or it can be indirect, threatening a species by disturbing the web of life in which the species exists. The blue whale, for instance, eats small sea animals called krill, which feed on algae that grow under sea ice. Rising temperatures have melted sea ice, reducing the algae population. This reduction in food supply has decreased the krill population by as much as 80 percent, which in turn could threaten the blue whale. Some scientists state that climate change has already contributed to the extinction of one species: the golden toad, a small, bright orange amphibian from Central America.

U•X•L Endangered Species *Fact Boxes and Classification: An Explanation*

Each entry in *U•X•L Endangered Species, 3rd Edition*, begins with a shaded fact box that contains the common name of the species, followed by its scientific name. The box lists the classification information for that species: phylum (or division), class, order, and family. It also lists the current status of that species in the wild according to the International Union for Conservation of Nature and Natural Resources (IUCN; see page xxix) and the Endangered Species List compiled under the U.S. Endangered Species Act (ESA; see page xxxi). (Note: For a listing of species whose status has changed since the publication of the 2nd edition, see page xxxv.) Finally, the box lists the countries or regions where the species is currently found and provides a locator map for the range of the species.

Classification

Biological classification, or taxonomy, is the system of arranging plants and animals in groups according to their similarities. This system, which scientists around the world currently use, was developed by 18th-century Swedish botanist (a scientist who studies plants) Carolus Linnaeus. Linnaeus created a multilevel system or pyramid-like structure of nomenclature (naming) in which living organisms were grouped according to the number of physical traits they had in common. The ranking of the system, going from general to specific, is: kingdom, phylum (or division for plants), class, order, and family. The more specific the level (closer to the top of the pyramid), the more traits shared by the organisms placed in that level.

Scientists currently recognize six kingdoms of organisms: Animalia (animals, fish, humans); Plantae (plants, trees, grasses); Fungi (mushrooms, lichens); Protista (bacteria, certain algae, other one-celled organisms having nuclei); Eubacteria (bacteria, blue-green algae, other one-celled organisms without nuclei); and Archaea (one-celled organisms found only in extreme environments such as hot or highly acidic water).

Every living organism is placed into one of these kingdoms. Organisms within kingdoms are then divided into phylums (or divisions for plants) based on distinct and defining characteristics. An example would be the phylum Chordata, which contains all the members of the kingdom Animalia that have a notochord (a rod, such as a backbone, that runs up an animal's back to support its body). Organisms in a specific phylum or division are then further divided into classes based on more distinct and defining characteristics. The dividing continues on through orders and then into families. Organisms that share a family often have the same behavioral patterns.

To further define an organism, Linnaeus also developed a two-part naming system—called binomial nomenclature—in which each living organism was given a two-part Latin name to distinguish it from other members in its family. The first name—italicized and capitalized—is the genus of the organism. The second name—italicized but not capitalized—is its species. This species name is an adjective, usually descriptive or geographic. Together, the genus and species form an organism's scientific name.

How similar organisms are separated by their scientific names can be seen in the example of the white oak and the red oak. All oak trees belong to the genus *Quercus*. The scientific name of white oak is *Quercus alba* (*alba* is Latin for "white"), while that of the red oak is *Quercus rubra* (*rubra* is Latin for "red"). In the past, scientists mainly took account of physical characteristics and behavior to group species together and give them scientific names. Now that scientists are able to compare species' DNA sequences, they also use this genetic information to classify species.

Each species or organism usually has only one scientific name under binomial nomenclature, which enables scientists worldwide who do not speak the same languages to communicate with each other about the species. However, as scientists learn more about species, they sometimes reclassify them based on new information. In such cases, a species will have a former name and a new name. Species can also end up with more than one name when scientists disagree about how they should be classified, with some scientists using one name and others preferring another. Alternate scientific names for a species are called "synonyms."

The scientific names provided for the species in *U•X•L Endangered Species, 3rd Edition*, are those used by the IUCN and the Endangered Species List. The Endangered Species List draws its taxonomic information from the Integrated Taxonomic Information System (ITIS). ITIS has also been consulted as a source for *U•X•L Endangered Species, 3rd Edition*, to determine accuracy of species' scientific names and taxonomies.

International Union for Conservation of Nature and Natural Resources (IUCN)

The International Union for Conservation of Nature and Natural Resources (IUCN), one of the world's oldest international conservation organizations, is a worldwide alliance of governments, government agencies, and nongovernmental organizations. It was established in Fontainebleau, France, on October 5, 1948. Working with scientists and experts, the IUCN tries to encourage and assist nations and societies around the world to conserve nature and to use natural resources wisely. As of December 2015, IUCN members represent 89 governments, 127 government agencies, and more than 1,000 nongovernmental organizations.

The IUCN has six volunteer commissions. The largest and most active of these is the Species Survival Commission (SSC). The mission of the SSC is to conserve biological diversity by developing programs that help save, restore, and manage species and their habitats. One of the many activities of the SSC is the production of the IUCN Red List of Threatened Species.

Available online, the IUCN Red List website has provided the foundation for *U•X•L Endangered Species, 3rd Edition*. The list presents scientifically based information on the status of threatened species around the world. Species are classified according to their existence in the wild and the current threats to that existence.

IUCN Red List categories

The IUCN Red List of Threatened Species places threatened plants, animals, fungi, and protists (organisms such as protozoans, one-celled algae, and slime molds) into one of nine categories:

activity or create an isolated refuge for the species in the chosen area. Once it has been established, however, any federal agencies planning to build on that land (a highway, for example) must seek the permission of the USFWS. Any other activities requiring federal permits must go through the USFWS as well. Private landowners are not affected, except that the designation alerts the public to the importance of the area in the species' survival. The ESA explicitly states that the economic interests of the human community must be given ample consideration in designating critical habitats and requires the balancing of species protection with economic development.

When a species is placed on the Endangered Species List, it is positioned in one of two categories:

- **Endangered:** A species that is in danger of extinction throughout all or a significant part of its range.
- **Threatened:** A species that is likely to become endangered in the foreseeable future.

The ESA outlaws the buying, selling, transporting, importing, or exporting of any listed species. Most important, the act bans the taking of any listed species within the United States and its territorial seas. "Taking" is defined as harassing, harming, pursuing, hunting, shooting, wounding, cutting, trapping, killing, removing, capturing, or collecting. The taking of listed species is prohibited on both private and public lands.

Violators of the ESA are subject to heavy fines. Individuals can face up to $100,000 in fines and up to one year's imprisonment. Organizations found in violation of the act may be fined up to $200,000.

On November 2, 2015, there were 2,246 species on the Endangered Species List. This total included 1,345 animals and 901 plants. The total also included 1,592 species found on U.S. territory or in U.S. waters, while the remaining 654 were species found in other countries.

Since its passage in 1973, the ESA has been continually targeted by its many opponents. Some of those opponents believe the ESA prohibits human progress, placing the rights of other species ahead of the rights of humans. There are many interest groups who lobby against the ESA: building and real estate development associations oppose the ESA because it could present some federal impediments to the large financial gains to be made in constructing new communities or facilities. Loggers, oil companies, farmers, fishers, hunters, fur traders, and others whose means of making a living are affected are also heavily represented in anti-ESA activism. Politicians, even those who nominally support the ESA, do not often find it politically advantageous to provide the necessary support and funding to rescue little-known animals or to oppose large and powerful companies.

In 1995 many Texans became upset on hearing news reports that said the USFWS might designate millions of acres of Texas land as critical habitat for the golden-cheeked warbler, an endangered bird. Designation of critical habitat is a required step for every species listed under the ESA. As a result of public outcry, U.S. senator Kay Bailey Hutchinson, a Republican from Texas, helped pass legislation that halted the USFWS's activities in the entire United States. The USFWS was prevented from designating new endangered or threatened species or designating critical habitat for existing species for a year. According to the USFWS, far less land was being proposed as critical habitat than news reports suggested, and critical habitat designation has no effect on private landowners anyway, a fact that the public often overlooks. When the moratorium (suspension of activity) was lifted in 1996, the agency faced delays and a backlog of proposed species to address.

In 2011 the nonprofit Center for Biological Diversity (CBD) concluded 10 years of lawsuits against the USFWS. The CBD had argued that the government agency was acting too slowly in listing new species. Under the eight years of President George W. Bush's administration (2001–2009), only 62 new species were listed, compared to 522 listed under the previous eight years during President Bill Clinton's administration (1993–2001). Meanwhile, the list of proposed species was getting longer as the USFWS took its time in making decisions. When the CBD and the USFWS made a settlement in 2011, the government agency agreed to decide on the backlog of 757 candidate species by 2018.

As recently as 2015, President Barack Obama's administration proposed making major changes to the ESA that would give states a larger role in the process of proposing new species for the ESA. It would also require that species be proposed only one at a time, rather than in bunches, which is currently done and saves time and steps. Opponents say that these changes will make it harder for citizens and organizations to propose new species as endangered.

Some of the species included in *U•X•L Endangered Species, 3rd Edition*, are losing the last few acres, streams, caves, or hillsides they require to survive; others stand only a few individual animals away from extinction. In the meantime, government agencies, wildlife organizations, politicians, and individuals often disagree on how best to balance the needs of humans and endangered species. Human activities are frequently the cause of endangerment, and human interests often conflict with those of other species. However, there are many examples in *U•X•L Endangered Species, 3rd Edition*, that illustrate how human efforts, including the protections of the ESA, can be critical in bringing species back from the verge of extinction.

Changes in Status from the 2nd Edition

Key: PE = Proposed Endangered; OFF = Delisted because of recovery;
LR–CD = Lower Risk, Conservation Dependent; TH = Threatened;
R = Rare (no longer used); NT = Near Threatened; VU = Vulnerable;
EN = Endangered; CE = Critically Endangered;
EW = Extinct in the Wild

Species that moved to a less threatened status, 2004–2016

Mammals

Armadillo, giant: EN to VU (IUCN)

Bat, gray: EN to NT (IUCN)

Bison, American: EN to TH (ESA)

Bison, European: EN to VU (IUCN)

Elephant, African: EN to VU (IUCN)

Ferret, black-footed: EW to EN (IUCN)

Lynx, Iberian: CE to EN (IUCN)

Markhor: EN to NT (IUCN); EN to TH (ESA)

Marmoset, white-eared: EN to VU (IUCN)

Monkey, Central American squirrel: EN to VU (IUCN)

Panda, red: EN to VU (IUCN)

Rat, giant kangaroo: CE to EN (IUCN)

Sea lion, Steller: EN to NT (IUCN)

Tamarin, golden lion: CE to EN (IUCN)

Birds

Booby, Abbott's: CE to EN (IUCN)

Cormorant, Galápagos: EN to VU (IUCN)

Eagle, bald: TH to OFF (ESA)

Macaw, Lear's: CE to EN (IUCN)

Magpie-robin, Seychelles: CE to EN (IUCN)

Parakeet, golden: EN to VU (IUCN)

Plover, piping: VU to NT (IUCN)

Warbler, Kirtland's: VU to NT (IUCN)

Woodpecker, red-cockaded VU to NT (IUCN)

Crustaceans

Shrimp, Kentucky cave: EN to VU (IUCN)

Insects

Dragonfly, Hine's emerald: EN to NT (IUCN)

Mollusks

Mussel, fat pocketbook pearly: CE to VU (IUCN)

Plants

Cypress, Saharan: CE to EN (IUCN)

Reptiles

Turtle, leatherback sea: CE to VU (IUCN)

Viper, meadow: EN to VU (IUCN)

Species that moved to a more threatened status, 2004–2016

Mammals

Fox, island gray: LR-CD to NT (IUCN); PE to EN (ESA)

Gazelle, dama: EN to CE (IUCN); PE to EN (ESA)

Gorilla: EN to CE (IUCN)

Hippopotamus, pygmy: VU to EN (IUCN)

Lemur, mongoose: VU to CE (IUCN)

Marmot, Vancouver Island: EN to CE (IUCN)

Mink, European: EN to CE (IUCN)

Numbat: VU to EN (IUCN)

Oryx, scimitar-horned: PE to EN (ESA)

Possum, mountain pygmy: EN to CE (IUCN)

Birds

Duck, Laysan: VU to CE (IUCN)

Ground-dove, purple-winged: EN to CE (IUCN)

Honeycreeper, crested: VU to CE (IUCN)

Kestrel, Mauritius: VU to EN (IUCN)

Murrelet, marbled: VU to EN (IUCN)

Pelican, Dalmatian: LR–CD to VU (IUCN)

Amphibians

Frog, Goliath: VU to EN (IUCN)

Fish

Catfish, giant: EN to CE (IUCN)

Sawfish, largetooth: EN to CE (IUCN)

Plants

Cactus, Tamaulipas living rock: VU to EN (IUCN)

Cycad, Natal grass: R to VU (IUCN)

Reptiles

Gharial: EN to CE (IUCN)

Tortoise, angulated: EN to CE (IUCN)

Turtle, Central American river: EN to CE (IUCN)

Words to Know

A

Adaptation: A genetically determined characteristic or inherited trait that makes an organism better able to cope with its environment.

Alpine: Relating to mountainous regions.

Arid: Land that receives very little rainfall annually and has a high rate of evaporation.

B

Biodiversity: The entire variety of life on Earth.

Biologist: A person who studies living organisms.

Botanist: A scientist who studies plants.

Brackish: A mixture of freshwater and saltwater; briny water.

Browse: A method of grazing in which an animal eats the leaf and twig growth of shrubs, woody vines, trees, and cacti.

C

Canopy: The uppermost spreading, branchy layer of a forest.

Captive breeding: A practice by which biologists (people who study living organisms) help a species reproduce in a controlled environment, such as a zoo, aquarium, or captive-breeding facility. Humans carefully select mating partners based on the individuals' genetics, behavior, and age, to find a match that will produce the healthiest offspring.

Carapace: A shell or bony covering on the back of animals such as turtles, lobsters, crabs, and armadillos.

Carnivore: An animal that eats mainly meat.

Carrion: The decaying flesh of dead animals.

Cetacean: An aquatic mammal that belongs to the order Cetacea, which includes whales, dolphins, and porpoises.

Chaparral: An ecological community of shrubby plants adapted to long, dry summers and natural forest-fire cycles, generally found in southern California.

Clear-cutting: The process of cutting down all the trees in a forest area at one time.

Clutch: A number of eggs produced or incubated at one time.

Competitor: A species that may compete for the same resources as another species.

Conservation: The management and protection of the natural world.

Conservationist: A person who works to manage and protect nature.

Convention on International Trade in Endangered Species of Wild Fauna and Flora (CITES): An international agreement by 143 nations to prohibit trade of endangered wildlife.

Critical habitat: A designated area considered necessary for the protection and preservation of a species that has been listed under the Endangered Species Act (ESA) in the United States. The area, either within the species' historical range or in an area similar to it, must provide an environment for normal behavior and reproduction so that the species may recover. The critical habitat designation does not prohibit human activity or create a refuge for the species. Once it has been established, though, any federal agencies planning to build or conduct activities within that area must seek the permission of the U.S. Fish and Wildlife Service (USFWS). The designation also serves to alert the public to the importance of the area in the species' survival.

Crustacean: A shellfish, such as a shrimp or crab, that has several pairs of legs and a segmented body with a hard outer shell.

Deciduous: Shedding seasonally; for example, a tree whose leaves fall off annually or a forest made up of trees that shed their leaves annually.

Deforestation: The loss of forests as they are rapidly cut down to produce timber or to make land available for agriculture.

Desertification: The gradual transformation of productive land into land with desertlike conditions.

Diurnal: Active during the day.

Domesticated: Animals trained to live with or be of use to humans.

Ecosystem: An ecological system, including all of its living things and their environment.

Ecotourism: Tourism, usually to a scenic natural place, that aims to raise awareness of threats and minimize environmental damage to the place.

Endangered: A classification indicating that a species is in danger of extinction in the foreseeable future.

Endangered Species Act (ESA): The legislation, passed by the U.S. Congress in 1973, which protects listed species.

Endangered Species List: The list of species protected under the U.S. Endangered Species Act.

Endemic species: A species native to, and found only in, a certain region.

Estivate: To hibernate (or sleep) through the summer.

Estuary: Coastal waters where a freshwater river empties into a saltwater sea or ocean.

Extinct: Refers to a species or subspecies that no longer exists because all of its living members have died.

Extirpated species: A species that no longer survives in the regions that were once part of its range.

Fauna: The animal life of a particular region, geological period, or environment.

Feral: An animal that has never been domesticated or has escaped from domestication and has become wild.

Fledge: When birds grow the feathers needed for flight.

Flora: The plants of a particular region, geological period, or environment.

Forage: To search for food.

Fragmentation: The breaking up of habitat into smaller areas that no longer border each other.

Gene: The basic biological unit of heredity that determines individual traits. Part of the DNA molecule, the gene is transmitted from parents to children during reproduction, and contains information for making particular proteins, which then make particular cells.

Genetic diversity: The variety of genes that exists among all the individuals of a particular species.

Gestation: Pregnancy.

Habitat: The environment in which specified organisms live.

Herbivore: An animal that eats mainly plants.

Hibernate: To spend the winter in an inactive state.

Historic range: The areas in which a species is believed to have lived in the past.

Hybrid: An animal or plant that is the offspring of two different species or varieties, resulting in a genetic mix.

Inbreeding: The mating or breeding of closely related individuals, usually within small communities. Inbreeding occurs when both parents have at least one common ancestor.

Indicator species: Plants or animals that, by their presence or chemical composition, give some distinctive indication of the health or quality of the environment.

International Union for the Conservation of Nature and Natural Resources (IUCN): An international conservation organization that publishes the IUCN Red List of Threatened Species.

Introduced species: Flora or fauna not native to an area, but introduced from a different ecosystem.

Invasive species: Species from a different ecosystem that cause harm when they are introduced into a new environment.

Invertebrate: An animal without a backbone.

Larval: The immature stage of certain insects and animals, usually of a species that develops by complete metamorphosis.

Lichen: A plantlike composite consisting of a fungus and an alga.

Marsupial: Mammals, such as the kangaroo and the opossum, whose young continue to develop after birth in a pouch on the outside of the mother's body.

Metamorphosis: A change in the form and habits of an animal during natural development.

Migration: The act of changing location (migrating) periodically, usually moving seasonally from one region to another.

Molting: The process of shedding an outer covering, such as skin or feathers, for replacement by a new growth.

Monogamous: Having just one mate for life.

Native species: The flora or fauna indigenous or native to an ecosystem, as opposed to introduced species.

Naturalist: A person who observes nature to find its laws.

Nocturnal: Most active at night.

Old-growth forest: A mature forest dominated by long-lived species (at least 200 years old), but also including younger trees; its complex physical structure includes multiple layers in the canopy, many large trees, and many large, dead, standing trees and dead logs.

Overhunting: Too much hunting of a particular species, resulting in a decline in the population of the species, which can lead to endangerment or extinction.

Perennial: A plant that lives, grows, flowers, and produces seeds for three or more continuous years.

Plumage: The covering of feathers on a bird.

Poaching: Illegally taking protected animals or plants.

Pollution: The contamination of air, water, or soil by the discharge of harmful substances.

Population: A group of organisms of one species occupying a defined area and usually isolated from similar groups of the same species.

Predator: An animal that preys on others.

Prehensile: Adapted for grasping or holding, especially by wrapping around something.

Pupal: An intermediate, inactive stage between the larva and adult stages in the life cycle of many insects.

Rain forest: A dense evergreen forest with an annual rainfall of at least 100 inches (254 centimeters); may be tropical (e.g., Amazon) or temperate (e.g., Pacific Northwest).

Range: The area naturally occupied by a species.

Recovery: The process of stopping or reversing the decline of an endangered or threatened species to ensure the species' long-term survival in the wild.

Reintroduction: The act of placing new members of a species into a habitat where that species had formerly disappeared.

Reserve: An area of land set aside for the use or protection of a species or group of species.

Rhizomatous plant: A plant having an underground horizontal stem that puts out shoots above ground and roots below.

Runoff: Water that drains away from the land's surface, such as after a heavy rain, bringing substances with it.

Savanna: A flat tropical or subtropical grassland.

Scavenger: An animal that feeds on carrion (dead animals) or scraps rather than hunting live prey.

Scrub: A tract of land covered with stunted or scraggly trees and shrubs.

Slash-and-burn agriculture: A farming practice in which forest is cut and burned to create new space for farmland.

Species: A group of individuals related by descent and able to breed among themselves but not with other organisms.

Steppe: Vast, semiarid grass-covered plains found in southeast Europe, Siberia, and central North America.

Subspecies: A population of a species distinguished from other such populations by certain characteristics.

Succulent: A plant that has thick, fleshy, water-storing leaves or stems.

Sustainable development: Methods of farming or building human communities that meet the needs of the current generation without depleting or damaging the natural resources in the area or compromising its ability to meet the needs of future generations.

Taproot: The main root of a plant growing straight downward from the stem.

Taxonomist: A biologist who classifies species on the basis of their genes, characteristics, and behavior.

Temperate: Characteristic of a region or climate that has mild temperatures.

Territoriality: The behavior displayed by an individual animal, a mating pair, or a group in vigorously defending its domain (territory) against intruders.

Trafficking: Dealing or trading in something illegal, such as protected animal and plant species.

Troglobite: A species that lives only in caves.

Tropical: Characteristic of a region or climate that is frost free, with temperatures high enough to support—with adequate precipitation—plant growth year round.

Tundra: A relatively flat, treeless plain in alpine, Arctic, and Antarctic regions.

Underbrush: Small trees, shrubs, or similar plants growing on the forest floor underneath taller trees.

Urban sprawl: The spreading of houses, shopping centers, and other city facilities through previously undeveloped land.

U.S. Fish and Wildlife Service (USFWS): A federal agency that oversees implementation of the Endangered Species Act.

Vegetation: Plants or the plant life of an area.

Vulnerable: A classification indicating that a species satisfies some of the risk criteria for endangerment, but not at a level that warrants its identification as endangered.

Wetland: A permanently moist lowland area such as a marsh or a swamp.

Wildlife biologist: A person who studies living organisms in the wild.

Amphibians

The axolotl, which lives in the canals and lakes near Mexico City, is threatened by pollution and other aspects of human activity.
© SERGIO GUTIERREZ GETINO/SHUTTERSTOCK.COM.

The axolotl has tiny teeth that it uses to grip food, which includes mollusks, worms, insect larvae, small crustaceans (shellfish such as shrimp or crabs), and small fish. The axolotl has traditionally been the main predator in its environment, although it can become a prey item when large nonnative fish are introduced into its habitat. It is also eaten by birds such as herons. Axolotls can live up to 15 years in the wild.

Habitat and current distribution

The axolotl is found only in the canals and wetlands (areas where there is a lot of water in the soil, such as swamps) of the central Mexican district of Xochimilco (pronounced so-chee-MEAL-co), including the area south of Mexico City. Axolotls are almost extinct in the wild. Scientific surveys in the first decade and a half of the 21st century found virtually none of the creatures, although fishers still occasionally catch them and sell them in local markets. Many axolotls are kept in captivity for the pet trade or for research purposes.

History and conservation measures

The axolotl has a long history in the area around Mexico City. Its name derives from the Nahuatl (pronounced NAH-wah-tull) words *atl*, meaning "water," and *xolotl*, meaning "monster." (Nahuatl was the language of the ancient Aztec people.)

Many factors have been identified as contributing to the reduction of the axolotl population. Human population growth has caused pollution of the lakes and canals around Mexico City. Population growth has also increased fishing for the axolotl, which are eaten by locals and used as medicine. Axolotls have also been captured to be sold as pets, although most pet axolotls are probably now bred in captivity. Foreign fish species, such as tilapia and carp, have been introduced into the axolotls' habitat, competing with them for food and sometimes preying on them.

There have been some efforts to control pollution in the Mexico City area, although high bacteria levels still threaten the axolotl. Because axolotls still exist in captivity, it is hoped that eventually the species can be reintroduced in the wild. Conservationists (people who work to manage and protect nature) believe, however, that the species currently faces too many threats to thrive in its former habitat.

Frog, California red-legged
Rana draytonii

PHYLUM: Chordata
CLASS: Amphibia
ORDER: Anura
FAMILY: Ranidae
STATUS: Vulnerable, IUCN
Threatened, ESA
RANGE: Mexico, USA (California)

Frog, California red-legged
Rana draytonii

Description and biology

The California red-legged frog is the largest native frog in the western United States, ranging from 2 to 5 inches (5 to 13 centimeters) in length. The frog's skin is rough and thick and mostly reddish brown or gray in color. It has dark spots with light centers on its back. Its upper abdomen is yellow, and its lower abdomen and hind legs are red. The frog's toes are only partially webbed (joined by tissues or membranes). It has vocal sacs, with which it makes sharp, low grunts during the weeks when it breeds. The California red-legged frog was once believed to be a subspecies of the northern red-legged frog (*Rana aurora*), but in 2004 scientists determined it to be a distinct species.

California red-legged frogs eat invertebrates (animals with no backbone), small mammals, and other amphibians. Tree frogs, mice, and insects are common food items. Adult frogs are nocturnal (active at night),

The California red-legged frog, native to Southern California and Mexico, is threatened by the small size and continued decline of its habitat. © JASON MINTZER/SHUTTERSTOCK.COM.

while younger frogs are active both day and night. Among the animals that prey upon California red-legged frogs are wading birds, snakes, and raccoons. When the frogs sense an enemy is near, they swim far out into the water to hide.

California red-legged frogs breed from late December to early April. Mating is through external fertilization. That means that males fertilize eggs after females lay them. The eggs are dark brown and about 0.08 to 0.11 inches (2 to 2.8 millimeters) wide. The female lays her eggs in masses of 2,000 to 5,000 eggs, which become attached to vegetation (plant life), such as cattails or bulrushes, at or near the surface of the water. In a week or two the eggs hatch, and dark-brown tadpoles (immature or newly hatched frogs) emerge. At the tadpole stage, the young frog has external gills and a rounded body with a long tail bordered by fins. It will remain in this form for 3.5 to 7 months. The tail and gills disappear and legs develop by the end of this period and the tadpole becomes a young frog.

Habitat and current distribution

California red-legged frogs live in rivers, streams, ponds, lakes, and wetland areas (areas where there is a lot of water in the soil, such as swamps or tidal flats) near the water's edge. They prefer standing ponds or slow-

Did You Know?

Frogs have been around for millions of years; in fact, their immediate ancestors roamed Earth with the dinosaurs. Over the years, frogs have evolved into many different species that have successfully adapted to almost every kind of climate and habitat. Although they have been around for a very long time—much longer than humans—frogs and other amphibians have been disappearing at a very fast rate worldwide since the 1980s.

Pollution is considered a likely factor in these declines because frogs take in much of the air they breathe through their skin and are sensitive to environmental pollutants. Other factors include loss of habitat and the introduction of invasive species that can prey on or outcompete native amphibians.

However, scientists now consider disease to be one of the biggest factors in frog declines. Amphibian chytridiomycosis, a disease caused by a fungus called *Batrachochytrium dendrobatidis* (*Bd*), affects a frog's ability to breathe and absorb water through its skin. Since its discovery in the 1990s, this fungus has caused the extinction of more than 100 frog and other amphibian species. Although it is not clear where the fungus originally came from, it is now present on all continents and was most likely spread by the trade of amphibians by humans. No known cure exists, but scientists are hopeful that immunization (the process of strengthening an organism's immune system against a disease) could help protect frog populations from *Bd*.

moving streams, and grasses, cattails, or other tall vegetation that can protect them from sun and predators.

The frogs have traditionally been found almost entirely in California. A study in the mid-1990s found that they had been driven from 70 percent of their original range. They are now mostly located in coastal drainage areas (areas where rainwater or melting snow flows from higher ground) in central California down to Baja California in Mexico. Some populations have been introduced in Nevada, though it is uncertain whether they are thriving.

The total adult population is thought to be greater than 10,000. California red-legged frogs are still common in parts of the San Francisco Bay area and Marin County.

History and conservation measures

Before the 19th century, the California red-legged frog could be found throughout most of California. It famously appeared in Mark Twain's 1865 short story, "The Celebrated Jumping Frog of Calaveras County."

A large gold rush beginning in 1848 brought thousands of miners into California's Central Valley. The miners tore up the mountain streams in their search for gold. This destroyed large portions of the California red-legged frogs' habitat. Later in the century, frog legs became a very popular food in San Francisco and the Central Valley. An estimated 80,000 frogs were killed for food each year. By the early 1900s they had become harder and harder to find. To keep up with the demand for frog legs, bullfrogs were brought into California at the end of the century. Bullfrogs quickly became predators of the California red-legged frog, seriously reducing the population once again. Bullfrogs remain in the California red-legged frogs' habitat and continue to prey upon the species.

California red-legged frogs face numerous threats today. By some estimates, developers and farmers have drained 90 percent of California's wetlands. The loss of habitat was worsened by a long-term, punishing drought in California that began in 2012 and may have been connected to the effects of climate change. Frogs are also threatened by exotic, non-native predators such as bass and mosquitofish. Bullfrogs continue to prey on California red-legged frogs and can also infect them with *Batrachochytrium dendrobatidis* (*Bd*) fungus, a deadly disease.

As a threatened species, the California red-legged frog has protections under both U.S. and California state law. In addition, the U.S. Fish and Wildlife Service (USFWS) has tried to protect the species by designating portions of its range as critical habitat. In areas considered critical habitat, U.S. agencies must consult with the USFWS before performing or funding actions that might destroy or negatively affect the habitat. Following various lawsuits and negotiations, the USFWS designated 1.6 million acres (647,000 hectares) as critical habitat for this frog in 2010.

The California red-legged frog was declared California's state amphibian in 2015 in an effort to raise awareness of the threats it faces. The National Wildlife Federation is working to encourage Californians to create their own small wetlands and native plant gardens, which can help provide more habitat for these frogs.

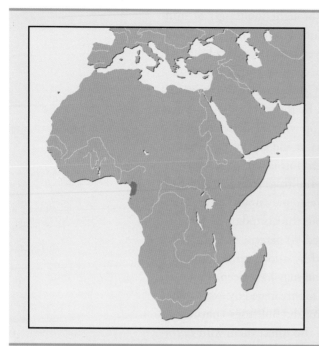

Frog, Goliath
Conraua goliath

PHYLUM:	Chordata
CLASS:	Amphibia
ORDER:	Anura
FAMILY:	Petropedetidae
STATUS:	Endangered, IUCN Threatened, ESA
RANGE:	Cameroon, Equatorial Guinea

Frog, Goliath
Conraua goliath

Description and biology

The Goliath frog is the largest frog in the world. It can weigh more than 7 pounds (3.2 kilograms) and measure almost 30 inches (76 centimeters) long with its legs extended. Its body alone can measure more than 12 inches (30.5 centimeters). The frog's upper body is greenish brown in color, allowing it to blend in well with the wet, moss-covered rocks on which it sits. Its underparts are pale orange or yellow. Its eyes can measure almost 1 inch (2.5 centimeters) in diameter. Males and females look very similar.

Adult Goliath frogs feed on insects, crustaceans (shellfish such as shrimp and crabs), fish, and amphibians (such as newts, salamanders, and smaller frogs). Goliath tadpoles (immature or newly hatched frogs) eat only one particular plant found near waterfalls and rapids in their range. Whereas smaller adults spend most of their time in the water, larger adults frequently come out to bask in sunlight on rocks. The frogs are more active during the night when they search for food along river edges.

The Goliath frog's eggs measure about 0.3 inches (0.8 centimeters) in diameter and are surrounded by a jellylike substance. After mating, a female Goliath frog lays her eggs attached to grass or other vegetation (plant life) along streams or the margin of rocky pools. Upon hatching, Goliath tadpoles are no larger than the tadpoles of other frog species. The tadpole stage, in which the young frog has external gills and a rounded body with a long tail bordered by fins, lasts about 90 days. The tail and gills disappear and legs develop by the end of this period.

Habitat and current distribution

The Goliath frog has a very small range. It inhabits only a strip of dense rain forest in coastal sections of Cameroon and Equatorial Guinea in

The Goliath frog has seen its population decline because it is trapped and hunted for food or by pet traders, and because of the effects of human activity on its habitat. © PAUL STAROSTA/TERRA/CORBIS.

Africa. This area measures about 150 miles (240 kilometers) long by 55 miles (89 kilometers) wide. Within this forest strip, the frog is found among only a few swift-moving rivers flowing to the coast. These rivers are clean and well oxygenated, with an average temperature of 65°F (18°C).

The total number of Goliath frogs in existence in the wild is unknown.

History and conservation measures

The Goliath frog was first identified in 1906. Since that time, private collectors have paid large sums of money to own a specimen. The government of Equatorial Guinea allows no more than 300 Goliath frogs to be exported from (taken out of) the country per year. The European Union also prohibits trade of this species, but no restrictions exist on the international trade of these animals in the rest of the world.

The primary threat to the Goliath frog is hunting. The species is considered a delicacy, and people have developed efficient methods of trapping the animals. The frog is also popular in the international pet trade because of its large size; it is often used in jumping contests. Another threat is destruction of the species' habitat when the rain forest is cleared for agriculture, logging, or human settlements. The construction of farms and homes also carries soil into the streams where the frog breeds, possibly harming tadpoles. When the International Union for Conservation of Nature and Natural Resources (IUCN) changed the Goliath frog's listing from threatened to endangered in 2004, it noted that the population of the species had declined 50 percent over the previous 15 years and projected that its population would decrease by a similar amount by around 2019.

Several nonprofit organizations are working to protect the Goliath frog. Biologists (people who study living organisms) are educating people who live near the frogs' habitat about the need to harvest the frogs responsibly in order to conserve the species. Conservation groups are planting trees to replace habitat lost by rain-forest clearing. Several Goliath frog habitats have been declared protected areas. This species does not breed successfully or survive well in captivity, so captive-breeding programs cannot be undertaken to restore it.

Newt, Luristan
Neurergus kaiseri

PHYLUM: Chordata
CLASS: Amphibia
ORDER: Caudata
FAMILY: Salamandridae
STATUS: Critically endangered, IUCN
RANGE: Iran

Newt, Luristan
Neurergus kaiseri

Description and biology

The Luristan newt sports a cheerful color scheme. The newt's body and tail are black with white blotches. An orange stripe runs down the center of its body and onto the tail. The arms and legs are orange with black spots, and the underside is orange. The animal's big black eyes bulge out. The newt is 4 to 5.5 inches (10 to 14 centimeters) long. Its bright colors warn predators that it is poisonous, and indeed its skin produces poisonous chemicals. In addition, the newt will give off a bad odor when threatened.

This newt lives in a dry habitat with hot summers and mild winters. In late fall through early spring, it inhabits cool, spring-fed streams. Then it crawls onto the rocky slopes surrounding these streams and estivates (enters a state similar to hibernation) until late fall. Biologists (people who study living organisms) know little about this secretive animal's

579

Luristan newts, like all other newts, are salamanders. But not all salamanders are newts. All salamanders belong to the same order (group) of animals, the Caudata. Animals in this group are amphibians with slim bodies, rounded snouts, short limbs at right angles from their bodies, and tails nearly as long as their bodies. Most are small, although the Chinese giant salamander can reach 6 feet (1.8 meters) long. Many live on land for most of the year but return to the water to breed. Young salamanders usually live in the water until they change into their adult form. The order Caudata includes 10 families. Newts belong to the family Salamandridae, which includes newts and animals called "true salamanders." These two groups are very similar. They are smaller than 8 inches (20 centimeters) long and brightly colored, with skin that gives off a toxic substance. One difference is that true salamanders usually have smooth, wrinkled skin, but the skin of newts is rough.

behavior on land but have observed them hiding in cracks of rocks and climbing up cliffs. No one knows what they eat, but a similar species eats small crustaceans (shellfish), insects, and snails.

Male newts court females on land near the water. The male waves its tail in front of the female, probably to release chemicals arousing her mating interest. The newts touch tails and the male deposits sperm near the female's body. She uses the sperm to fertilize 45 to 60 eggs, which she lays and attaches to rocks underwater. Newt tadpoles are grayish brown with black spots and external gills. Three to four months after hatching, they develop adult coloration, their gills disappear, and they move to dry land. They reach sexual maturity two to four years later. This species' life span in the wild is not known, but in captivity it lives six to eight years.

Habitat and current distribution

The Luristan newt lives only in the southern Zagros Mountains of Luristan (also spelled Lorestan), a province of Iran. In 2009 the International Union for Conservation of Nature and Natural Resources (IUCN) reported that fewer than 1,000 mature individuals remained in the wild, in only four streams. However, a 2014 survey by Iranian government biologists estimated a population of at least 9,000 adults at 20 sites.

History and conservation measures

First identified in 1952 and living in remote, barely inhabited areas, the Luristan newt has been little studied until recently. The IUCN declared the species critically endangered in 2006, stating that its population had declined by 80 percent over the previous 10 years. The Luristan newt appeared on a 2012 IUCN list of the 100 most threatened species in the world.

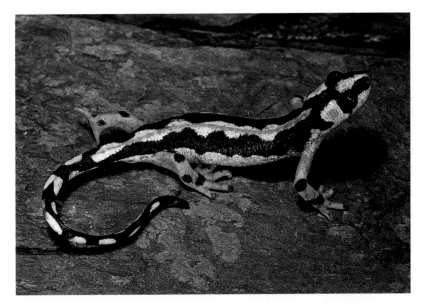

The Luristan newt, which is native to Iran, is threatened by both the pet trade and loss of habitat. © PAUL STAROSTA/TERRA/CORBIS.

The biggest threat to this species has been illegal collection for the international pet trade. Hobbyists want the newt for its beauty and rarity. However, this threat has greatly lessened since the species' 2010 listing on Appendix I of the Convention on International Trade in Endangered Species of Wild Fauna and Flora (CITES; an international treaty to protect wildlife). Species on this list cannot legally be bought and sold. Captive breeding is allowed, however, and such a program at the Sedgwick County Zoo in Wichita, Kansas, has been very successful.

Various other threats may exist. Nonnative fish species introduced into streams could eat the newt's eggs and tadpoles. Illegal waste disposal and agricultural chemicals lessen the streams' purity. Water use reduces water levels, and severe droughts dry up the streams entirely. Firewood collection could reduce the newt's hiding spots on land as well.

The authors of the 2014 Iranian government study recommend expanding a protected forest to include the newt's habitat and educating local communities about the animal's importance. They also suggest that because their study revealed a much higher population and a larger range than earlier reports, the IUCN should reassess its critically endangered designation.

Salamander, California tiger
Ambystoma californiense

PHYLUM: Chordata
CLASS: Amphibia
ORDER: Caudata
FAMILY: Ambystomatidae
STATUS: Vulnerable, IUCN
Endangered, ESA (Sonoma
County and Santa Barbara
County populations)
Threatened, ESA (other
populations)
RANGE: USA (California)

Salamander, California tiger
Ambystoma californiense

Description and biology

California tiger salamanders have wide bodies and round snouts. Their body color is black or dark gray, and their backs and sides have white or pale yellow spots. The belly is white or pale yellow and can be patterned with black. The salamander's small brown eyes protrude, or stick out, from its head, and its wide mouth is outlined in yellow. Males can reach a length of 8 inches (20 centimeters) and females 7 inches (18 centimeters). They can live up to 15 years.

These secretive amphibians spend most of their lives underground, living in small-mammal burrows located in grasslands and oak woodlands. They come out at night to feed on earthworms, snails, insects, and even small frogs and mice. When the rainy season starts in late fall, the salamanders migrate as a group at night to vernal pools (ponds that fill with rain in winter and spring but are dry for the remainder of the year).

The California tiger salamander, found in several areas of Northern California, is at risk because of the loss of its habitat and breeding areas caused by urban and agricultural development. © SEBASTIAN KENNERKNECHT/MINDEN PICTURES/CORBIS.

Females lay eggs in the pools, attaching them to underwater vegetation (plant life). The adult salamanders then return to their usual habitat, leaving the eggs to hatch two to four weeks later. Tadpoles remain in the ponds until they are fully developed in late spring and then move to land.

Habitat and current distribution

The California tiger salamander is found in central California, including Sonoma County, the San Francisco Bay area, the Central Valley, the southern San Joaquin Valley, the Central Coast range, and Santa Barbara County. Biologists (people who study living organisms) divide the species into three groups: Sonoma County salamanders, Santa Barbara salamanders, and central California salamanders. There are at least 10,000 California tiger salamanders, but biologists have been unable to determine a more exact number because the salamanders are seldom seen aboveground.

History and conservation measures

Tiger salamanders, the largest of the land-dwelling salamanders, live throughout the United States. The California tiger salamander was recognized as a separate species only in 1991. This species requires both vernal ponds and grasslands or oak woods for its habitat. Since 1900, however, 80 percent of its vernal pond habitat and 75 percent of its grassland habitat has been lost to agricultural and urban development. In Sonoma County, for instance, office buildings and roads now occupy 95 percent of the salamanders' habitat. Urban and agricultural development also causes habitat fragmentation, in which larger continuous habitats become divided into smaller, more isolated sections. This prevents animals from moving to new breeding areas or returning to established ones. Salamanders may die crossing roads, and road runoff (water that drains away, bringing substances with it) can damage and pollute vernal ponds. Introduced species, such as bullfrogs and mosquito fish, can also pose a threat because they eat the salamanders' larvae.

In 2000 the U.S. Fish and Wildlife Service (USFWS) listed the Santa Barbara County population of the California tiger salamander as endangered. It listed the Sonoma County population as endangered in 2002 and the central California population as threatened in 2004. The USFWS is developing species recovery plans (plans promoting the conservation of species) for each of the three populations. These plans call for buying and protecting habitat for the California tiger salamander. As of 2015, draft plans for the Sonoma County and Santa Barbara County salamanders had been released, and a plan for the central California population was expected to follow in 2017.

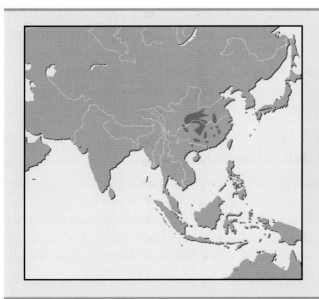

Salamander, Chinese giant
Andrias davidianus

PHYLUM: Chordata
CLASS: Amphibia
ORDER: Caudata
FAMILY: Cryptobranchidae
STATUS: Critically endangered, IUCN
Endangered, ESA
RANGE: China

Salamander, Chinese giant
Andrias davidianus

Description and biology

The Chinese giant salamander is the largest salamander and the largest amphibian on Earth (salamanders resemble lizards but have smooth, soft, moist skin). It can grow up to almost 6 feet (1.8 meters) in length and weigh up to 110 pounds (49.9 kilograms). Its head is broad and flat with a broad mouth. It has four short limbs and a tail measuring more than half of its total length. The Chinese giant salamander has smooth, rounded bumps (called tubercles) on its snout, at the edge of its eyes, and on other parts of its head. Thick skin folds with larger tubercles appear on the sides of its body. The upper part of the salamander's body is dark brown or pale brown in color with irregular black patches. It is lighter in color underneath.

The Chinese giant salamander is a carnivore (an animal that eats mainly meat), feeding on crabs, fish, frogs, shrimp, mollusks, and aquatic insects.

During the breeding season, which peaks in July and August, a female Chinese giant salamander lays hundreds of eggs in an underwater cave. Each egg is about 0.9 inches (2.2 centimeters) wide. The male that fertilizes the eggs then protects the cave until the eggs hatch in 12 to 15 weeks. The hatchlings, or newborn salamanders, are about 1.2 inches (3 centimeters) long.

Habitat and current distribution

The Chinese giant salamander can be found in tributaries of the Pearl (Zhu), Yellow (Huang), and Yangtze (Chang) Rivers in China. It lives in 12 separate areas in its range, but these populations are fragmented (broken into smaller areas that no longer border each other). Biologists (people who study living organisms) estimate that the species' population has decreased more than 80 percent since the 1950s.

The Chinese giant salamander is at risk because of the decline of its habitat. It is also hunted for its meat and for its use in traditional medicine. © TOM MCHUGH/SCIENCE SOURCE.

The Chinese giant salamander inhabits mountain streams at elevations below 4,920 feet (1,500 meters). In these areas, plant cover is extensive and river water is shallow, cold, clear, and fast moving. Deep pools and caves are abundant. The salamander seeks shelter in dark, muddy caves during the day and emerges to search for food at night.

History and conservation measures

The primary threat to the Chinese giant salamander is hunting. The meat of this salamander is said to be smooth, white, delicious, and high in nutrients. In addition, humans in the salamander's range use other parts of its body to create medicines. Another threat to the salamander is the pollution and destruction of its natural habitat due to the construction of dams, farming, mining, and other human activities.

In 1989 the Chinese government added the Chinese giant salamander to its list of protected animals. After this, many Chinese provincial governments also passed legislation to ban the killing of the salamander. In the early 21st century this salamander is widely bred in commercial farms in rural China, where it continues to be sold for its meat and other uses. Salamanders are sometimes poached (hunted illegally), however, in the wild in order to stock these farms.

Thousands of farmed salamanders have been released in at least 11 Chinese provinces as a way to increase the species' population in the wild. Conservationists (people who work to manage and protect nature) are concerned that this practice poses a new threat to the Chinese giant salamander, however. Farm-bred salamanders have caused deadly disease outbreaks among wild populations and may introduce inbred genes (genes of animals that are closely interrelated) to wild populations. Inbreeding (animals mating with relatives) occurs when there are too few individuals in a population. Inbred offspring of farm-bred salamanders may be more likely to develop genetic diseases. When these offspring are released into the wild, such genetic diseases can become a problem in the wild population as well.

Salamander, Texas blind
Eurycea rathbuni (also *Typhlomolge rathbuni*)

PHYLUM: Chordata
CLASS: Amphibia
ORDER: Caudata
FAMILY: Plethodontidae
STATUS: Vulnerable, IUCN
Endangered, ESA
RANGE: USA (Texas)

Salamander, Texas blind
Eurycea rathbuni (also *Typhlomolge rathbuni*)

Description and biology

The Texas blind salamander, which inhabits underground caves, has whitish, transparent skin. Its larger organs are visible through its sides and belly, giving its body a pinkish tinge. It has red external gills and tiny gray dots covering its upper body. Two dark spots under the skin on the salamander's head may have been eyes at one time in this species' history. Its body is short and slender, and its large head has a wide, flattened snout. An average adult has a head and body length of about 5 inches (13 centimeters). Its tail, which tapers at the tip, is about the same length as the head and body. The salamander's long, slender legs resemble toothpicks.

The Texas blind salamander is a major predator in its underground habitat. It uses vibrations and smell to hunt invertebrates (animals with no backbone) such as shrimp and snails. If the salamander is brought

The Texas blind salamander, found only in San Marcos, Texas, is affected by pollutants and changes in water quality in its habitat. © DANTE FENO-LIO/SCIENCE SOURCE.

to the surface through a spring or well, however, it is an easy prey for fish.

Biologists (people who study living organisms) know very little about this salamander's reproductive habits. They believe that females can lay more than 35 eggs at a time and that they are able to mate throughout the year. In captivity, the Texas blind salamander has been known to live more than five years.

Habitat and current distribution

The Texas blind salamander is found only in the San Marcos Pool of the Edwards Aquifer in Hays County, Texas. (An aquifer is an underground layer of sand, gravel, or spongy rock that collects water.) Biologists have no estimate of the salamander's total population.

This salamander lives in the perpetual darkness of underground streams and caves. The water of its habitat is usually very clean and has a constant temperature about 72°F (22°C).

History and conservation measures

The Texas blind salamander was first identified in 1896. By the 1960s it had begun to decline in number. The main reason was over-collection. Many scientists and hobbyists captured the salamander, fascinated by its physical appearance and ability to live in a cave environment. To protect the salamander from further collection, the only entrance to its habitat, Ezell's Cave, was declared a nature preserve.

The survival of this salamander depends on the quality of its water habitat. Farms and increasing urban development in its range now threaten the water. The water level in the aquifer continues to decrease as more and more water is used for human consumption and for crop irrigation. In addition, pollution from both urban areas and farms threatens to seep into the aquifer, destroying the Texas blind salamander's fragile ecosystem (an ecological system including all of its living things and their environment).

The species is listed as endangered and protected by the laws of the U.S. government and the state government of Texas. Research is being conducted on the Texas blind salamander to ensure its survival. A captive-breeding program has been ongoing since the 1970s at the San Marcos National Fish Hatchery, now called the San Marcos Aquatic Resources Center (SMARC). SMARC also maintains a captive population of wild-caught Texas blind salamanders to protect the species in case the wild population suffers unexpected declines. As of June 2015, SMARC had a protected population of 143 wild-caught salamanders, as well as 127 captive-bred offspring.

Toad, Houston
Anaxyrus houstonensis (also *Bufo houstonensis*)

PHYLUM: Chordata
CLASS: Amphibia
ORDER: Anura
FAMILY: Bufonidae
STATUS: Endangered, IUCN
Endangered, ESA
RANGE: USA (Texas)

Toad, Houston

Anaxyrus houstonensis (also *Bufo houstonensis*)

Description and biology

The Houston toad is a medium-sized toad, 2 to 3.5 inches (5 to 9 centimeters) long. Males are slightly smaller than females. The toad is usually light brown or gray in color. Sometimes it has green patches. It has small, dark-brown to black spots on its pale underside.

Adult Houston toads feed mainly on insects, such as ants and beetles. Tadpoles (toads newly hatched or in their larval stage) eat algae and pine pollen. Some snakes and turtles may prey on the toad, and certain fish may prey on its eggs.

During mating season, males make a high-pitched trill to attract females. This calling can occur from December to June. Breeding takes place after the air temperature reaches around 57°F (14°C). Females lay their eggs between mid-February and late June. Each female will produce 500 to 6,000 eggs. In order for tadpoles to develop, breeding pools have to remain intact for at least 60 days.

The Houston toad is no longer found in the Houston area because of the effects of drought and urban development on its habitat. PAIGE NAJVAR/U.S. FISH AND WILDLIFE SERVICE.

Habitat and current distribution

The Houston toad once lived throughout the central coastal region of southeastern Texas. It disappeared from the Houston area in the 1960s. Biologists (people who study living organisms) believe the species currently exists in up to nine counties near its former range, with the largest concentration in Bastrop County. The total population there was estimated to be between 100 and 200 toads in 2003. However, a 2011 survey carried out in Bastrop County and surrounding counties only found 12 Houston toads. All Houston toad populations are small and fragmented (broken into smaller areas that no longer border each other).

The Houston toad occupies a variety of aquatic habitats, including lakes, ponds, roadside ditches, flooded fields and pastures, and temporary rain pools. Because it cannot dig burrows very well, the toad inhabits areas with sandy soil, such as pine forests. When not mating, the toad finds shelter in the sand, in burrows, under logs, or in leaf debris.

History and conservation measures

The Houston toad was discovered in the 1940s. Just one decade later, because of severe droughts that struck Texas, it was thought to be extinct. In 1965 it was rediscovered in Bastrop State Park.

This toad does not adapt well to dry and warm conditions, so these droughts severely reduced its population. Since then, the number of Houston toads has been further reduced as pine forests have been cleared to create farms and communities. The runoff (water that drains away, bringing substances with it) of insecticides and herbicides used on farms and in residential areas also threatens to destroy what remains of the toads' habitat.

Another threat to the Houston toad is red fire ants introduced to Texas from other countries. The ants eat young toads under 10 days old. They also reduce the amount of food available for adult toads because the ants eat the same types of insects and small organisms.

Conservation efforts for the Houston toad include protecting its remaining habitat and reintroducing it into areas in its former range. Scientists continue to study the species to learn more about its biology, population numbers, and habitat requirements, as well as how the toad is affected by certain land management practices.

Toad, Wyoming
Anaxyrus baxteri (also *Bufo baxteri*)

PHYLUM: Chordata
CLASS: Amphibia
ORDER: Anura
FAMILY: Bufonidae
STATUS: Extinct in the wild, IUCN
Endangered, ESA
RANGE: USA (Wyoming)

Toad, Wyoming
Anaxyrus baxteri (also *Bufo baxteri*)

Description and biology

The Wyoming toad is one of the four most endangered amphibians in the United States. In fact, it is considered extinct in the wild. This toad is rather small, having a head and body length just over 2 inches (5 centimeters). It is dark brown, gray, or greenish in color with dark blotches. Its belly is often spotted and its upper body has numerous rounded warts. Males, which tend to be smaller than females, have a darker throat. This toad eats a variety of insects, including ants and beetles.

During the fall and winter, the toad hibernates (spends the winter in an inactive state), often in rodent burrows. In May, males move to breeding sites along the borders of bays, ponds, and wet meadows, where water is shallow and vegetation (plant life) plentiful. The males attract females with their calls. Breeding takes place up to mid-June. After mating, a female Wyoming toad will lay 2,000 to 5,000 black eggs in jellylike strings, often tangled among vegetation. These eggs hatch within one week. The tadpoles (larval stage of a toad) metamorphose, or change, into an adult stage within 4 to 6 weeks.

Habitat and current distribution

Wyoming toads are found only at one site in the wild: Mortenson Lake National Wildlife Refuge, approximately 20 miles (32 kilometers) from Laramie, Wyoming. All toads at this lake were bred in captivity and released into the lake as tadpoles.

In 2013 biologists (people who study living organisms) found 20 full-grown adult Wyoming toads at Mortenson Lake, 79 young toads, and 408 very young toads. About 500 Wyoming toads are in captivity.

History and conservation measures

The Wyoming toad was discovered in 1946. Despite its narrow range, it seemed to exist in great numbers. In the early 1970s, however, its pop-

The Wyoming toad is nearly extinct in the wild, but it survives in captivity due to conservation programs. © SUZANNE L. & JOSEPH T. COLLINS/SCIENCE SOURCE.

ulation began to decrease drastically, and by the mid-1980s biologists thought it was extinct. The toad was rediscovered at Mortenson Lake in 1987. In 1995 biologists began breeding the toad in captivity and releasing tadpoles into Mortenson Lake, which is part of a national wildlife refuge. Although more than 160,000 tadpoles have been released, very few survive to mature adulthood.

Perhaps the biggest threat facing the Wyoming toad is its small population size, combined with the fact that it lives in only one place in the wild. One catastrophe, whether natural or human-caused, could completely destroy the entire population. Another major threat is an infectious disease caused by a fungus known as *Batrachochytrium dendrobatidis* (*Bd*), which has killed large numbers of amphibians worldwide and is probably responsible for the deaths of most of the Wyoming toads since the captive-breeding program began. The third major threat is that existing regulations do not fully protect this species. Conservationists (people who work to manage and protect nature) believe that for the species to survive, it should be reintroduced into wetlands (areas where there is a lot of water in the soil, such as swamps) along a Wyoming river as well as being reintroduced at Mortenson Lake, but these lands are privately owned. In order to release toads in areas that are held privately, the government will need to purchase the land or receive permission from landowners.

Because so few toads remain in the wild, biologists are focusing on maintaining a healthy captive population. This includes breeding many toads, controlling disease among them, and making sure they are genetically diverse. Biologists are also continuing to study the species' habits in the wild and investigating how to control the *Bd* fungus in other types of amphibians.

Corals

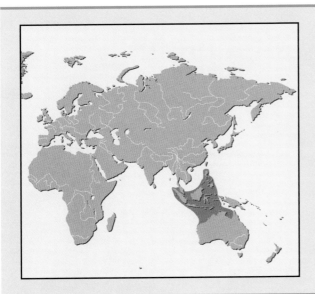

Coral, branching frogspawn
Euphyllia paradivisa

PHYLUM: Cnidaria
CLASS: Anthozoa
ORDER: Scleractinia
FAMILY: Caryophylliidae
STATUS: Vulnerable, IUCN
Threatened, ESA
RANGE: American Samoa, Australia,
Indonesia, Malaysia, Philippines, Samoa,
Singapore, Thailand

Coral, branching frogspawn
Euphyllia paradivisa

Description and biology

Branching frogspawn corals received their name because their tentacles branch out and look like a group of frog eggs, or spawn. Each individual coral, called a polyp, has a very hard, cup-shaped outer shell, the corallite. Out of the corallite grows a cylinder-shaped body, with tentacles at the top. The branching frogspawn coral's tentacles can extend for 6 inches (15 centimeters). They are usually a pale, greenish gray but occasionally they are pink. The tips of the tentacles are shaped like little knobs and are lighter in color. Branching frogspawn coral polyps grow next to each other, attached to hard objects on the ocean floor. The polyps themselves form a branching shape.

Like other reef corals, the branching frogspawn coral has algae called zooxanthellae (zoh-uh-zan-THEH-lee) living within its tissues. Both coral and algae benefit from this arrangement. The coral protects the algae and provides waste products that the algae use for photosynthesis

This coral got its name because of its tentacles, which branch out and look like a group of frog eggs, or spawn. © BLICKWIN-KEL/ALAMY.

(the process of converting energy from the sun into chemical energy, in sugar form). The coral benefits because it feeds on the sugars the algae produce through photosynthesis. Zooxanthellae also give the coral its color. The coral's tentacles also shelter some shrimp species, which do not harm the coral.

Scientists do not know how this species of coral reproduces. Some similar species have female colonies, which release bundles containing eggs, and male colonies, which release clouds of sperm. The egg bundles break open in the water and are fertilized by the sperm. In another similar species, male corals release sperm cells, and female coral polyps take in these sperm cells, fertilize them internally, and release coral larvae into the water. With either type of reproduction, the larvae float in the water until finding a hard surface on the reef, where they attach.

The life span of the branching frogspawn coral is unknown.

Did You Know?

Corals are animals, defined as living organisms that do not make their own food. Each individual coral, called a polyp, is a soft-bodied creature usually no bigger than the width of a matchstick. Its body consists of a mouth, tentacles around the mouth that sting and capture food, and a digestive tract. Polyps make a hard outer skeleton of calcium carbonate that attaches to rocks or to other polyp skeletons on the ocean floor. Together, thousands of these skeletons form coral reefs. The world's largest coral reef, Australia's Great Barrier Reef, covers about 134,350 square miles (348,000 square kilometers).

As a group, corals that form reefs are approaching extinction rapidly. Climate change is considered to be the main reason. Very small increases in water temperature, due to global warming, cause corals to become stressed and much more fragile.

Another climate change–related problem, ocean acidification, occurs because the ocean absorbs much of the carbon dioxide (CO_2) in the air. As the level of carbon dioxide rises, the ocean becomes more acidic. This makes it more difficult for corals to grow their hard skeletons.

Habitat and current distribution

This coral occurs in a region along the equator where the western Pacific and eastern Indian Oceans meet. This area, called the Coral Triangle, houses half of the world's coral reefs and 75 percent of its coral species. Branching frogspawn coral colonies occur on reefs in areas protected from waves, at depths of 6.5 to 82 feet (2 to 25 meters).

This coral is rare, although scientists estimate there are tens of millions of colonies of the species.

History and conservation measures

Corals of the genus (a group with similar characteristics) *Euphyllia* date from the Eocene epoch (56 million to 33.9 million years ago) in the Indo-Pacific. The branching frogspawn coral was first identified as a separate species in 1990. Popular in aquariums because of its attractive appearance, it can be grown in the ocean especially for aquarium use. However, it is also taken directly from the ocean instead of being grown only to sell. International trade in this species is restricted but not forbidden. Because the branching frogspawn coral species is naturally rare, its biggest threat is over-collection for the aquarium trade.

Euphyllia corals are also at risk because of climate change. Scientists have predicted that the Coral Triangle region will suffer the worst impact of any region from climate change during the 21st century. When ocean temperatures become warmer than the corals' preferred temperature, the corals expel the algae that provide most of their nutrients as well as the corals' color—an occurrence known as coral bleaching. Some *Euphyllia* corals in the region have already become bleached because of higher ocean temperatures. Another threat to corals is that the chemistry of the oceans' water is changing. The change is happening because the ocean absorbs one-quarter of the carbon dioxide (CO_2) that is released into the air from humans' extensive use of fossil fuels, such as oil, natural gas, and coal. So as the air's carbon dioxide levels increase, the levels in the ocean increase too. This increased carbon dioxide content makes ocean water more acidic, which harms corals as well as other sea life.

In 2012 the U.S. Fish and Wildlife Service (USFWS) proposed listing the branching frogspawn coral as endangered under the U.S. Endangered Species Act. After heavy opposition from the aquarium industry, however, the USFWS listed the species with the less protected status of threatened.

The countries in the Coral Triangle made an agreement in 2009 to protect the ocean ecosystem (an ecological system including all of its living things and their environment) in their areas and conserve the species living there. This agreement includes efforts to adapt to climate change.

Coral, elkhorn
Acropora palmata

PHYLUM: Cnidaria
CLASS: Anthozoa
ORDER: Scleractinia
FAMILY: Acroporidae
STATUS: Critically endangered, IUCN
Threatened, ESA
RANGE: Bahamas, Caribbean, Gulf of
Mexico, USA (Florida)

Coral, elkhorn
Acropora palmata

Description and biology

Elkhorn coral is one of the most important corals in the Caribbean. This species grows in colonies that look like elk antlers, giving the coral its name. Each sturdy, yellowish-brown branch can measure up to 20 inches (50 centimeters) across. Colonies of branches become at least 6.5 feet (2 meters) in height and 13 feet (4 meters) wide. Together, these colonies form dense thickets housing colorful fish and other marine animals.

In the soft tissues of each tiny coral polyp live a type of algae called zooxanthellae (zoh-uh-zan-THEH-lee). The coral and algae benefit each other. The coral protects the zooxanthellae and the algae use the coral's waste products for photosynthesis, the process whereby algae and plants convert sunlight into energy. In turn, this photosynthesis produces

Did You Know?

Corals are probably the best-known foundation species, which are species that provide critical shelter and habitat for other plant and animal life. Corals live on marine seabeds and secrete calcium carbonate to protect their soft bodies. The calcium carbonate hardens into hard structures, or coral reefs.

Coral reefs become home to, and protection for, numerous species, such as crabs, shrimp, oysters, clams, fungi, starfish (also known as sea stars), sea urchins, anemones, jellyfish, turtles, and snails. Reefs also protect coastlines and the species that live along them from storms and floods. When coral is threatened, all the species that live on coral reefs are also threatened. Protecting a foundation species also means protecting an entire ecosystem (an ecological system including all of its living things and their environment).

carbohydrates that provide most of the coral's food. Elkhorn corals also capture and eat small organisms, such as plankton.

Elkhorn coral reproduces both asexually and sexually. In asexual reproduction, the species' most common method, branches break away from a colony and reattach on the ocean floor elsewhere. Sexual reproduction occurs once a year in August or September. The coral colony releases both sperm and eggs into the water. The sperm and eggs join together, making larvae that attach to the ocean floor several days later.

Elkhorn colonies grow at a rate of 2 to 4 inches (5 to 10 centimeters) a year and reach maximum size at 10 to 12 years. The life span of each individual polyp is not known.

Habitat and current distribution

The elkhorn coral occurs on reefs in southern Florida, the Gulf of Mexico, and throughout the Caribbean, extending south to Venezuela. It is found in shallow waters where there are waves, at an average depth of 11.5 feet (3.5 meters). Its preferred water temperature is 70 to 84°F (21 to 29°C). Scientists have not estimated the total population of this coral.

History and conservation measures

This coral species originated sometime between 33 million and 55 million years ago. Elkhorn coral had been the most common species of coral in the Caribbean. Then, in the 1970s and 1980s, its colonies began suffering from white band disease, an illness that produces a strip of dead, white tissue that moves from the coral's base up to its tips. Up to 98 percent of elkhorn coral had died by 2005, and since then a similar disease, white pox, has killed 50 percent of the remaining populations studied by scientists.

A major threat to elkhorn coral is increased water temperatures caused by climate change. © JOHN A. ANDERSON/SHUTTERSTOCK .COM.

The other major threat to elkhorn coral is increased water temperature caused by climate change. The ocean temperature has risen by 1.3°F (0.7°C) since the early 20th century, and scientists fear it could rise as much as 8.6°F (4.8°C) by 2100. When water temperatures exceed corals' preferred temperatures, they become stressed and expel their zooxanthellae. Without these algae, they become white, or bleached, and are at much higher risk of death.

The elkhorn coral was listed as threatened under the U.S. Endangered Species Act in 2006 and as critically endangered by the International Union for Conservation of Nature and Natural Resources (IUCN) in 2008. Although the U.S. National Marine Fisheries Service proposed in 2012 that the species be reclassified as endangered, a more serious listing, it determined in 2014 that it would remain listed as threatened.

To save this important coral, scientists are studying the diseases affecting it and developing strategies to combat these diseases. As the emission of carbon dioxide into the atmosphere has been identified as one of the major triggers for climate change, another top priority for scientists is to advocate for national and international policies to decrease these emissions. They also plan to supplement the existing elkhorn coral population by cultivating the species in underwater nurseries and then planting them in the ocean.

Fish

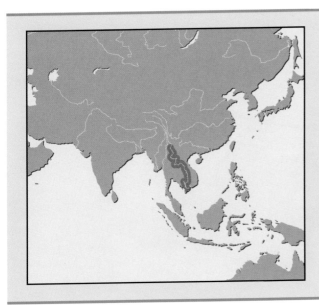

Catfish, giant
Pangasius gigas (also *Pangasianodon gigas*)

PHYLUM: Chordata
CLASS: Actinopterygii
ORDER: Siluriformes
FAMILY: Pangasiidae
STATUS: Critically endangered, IUCN
Endangered, ESA
RANGE: Cambodia, Laos, Thailand,
Vietnam

Catfish, giant
Pangasius gigas (also *Pangasianodon gigas*)

Description and biology

The giant catfish, often called the Mekong or Thailand giant catfish, is one of the largest freshwater fish in the world. This light gray to off-white fish can grow to almost 10 feet (3 meters) long and weigh up to 660 pounds (300 kilograms). The fish has smooth skin. Young giant catfish have barbels (slender feelers extending from the head near the mouth) that disappear when the fish becomes an adult. Adult giant catfish lack teeth. They live in deep waters in large rivers, feeding on algae from stones in the riverbed.

The giant catfish migrates up and down the Mekong River and rivers connected to it in Southeast Asia. Biologists (people who study living organisms) know little about the species' life cycle or migration patterns. Some adult fish move from the Mekong into and then out of a connected lake at the end of November, swimming upstream. They spawn (lay eggs) in northern Thailand and in Laos in June. Spawning adults

The giant catfish is native to the basin of the Mekong River in Southeast Asia. © LEONID SEREBRENNIKOV/ALAMY.

average 6 to 8 years of age and weigh 330 to 550 pounds (150 to 250 kilograms). The giant catfish can live for more than 60 years.

Habitat and current distribution

The giant catfish is found in the Mekong River, rivers that flow into the Mekong, and lakes connected to these rivers in Thailand, Laos, and Cambodia. It is very rare in Vietnam. The population size in the wild is estimated to be only a few hundred.

History and conservation measures

The giant catfish was fished for food for centuries. In the late 1880s thousands were being caught each year. This level dropped to hundreds by the 1930s, dozens in the 1990s, and fewer than 10 since 2000. Biologists say that the total population of the fish has decreased by at least

95 percent since the early 20th century. The International Union for Conservation of Nature and Natural Resources (IUCN) listed the species as critically endangered in 2003.

Overfishing caused the original huge decline. Now, fishing for wild-caught giant catfish is banned. Since the 1990s the biggest threat to this enormous fish has been human-caused changes to the Mekong River, particularly the construction of dams along the river to supply hydroelectricity and water to growing communities and farms. These dams alter the flow of the Mekong, change the river's sediment (dirt and rocks settling on the river's bottom), and prevent the catfish from migrating upstream to spawning areas. Conservationists (people who work to manage and protect nature) believe that one planned dam could cause the species to go extinct because it may block the fish's migration entirely. People also affect the river by using dynamite to dredge shallow areas in order to improve conditions for boats.

The Thai government has been breeding and raising giant catfish since the 1980s. These fish thrive when released into lakes and reservoirs, and it is legal to fish for the species there on a limited basis. They do not breed in the lakes, however, and captive-bred fish do not survive when released into the Mekong River.

Conservation groups have three goals: to maintain the wild population and expand its range, to preserve the fish's habitat, and to keep a genetically diverse population in captivity. Government and nonprofit groups study and monitor the fish. Conservationists say that governments need to make sure fishers do not catch the species intentionally. Keeping migrating giant catfish safe is urgent, but it will be difficult because it may not be possible to build dams that are safe for them. Still, conservationists say it is possible to save the fish because it is still found along the length of the Mekong River, still spawns, and is still genetically diverse.

Did You Know?

The traditional Thai New Year's celebration, called Songkran, begins April 13. From this time until the end of May, farmers in the northern regions of Thailand used to undertake an ancient ritual. They left their fields and went to the banks of the Mekong River. They took to the waters in long wooden boats and, armed with large nets, sought to catch giant catfish.

Mekong villagers in these northern areas consider the catfish sacred. Before the fishing could begin, rituals would be performed. In ancient times, pig or chicken sacrifices were offered to the Spirit of the Water and the Spirit of the Fish. Boats, nets, and fishers were all blessed. Celebrations with food, drink, music, and dancing often lasted more than three weeks. Now that the giant catfish population has nearly disappeared from the Mekong River, these celebrations have changed. Although they still include plenty of feasting, the festivities now have a beauty contest and boat races on the river.

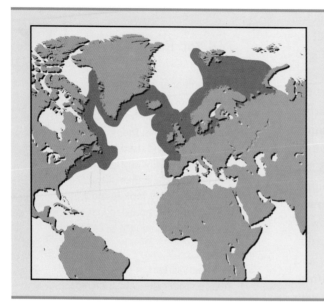

Cod, Atlantic
Gadus morhua

PHYLUM: Chordata
CLASS: Actinopterygii
ORDER: Gadiformes
FAMILY: Gadidae
STATUS: Vulnerable, IUCN
RANGE: Atlantic Ocean (northeast, northwest)

Cod, Atlantic
Gadus morhua

Description and biology

The Atlantic cod (sometimes called the North Sea cod) has been one of the world's major food fishes for centuries and is especially popular among people in Europe and the Americas. Tens of thousands of tons of this fish are caught every year, and thousands of people earn their living in the cod market. Atlantic cod are large fish: an average adult is over 4 feet (1.2 meters) long and weighs about 60 pounds (27 kilograms). Exceptionally large cod have been known to grow to about 6 feet (1.8 meters) and 210 pounds (95 kilograms). The Atlantic cod ranges from a dark greenish-gray to orange-brown in color. The upper body has spots across it, and there is a white line running from side to side. The fish has a stout body, a large head, and a long barbel (slender feeler) on its chin. Its fins—three dorsal (rear) fins and two anal fins—are all rounded in shape. Its belly is white.

The Atlantic cod is omnivorous (eats animals and plants). It generally feeds at dawn and at dusk. Young cod feed at the bottom of the

Did You Know?

Since the late 1980s, many ocean fish populations have seriously declined. Besides Atlantic cod, other species threatened by overfishing include orange roughy, Chilean sea bass, bluefin tuna, and several species of sharks. The populations are threatened by loss of habitat, pollution, and fishing practices that are not sustainable—that is, they allow fishers to take so many fish that the remaining population is unable to reproduce fast enough to make up for the ones taken.

Although the prospects for many of the endangered fish have seemed bleak, there is at least one case in which government-enforced fishing restrictions have successfully corrected the problem. The swordfish (*Xiphias gladius*) population in the North Atlantic has experienced a dramatic recovery. In 1999 it was determined that the population had dropped to one-third of what it would have been without fishing. To continue existing fishing practices meant certain extinction for the species. A plan was enacted that limited fishing quotas to 11,025 tons (10,000 metric tons) per year. In addition, the United States closed 132,670 square miles (343,610 square kilometers) of swordfish habitat in the Atlantic to longline fishing, in which the fishing line can be a couple of miles long and has baited hooks placed at intervals along its length. Within just three years, the swordfish population rose to about 94 percent of the number that scientists believed would ensure the survival of the species if controls on commercial fishing were kept in place. As of 2012, swordfish numbers in the North Atlantic were continuing to grow, and the number of swordfish caught was being kept at a sustainable level. Not all recovery plans for fish species have been so successful.

ocean floor on small crustaceans (shellfish), such as shrimp or amphipods. Adults eat a great variety of mollusks, crabs, lobsters, and fish. Although cod do not form large schools for traveling, they do form small groups when they are hunting for food.

Cod travel long distances to their spawning grounds (the places where they lay their eggs) each year. Spawning generally takes place in the winter. The older a female cod becomes, the more eggs she will produce—a younger female may produce three million eggs, while an older female may produce nine million eggs, in a season. Cod reach sexual maturity between the ages of 2 and 4, and they may live to be about 20 years old.

Habitat and current distribution

Cod live in a variety of habitats near the shore and in the ocean depths. They are called groundfish because they stay near the bottom of the ocean much of the time. During the day, large schools of cod swim between 100 and 260 feet (30 and 80 meters) from the bottom. Most of the time, cod are found at depths between 500 and 650 feet (150 and 200 meters). They prefer cool waters of about 23°F (–5°C) but can be found in waters at a wide range of temperatures up to 68°F (20°C).

Atlantic cod occur on both sides of the North Atlantic Ocean. In the western North Atlantic, they occur from Greenland in the north down to North Carolina in the south. In the eastern North Atlantic, they occur from Iceland in the north down to the Norwegian Sea, to the Barents Sea and Spitsbergen (both north of Norway), and southward to the Baltic Sea and Bay of Biscay (on the west coast of France). The species is widespread all around the coasts of Britain and Ireland. In the waters off the United States, cod are managed as two commercial and recreational stocks: the Gulf of Maine and the Georges Bank (off the coast of Massachusetts) stocks.

The Atlantic cod is omnivorous—it eats both animals and plants. © HANS LEIJNSE/NIS/MINDEN PICTURES/CORBIS.

History and conservation measures

For centuries, abundant cod populations provided tons of food as well as reliable employment in cod fishery to thousands of fishers in Europe, Greenland, Canada (particularly Newfoundland), and the United States. Then, in the late 1980s, the cod fishery in most of the western Atlantic collapsed as a result of overfishing. The Atlantic cod population was in such decline that by 1992 moratoriums (enforced prohibitions) on cod fishing were in place throughout the northwestern part of the species' range. Even with the moratoriums, the stock in many places of the western sector has never recovered. The cod in the areas around Greenland and Newfoundland experienced a 97 percent decline in population. Protected areas for cod and their vulnerable habitat were created off the coast of New England. But Canada's once-thriving cod industry collapsed, and in April 2003 the Canadian government listed the Atlantic cod as an endangered species. A decline in the northeastern Atlantic cod population occurred later, with the fishing industry in Europe beginning to collapse by the early years of the 21st century. In 2001 the stock was at such a low point that a large part of the North Sea was closed to cod fishing.

Overfishing was responsible for the huge decline in the cod population, but the failure to recover stems from other very serious problems. Destruction of ocean habitat is one area of concern. A fishing technique known as bottom trawling, in which fishers scour the ocean floor for fish, removes the cod's food sources and also eliminates places for young cod to hide along the ocean floor, so that they become easy prey for other fish. Pollution and climate changes are also likely affecting the fish's comeback. Some species of seals, which are natural predators of the cod, are being blamed for the cod population's failure to recover.

Scientists do not understand what is causing some of the deaths and illnesses among cod. Many fish appear to be starving to death; they are found in very frail condition with lean bodies. Others appear to have developed a different body shape, perhaps to adapt to difficult conditions. In April 2003 hundreds of tons of Atlantic cod froze to death in the seas off eastern Newfoundland, and the incident remains unexplained. Scientists have also noted a mysterious lack of older fish in the cod population.

Since Canada imposed a moratorium on cod fishing in 1992, some populations of cod have begun to recover, whereas others continue to decline. There are numerous recovery plans in the United States, although in 2015 groups that represent fishers were successful in having the cod's protected habitat in New England scaled back. Recovery plans are in place in other countries as well. In May 2003 the European Commission met to launch a revised recovery plan for cod. (Europe had already limited fishing in a temporary emergency plan.) The cod catch in the seas off Europe was to be strictly controlled for a period of 10 years, with quotas set so that each year there would be 30 percent more adult cod than the year before. Late in 2010, however, the European Commission reported that the stock of cod continued to decline in key areas of the Atlantic Ocean. The commission ran into difficulty in reducing the quota amounts because fishers in some countries argued that the restrictions on fishing endangered their jobs.

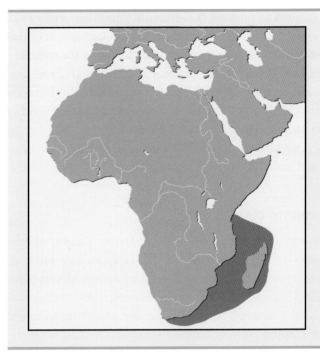

Coelacanth
Latimeria chalumnae

PHYLUM: Chordata
CLASS: Sarcopterygii
ORDER: Coelacanthiformes
FAMILY: Coelacanthidae
STATUS: Critically endangered, IUCN
RANGE: Comoros, Kenya, Madagascar, Mozambique, South Africa, Tanzania

Coelacanth
Latimeria chalumnae

Description and biology

Biologists (people who study living organisms) call the coelacanth (pronounced SEE-luh-canth) a "living fossil." This fish is the only living member of an order that was abundant 80 million to 370 million years ago. A stocky fish, it is brown to steel blue in color. It has large, rough scales and muscular lobes at the base of its fins. The coelacanth grows to a length of 5 feet (1.5 meters) and can weigh up to 150 pounds (68 kilograms). It is a passive drift feeder; when it eats, it moves slowly and feeds on floating lantern fish, cuttlefish, other reef fish, squids, and octopuses. The coelacanth has a hinged joint in its skull that allows it to open its mouth wide to eat the larger fish it finds.

Like its relative the lungfish, the coelacanth can sense electric fields through an electroreceptive organ in its snout. When it encounters an electric field, it assumes an unusual "headstanding" position: it tilts so its head points downward and its tail points upward. Biologists believe this might be a technique the fish uses to detect prey hiding in the seabed.

A female coelacanth does not lay eggs but gives birth to fully formed young after a gestation (pregnancy) period of over 12 months. Between 5 and 26 offspring are born at a time, each measuring about 15 inches (38 centimeters) long at birth. Young coelacanths most likely live in caves and hunt at night. The fish reach sexual maturity at about 12 to 15 years of age and may live up to 80 years.

Habitat and current distribution

Coelacanths have been found in the western Indian Ocean, off the coasts of Kenya, Tanzania, South Africa, Madagascar, Mozambique, and the Comoros (a group of islands between northeastern Mozambique and northwestern Madagascar). The greatest concentration of these fish seems to be around Comoros, especially near the western coast of the island of Grande Comore.

Biologists have found it difficult to determine the exact number of coelacanths currently in existence. They estimate the total population around the Comoros to be between 300 and 400 individuals. Surveys have confirmed the presence of coelacanths along the South African and

The coelacanth, considered a "living fossil" because its features are similar to those of prehistoric fish, is threatened by deepwater fishing in its ocean habitat. © ALESSANDRO-ZOCC/SHUTTERSTOCK.COM.

Tanzanian coasts as well, although in far smaller numbers. No surveys have been carried out along the coasts of the other countries where the fish is believed to occur, but occasional specimens have been accidentally caught by fishers.

Coelacanths inhabit volcanic-rock caves and steep, rocky drop-offs at depths between 500 and 800 feet (150 and 240 meters). Some of these fish have been recorded at depths of almost 2,300 feet (700 meters). They congregate in caves during the day and emerge at night to hunt for food. A single coelacanth may cover a stretch of coastline over 5 miles (8 kilometers) in length in one night.

History and conservation measures

In 1938 an unusual fish was caught by fishers off the eastern coast of South Africa. James L. B. Smith, a British amateur ichthyologist (a scientist who studies fish), identified it as a coelacanth. This was surprising, as scientists had thought this fish had been extinct for 70 million years. In 1952 biologists found coelacanths living and breeding off the coast of the Comoros. A second species of coelacanth (*Latimeria menadoensis*) was also discovered off the coast of Indonesia in 1997, and scientists suggest that the two species have been separated for at least several million years.

Word of these discoveries soon spread. Museums and private collectors have sought the elusive fish, paying high prices for their capture. In 1989 the fish was listed on Appendix I of the Convention on International Trade in Endangered Species of Wild Fauna and Flora (CITES; an international treaty to protect wildlife). This banned the trade of the fish between nations that had signed the treaty. As of the mid-2010s, the main threats to the coelacanth include habitat loss and bycatch (accidental catches of this fish when fishing for other species), but these threats are not considered to be severe.

The Coelacanth Conservation Council, established in 1987 in Moroni, Grande Comore, promotes public education programs, coordinates research, and organizes protection efforts for the endangered coelacanth. In 2002 South Africa also instituted a program that coordinates research on the species. In addition, a marine park was created in Tanzania, and the Mohéli Marine Park in the Comoros has been attempting to halt destructive fishing and conserve marine habitats.

Eel, American
Anguilla rostrata

PHYLUM: Chordata
CLASS: Actinopterygii
ORDER: Anguilliformes
FAMILY: Anguillidae
STATUS: Endangered, IUCN
RANGE: Caribbean, Colombia, eastern North America, Greenland, Gulf of Mexico, Venezuela

Eel, American
Anguilla rostrata

Description and biology

The adult American eel is a slender fish that grows up to 5 feet (1.5 meters) long and weighs as much as 16.5 pounds (7.5 kilograms). It is greenish brown, fading to yellowish on its underside, and its long body gives it a snakelike appearance. Adult American eels are sometimes referred to as yellow eels.

The American eel is catadromous (pronounced cuh-TAH-druh-muhs), which means that it spends its life in freshwater but goes to saltwater to spawn (lay eggs). In fact, this species has a very complicated life cycle. The eels hatch in the Sargasso Sea, a massive span of warm water in the North Atlantic off the coast of the United States. Once the eggs hatch, the larvae are in the leptocephalus (pronounced lep-tuh-SEH-fuh-luhs) stage.

Did You Know?

The American eel and other eel species are seriously threatened by dams, which prevent them from traveling upstream to suitable habitat. To try to conserve eels, many dams have installed eel ladders, which help eels get around or over the dam.

Hydroelectric dams on the St. Lawrence River, for example, are fitted with a series of chutes that are installed to zigzag, allowing eels to more easily climb the steep dam in stages. Alternate designs that are being tested on the Hudson River involve tubes filled with netting, which end in a holding bucket. Volunteers count the numbers of eels in the bucket and then release the eels upstream.

Eel ladders can help eels get upstream, but when the eels come back downstream, they are often caught in and killed by the dams' turbines. Ladders can help preserve some eels, but other conservation efforts are also necessary to preserve dwindling eel populations.

American eel leptocephali (which means "slender heads") are leaf shaped, flat, and transparent. They swim and drift with the Gulf Stream (a warm ocean current that flows northeast along the coast of North America) until they reach northern coastal waters. Along the way they grow through two more stages, during which they are referred to as glass eels and elvers. They continue to grow and reach their adult form in freshwater creeks, rivers, and river-fed lakes and ponds, although some stay in coastal lagoons and estuaries (coastal waters where a freshwater river empties into a saltwater sea or ocean). Then, after 10 to 20 years, they swim thousands of miles back to the Sargasso Sea, where they spawn and then die.

Habitat and current distribution

The American eel's complicated life cycle and extensive migration means that it lives in widely varied habitats and locations at different points in its life cycle. It is found throughout the western Atlantic, from Greenland and Canada to Florida and the Yucatán Peninsula, the Caribbean, Central America, and the northern part of South America, as well as throughout the eastern United States, including the Great Lakes, the Mississippi River, and other waterways. It is believed that all eels in this range return to the Sargasso Sea to spawn.

Eels were once extremely common. In Lake Ontario in the 1800s, naturalists (people who observe nature to find its laws) reported "hundreds of wagonloads" of eels near Niagara Falls. Their numbers declined steeply starting in the late 20th century. For example, the largest average yearly eel catch in Florida peaked in the late 1970s at around 235 tons (213 metric tons). In the 1980s there were more than a million eels per year making the climb up the eel ladders of the Moses-Saunders Power Dam on the St. Lawrence River between New York and Ontario. This number had dropped to about 4,000 by the late 1990s and then to close to zero by 2001. In 2004 the numbers began increasing again.

History and conservation measures

American eels were widely fished for food by native peoples in the Americas. They continue to be commercially fished today. Although they are not much consumed in North America anymore, large numbers are ex-

The American eel, found in freshwater and coastal water from Greenland to South America, faces changes in its habitat due to development and climate change as well as threats from the turbines operated by hydroelectric dams. © OLIVER LUCANUS/NIS/MINDEN PICTURES/CORBIS.

ported to Asia and Europe, where they are popular as food and often farmed. Glass eels are also fished for use as bait for striped bass. Eel skin is also a popular material for making wallets and other leather products.

The American eel faces pressure from overfishing and from parasites and pollution. The largest threat to the species, however, appears to be the damming of rivers and the resulting destruction of habitat. Dams can prevent eels from migrating upstream to find suitable habitat, and eels are often killed when passing downstream through the turbines of hydroelectric dams (which create electricity from water power).

In an effort to conserve the eels, Canada has placed upper limits on eel harvests, although the population has declined so quickly that these harvest limits have never been reached. The United States denied the American eel protection under the Endangered Species Act in 2007 but began reconsidering the species' classification in 2011.

Pupfish, desert
Cyprinodon macularius

PHYLUM: Chordata
CLASS: Actinopterygii
ORDER: Cyprinodontiformes
FAMILY: Cyprinodontidae
STATUS: Vulnerable, IUCN
Endangered, ESA
RANGE: Mexico, USA (Arizona and California)

Pupfish, desert
Cyprinodon macularius

Description and biology

The desert pupfish is one of at least 35 species and subspecies of pupfish. Most are threatened with extinction. The desert pupfish is small, ranging in size from 0.8 inches (2 centimeters) to 3 inches (7.6 centimeters) long. It is mainly silver in color with six to nine dark bands on its sides. This pupfish has a short, scaled head with an upturned mouth.

The desert pupfish feeds primarily on brown and green algae. It becomes dormant during cold winter months, burrowing in mud at the bottom of its water habitat. When the weather and the water warms, the fish is active again and begins to mate. Breeding males turn iridescent blue in color and fight each other over the right to mate with receptive females. After having mated, females begin spawning (laying eggs) at the end of February. The males protect the eggs until they hatch three days later. Spawning continues throughout the summer.

The desert pupfish, native to the southwestern United States and Mexico, has seen its habitat severely limited by industrial and agricultural development as well as the introduction of nonnative species. © TOM MCHUGH/SCIENCE SOURCE.

The average life span of a desert pupfish is six to nine months, although some survive more than one year. Many die when intense summer heat dries up their streams and pools.

Habitat and current distribution

The desert pupfish inhabits the shallow waters of desert pools, marshes, streams, and springs below 5,200 feet (1,585 meters) in elevation. It can tolerate very warm and very salty waters. There are only 11 known populations of the fish in the wild: 5 in California, 5 in Mexico, and 1 in Arizona. Biologists (people who study living organisms) have no estimates of the desert pupfish's total population. However, as of 2010, more than one million desert pupfish had been relocated from breeding ponds to natural habitats.

History and conservation measures

The desert pupfish was once common in the Sonoran and Mojave Deserts of Southern California, southern Arizona, and northwestern Mexico. The desert pupfish population has declined because human populations have increased in its range, turning desert areas into communities. As a result, the fish's water habitat has become polluted or has been drained.

The pupfish has also been threatened by introduced predators and competitors such as mosquito fish, crayfish, bullfrogs, and snails.

The U.S. Fish and Wildlife Service (USFWS) adopted a species recovery plan in 1993 and conducted a review of progress made in 2010. According to the USFWS, populations of the desert pupfish have remained relatively stable. However, introduced predators and competitors and the human demands for water continue to threaten the species. The USFWS continues to study and monitor the fish. It also manages programs to breed the desert pupfish in captivity for reintroduction.

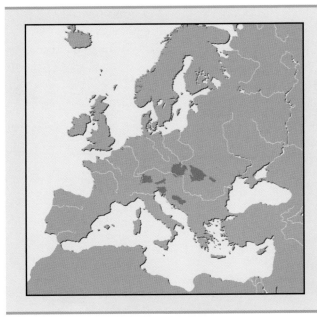

Salmon, Danube
Hucho hucho

PHYLUM: Chordata
CLASS: Actinopterygii
ORDER: Salmoniformes
FAMILY: Salmonidae
STATUS: Endangered, IUCN
RANGE: Austria, Bosnia and Herzegovina, Croatia, Czech Republic, Germany, Hungary, Montenegro, Poland, Romania, Serbia, Slovakia, Slovenia, Ukraine

Salmon, Danube
Hucho hucho

Description and biology

The Danube salmon, also known as the huchen, is the largest member of the salmon family. It can grow to almost 6 feet (1.8 meters) long and weigh 155 pounds (70 kilograms). It has a slender, cigar-shaped body. Its broad mouth contains a dense arrangement of teeth. This fish is highly predatory, feeding on fish, amphibians, reptiles, waterfowl (waterbirds), and small mammals.

Male Danube salmons become sexually mature at the age of four; females become sexually mature a year later. In the spring, the fish make short migrations upstream, where the females spawn (lay eggs) on the gravel bottoms of mountain rivers at temperatures between 42.8°F and 50°F (6°C and 10°C). After hatching, the young salmons develop very fast. After one year, they measure about 5 inches (12.7 centimeters) in length; by the end of their second year they have grown to almost 12 inches (30.5 centimeters) in length.

The Danube salmon, found in central and eastern Europe, is at risk from the effects of hydroelectric dams on its river habitat.
© BLICKWINKEL/ALAMY.

Habitat and current distribution

The Danube salmon was common in almost all rivers of the Danube watershed (the entire region drained by the Danube River) in central and eastern Europe. As of 2014, it could be found only in fragmented (broken into smaller areas that no longer border each other) populations in about 33 percent of its former habitat range. Breeding populations are known to exist in Bosnia and Herzegovina, Croatia, Germany, Montenegro, Poland, Serbia, and Slovenia. However, most of the Danube salmon's populations do not reproduce naturally; they depend on programs that breed and hatch the fish to restock the waterways. The Danube salmon has been introduced to waters outside of its original range in Belgium, France, northern Germany, Morocco, Spain, Sweden, and North America, though these populations probably only survive through restocking of captive-bred fish.

Danube salmons prefer cold, freshwater streams rich in oxygen and containing both rapid sections and deep pools lined with pebbles.

History and conservation measures

The greatest threat to the Danube salmon is the destruction of its habitat. Throughout the species' range, dams and canals have been built, preventing the fish from swimming to spawning grounds. Its habitat has been poisoned in many areas because sewage and industrial wastes have been pumped into rivers and streams. In addition, the runoff (water that drains away, bringing substances with it) of pesticides from nearby farms has also poisoned many waterways. To help save the Danube salmon from extinction, conservationists (people who work to manage and protect nature) urge that sewage dumping and pesticide use be controlled throughout the fish's range. They also consider the proposed construction of new hydroelectric power plants to be a great threat to the survival of the Danube salmon, particularly in eastern Europe. Hydroelectric power plants require dams and change the natural river environment both upstream and downstream.

Overfishing is a secondary threat to this salmon. Even though the Danube salmon cannot be taken without a permit and the fishing season has been shortened, its numbers continue to decline. Global climate change is also a potential threat to the species. Danube salmon populations may be seriously harmed by increases to river water temperatures and changes in water flow rates related to global warming.

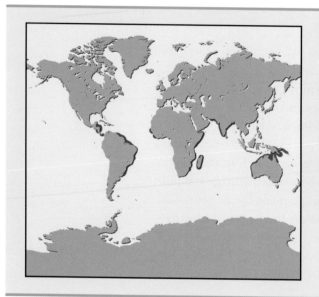

Sawfish, largetooth
Pristis pristis

PHYLUM: Chordata
CLASS: Chondrichthyes
ORDER: Pristiformes
FAMILY: Pristidae
STATUS: Critically endangered, IUCN Endangered, ESA
RANGE: Australia, Bangladesh, Belize, Brazil, Colombia, French Guiana, Guinea-Bissau, Guyana, Honduras, India, Madagascar, Mozambique, Nicaragua, Pakistan, Panama, Papua New Guinea, Sierra Leone, Somalia, Suriname

Sawfish, largetooth
Pristis pristis

Description and biology

Sawfish are large rays (flat, shark-related fish that live along the ocean floor) with long, flat, tooth-studded snouts resembling saws. The snout, usually between one-quarter and one-fifth of the sawfish's total length, is edged with 14 to 22 specially developed scales that look and act like teeth. The sawfish uses its snout like a sword to slash at and kill or stun prey (usually small fish), to fend off enemies, and to forage (search for food) in the seabed or river bottom for crabs or clams.

An adult largetooth sawfish measures from about 9.8 to 23 feet (3 to 7 meters) in length and can weigh over 1,325 pounds (600 kilograms). It looks like a flattened shark except for its distinctive saw-shaped snout. The fish is dark yellow to gray in color, with a white or cream-colored underside. Sawfish have wide, triangular pectoral (front) fins and tall, pointed dorsal (back) fins. Openings behind their eyes, called spiracles, are used to breath by inhaling water, from which they get oxygen. Their

The largetooth sawfish, with its distinctive bladelike snout, is prone to getting tangled in fishing nets. COURTESY OF SIMON FRASER UNIVERSITY.

eyesight is good, but in the dark water at the bottom of rivers they use other senses as well. For example, their snouts are so sensitive that sawfish can actually feel the heartbeat of their prey in the water.

Sawfish are believed to mate every other year. They produce baby fish, rather than laying eggs as most other fish do. The female produces anywhere from 1 to 12 young at a time. Sawfish pups are around 2.5 feet (0.76 meters) long at birth. They are born with a protective covering over their saws, probably to prevent injury to the mother during birth. Their saws harden quickly, however, and the covering dissolves. They can begin to hunt small prey soon after birth. The largetooth sawfish reaches maturity at about 10 years of age and lives about 25 to 30 years.

Habitat and current distribution

The largetooth sawfish can move between freshwater and saltwater. It spends most of its time lying on the muddy bottoms of areas with brackish (mixture of freshwater and saltwater) water, such as bays or the mouths of rivers.

In the early 21st century, largetooth sawfish populations were located in the eastern Atlantic, western Atlantic, eastern Pacific, and Indo-West Pacific regions. In the eastern Atlantic, since 2000 the species has only been seen in the West African countries of Sierra Leone and Guinea-Bissau. In the western Atlantic region, they are found in freshwaters in Central and South America. In the eastern Pacific, the fish appears in Colombia, Nicaragua, and Panama. The Indo-Pacific region has few, if any sawfish left, except in Australia, which has the largest population in the world. Overall, the total number of largetooth sawfish is unknown.

History and conservation measures

Until 2013 biologists (people who study living organisms) divided the largetooth sawfishes into three distinct species: *Pristis perotteti*, *Pristis microdon*, and *Pristis pristis*. After 2013 they recognized all three as the same species: *Pristis pristis*.

The largetooth sawfish became critically endangered because of overfishing. People used the fins for soup, the snouts for souvenirs, the skins for leather, and other parts of the fish for traditional medicine (health practices used by specific cultures since before the time of modern medicine). Although international trade in this species is now banned, many countries do not enforce this law effectively. Perhaps the most severe threat to this species is accidental. They often get caught by mistake in fishing nets intended for catching other species of fish. The sawfish's snout can become hopelessly entangled in such nets.

Loss and disruption of habitat affects the largetooth sawfish as well. The animal is also threatened by development of farms and towns near waters where the fish live, altering the size or course of rivers, boating, and other human-caused changes to the water.

Australia has extensive protections for the largetooth sawfish. For instance, fisheries that catch sawfish must release them and report the catch. To save this species, conservationists (people who work to manage and protect nature) believe that governments in other countries need to honor the ban on international trade in largetooth sawfish, make and enforce their own regulations, and educate people about this now-rare species.

Sculpin, pygmy
Cottus paulus

PHYLUM: Chordata
CLASS: Actinopterygii
ORDER: Scorpaeniformes
FAMILY: Cottidae
STATUS: Critically endangered, IUCN
Threatened, ESA
RANGE: USA (Alabama)

Sculpin, pygmy
Cottus paulus

Description and biology

The pygmy sculpin is a small freshwater fish, averaging less than 2 inches (5 centimeters) long. It has a large head and its fins have yellowish splotches or spots. Young pygmy sculpins have a black head and a grayish-black body. The adult sculpin has a lighter body and a white head with a few dark spots. These fish feed on a variety of insects, snails, and small crustaceans (shellfish) such as crabs.

Male and female pygmy sculpins both darken in color while breeding. Males become almost black and have a reddish-orange tinge along their dorsal (back) fin. Females may spawn (lay eggs) at any time during the year, but do so mostly in spring and summer. Sometimes two or three females form a communal (shared) nest by laying all their eggs on the underside of a single rock. A nest may include more than 200 eggs. Biologists (people who study living organisms) believe a male then guards this nest until the eggs hatch.

The pygmy sculpin is found in Coldwater Spring in Calhoun County, Alabama. © DR. CAROL JOHNSTONE / ALABAMA DEPARTMENT OF CONSERVATION AND NATURAL RESOURCES.

Habitat and current distribution

Pygmy sculpins are found only in Coldwater Spring in Calhoun County, Alabama. The fish exists in an area of less than 3.8 square miles (9.84 square kilometers). Biologists estimate that about 2,500 sculpins inhabit the spring run (small stream or brook) and 25,000 inhabit the spring pool. Both the pool and the run have sand and gravel bottoms. The temperature of the water in each is a constant 61°F to 64°F (16°C to 18°C).

History and conservation measures

The pygmy sculpin was discovered in 1968. Because of its restricted range, it is especially vulnerable. Even though its population numbers seem high, the species could be wiped out if a natural or human-made disaster occurs at its site. The U.S. Fish and Wildlife Service (USFWS) began a species recovery plan in 1991. According to the service, the species continues to be vulnerable even though its population size, range, and habitat have remained stable.

Conservationists (people who work to manage and protect nature) believe the pygmy sculpin is indeed in danger. Evidence indicates that the aquifer (underground layer of sand, gravel, or spongy rock that collects water) that feeds the Coldwater Spring is becoming polluted. Although the water quality in the 90-square-mile (230-square-kilometer) area that feeds the aquifer has deteriorated, the water quality in the spring itself has not been harmed.

Conservationists recommend developing a disaster recovery plan for the pygmy sculpin that would create an alternate population of the species in case its habitat suffered a catastrophe. This could be done either by keeping a number of individuals protected in an aquarium or by introducing the species to a new habitat in another pool or pond in the area. Keeping an aquarium population would also provide an opportunity to educate local people about the species and the threats it faces.

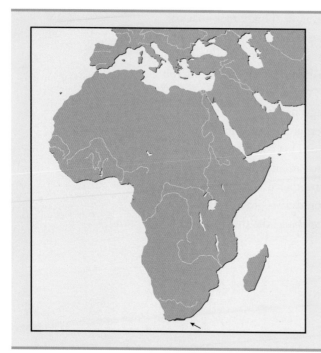

Seahorse, Knysna
Hippocampus capensis

PHYLUM: Chordata
CLASS: Actinopterygii
ORDER: Gasterosteiformes
FAMILY: Syngnathidae
STATUS: Endangered, IUCN
RANGE: South Africa

Seahorse, Knysna
Hippocampus capensis

Description and biology

The Knysna (pronounced NIZE-nuh) seahorse, also called the Cape seahorse, has the slender, curved shape of most seahorses. It is small and delicate and ranges between 2.1 and 4.7 inches (5.3 and 12 centimeters) in length. A series of bony rings encases its body. In color, it is greenish brown with some scattered darker spots. It has a short snout and a smoothly curving neck but lacks the crown found in some seahorse species.

The Knysna seahorse's tail is muscular, with short, blunt spines. The seahorse uses its tail to anchor itself to sea plants. This is an important function because the creature is not a strong swimmer, having only a single dorsal (back) fin for propulsion. If they do not have plants to attach themselves to, seahorses can be swept away by strong currents and other underwater disturbances. The tail is longer in the male, which uses it to grasp the female during mating.

During the complicated mating process, the female Knysna seahorse, as is the case with other seahorses, transfers her eggs into a pouch on the male's body. The male then fertilizes the eggs, and the embryos develop in the pouch. After two or three weeks, the male releases the baby seahorses. Juveniles are vulnerable during the period that they grow in the open water because they receive no parental protection. It takes Knysna seahorse juveniles about a year to reach sexual maturity.

Knysna seahorses use their ability to change color to hide and to surprise prey, which they swallow whole. As with other seahorses, they have no teeth and no stomach. They eat mostly small crustaceans (shellfish), which they find attached to underwater plants or in the water itself.

Did You Know?

An estuary is a body of water found where a river meets the sea. Plants and animals that live in estuaries are adapted to brackish water—that is, a mixture of freshwater and saltwater. For instance, whereas many fish can survive only in saltwater *or* freshwater, the Knysna seahorse, native to estuaries, is able to live in water that is very salty or only somewhat salty.

Estuaries are attractive sites for human development. Access to the ocean from a river is good for trade, while the fresh river water can be used for drinking. Many major cities, such as New York and Tokyo, are built on estuaries. Human development, however, can damage delicate estuary environments for other species.

Habitat and current distribution

Knysna seahorses are found in the Knysna, Swartvlei, and Keurbooms estuaries (coastal waters where a freshwater river empties into a saltwater sea or ocean) in South Africa. They can tolerate a wide range of salinity, or saltiness, in the water. The Knysna seahorse lives at depths from 19.5 inches to 65.5 feet (0.5 to 20 meters). It prefers areas with underwater vegetation (plant life), such as marine eelgrass.

The population was estimated to range between 124,000 and 360,000 individuals in a survey conducted in 2003. As of 2010, the population still appeared to be healthy but comprehensive surveys had not been carried out to verify this.

History and conservation measures

Knysna seahorses have the smallest range of any seahorse and are often considered the most endangered seahorse in the world. They are also the only seahorse that is primarily at risk as a result of habitat destruction.

The Knysna seahorse is at risk due to the effect of human activity on its habitat in the estuaries of South Africa. © TIM ROCK/LONELY PLANET/GETTY IMAGES.

The Knysna estuary, which is the primary habitat of this seahorse, is heavily and increasingly used by humans for trade, housing, and recreation. Deposits of silt (mineral particles) and pollutants threaten the seahorses living there, while boating can damage the eelgrass essential to the Knysna seahorse's survival. Other alterations in habitat, such as changes in water temperature or decreases in water levels, can also threaten the seahorses.

Seahorses also face threats from collection. Humans capture them to be pets or for folk medicine. Folk medicine practitioners claim that seahorses can be used to treat asthma, skin conditions, and baldness in humans.

South Africa officially protects seahorses in the Knysna estuary. It is illegal to catch them without a permit or to disturb their natural environment. In addition, in 1998 scientists began a conservation breeding program, hoping to protect the species for the future. Conservationists (people who work to manage and protect nature) believe that more research into the behavior of, and threats to, the Knysna seahorse is needed to increase the effectiveness of conservation programs.

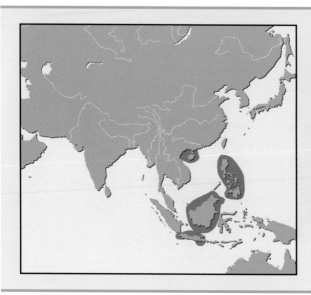

Shark, Borneo
Carcharhinus borneensis

PHYLUM: Chordata
CLASS: Chondrichthyes
ORDER: Carcharhiniformes
FAMILY: Carcharhinidae
STATUS: Endangered, IUCN
RANGE: Pacific Ocean (northwest and western central)

Shark, Borneo
Carcharhinus borneensis

Description and biology

The Borneo shark is a very rare species, little known to humans. It is not a large or dangerous shark. An adult measures about 27 inches (70 centimeters). In coloring, it is brown across the upper part of its body and white underneath. The markings on the shark are not very noticeable. The tips of its dorsal (near the back) fins are dusky, and it has light edges on its anal fin. Wildlife biologists (people who study living organisms in the wild) do not have much information on the reproductive or other behavior of this species, but Borneo sharks are known to form strong male-female pairs. Fertilization is internal—Borneo sharks do not lay eggs for external fertilization as do most fish. When the female gives birth, just a few young are born, and they are developed at the time of birth.

Habitat and current distribution

The Borneo shark is native to several coastal areas of the Pacific Ocean, the Indonesian Sea, and the South China Sea. It has been found in tropi-

Did You Know?

Sharks have been around in largely the same form for at least 400 million years. Unlike most fish species, they have no bones. Instead, their skeletons are made up of cartilage, a strong but slightly elastic tissue. Sharks also lack a swim bladder, the air-filled balloon-like organ that keeps most fish upright. Without a swim bladder to keep them afloat, sharks will sink if they are not swimming. Most sharks must keep moving constantly because as they move forward with an open mouth, the water passing across their gills serves as their breathing. All sharks have jaws, and many have up to 1,000 teeth arranged in rows. When the teeth are lost, new ones grow in to replace them.

Sharks play a crucial role as predators in ocean ecosystems (an ecological system including all of its living things and their environment). To save their energy, many sharks eat old, sick, or otherwise damaged fish—often whole schools of them—thus getting rid of the weaker populations and freeing up resources for the strong.

Since the 1950s the world's shark population has been in serious decline. The main reason for this is overfishing. Nearly 100 million sharks are killed each year by fishing operations. The majority of these are killed in a cruel practice called "finning." People catch a live shark, cut off its fin, and then throw the maimed fish back into the water. The shark, unable to swim without its fin, plummets helplessly to the bottom of the ocean and suffocates or bleeds to death.

Shark fins are very popular in Asia. Nearly all the shark fins collected are consumed in China, where they are used in shark fin soup, which is thought to work as an aphrodisiac (something that arouses sexual desire).

As of 2014 one-quarter of all shark and closely related ray species were threatened with extinction, according to the International Union for Conservation of Nature and Natural Resources (IUCN). Sharks do not reach sexual maturity until late in life (often at the age of 15), and they have long gestation (pregnancy) periods. Reproduction becomes rare because young sharks are caught by fishers and never have a chance to give birth. Thus, the shark populations have been unable to recover.

Since 2003 the annual global shark catch has been decreasing, perhaps because of smaller populations. However, there is hope for sharks. Demand for shark fin soup has been declining in China. In 2009 China's best-known athlete, basketball player Yao Ming, said he would not eat shark fin soup anymore out of concern for the sharks. In 2012 the Chinese government banned shark fin soup at its official banquets. In addition, the European Union has banned shark finning, and the state of California has banned the trade of shark fins. Also, new marine reserves have been established in several countries to provide some needed protection for sharks.

cal areas off the island of Borneo and the coast of China. Some scientists believe it may also occur off the island of Java and around the Philippines. Because these sharks are very difficult to locate and observe, wildlife biologists do not know the exact population of the species.

History and conservation measures

All that is known of the Borneo shark was learned from only five specimens, four of which were found in Borneo and one in China. These five specimens were all found before 1938. There were surveys of the shark collections in the markets of Malaysia, Thailand, Singapore, and China in the 1990s, and there were no records of any Borneo sharks among them. After many decades in which no Borneo sharks had been seen in the wild, researchers from the Malaysian University of Sabah reported a sighting in 2007.

The primary threat to the Borneo shark is believed to be fishing. Nearly 100 million sharks of all species are killed each year for their fins and meat.

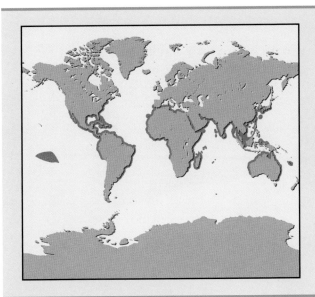

Shark, great hammerhead
Sphyrna mokarran

PHYLUM: Chordata
CLASS: Chondrichthyes
ORDER: Carcharhiniformes
FAMILY: Sphyrnidae
STATUS: Endangered, IUCN
RANGE: Warm coastal waters worldwide, including the Atlantic, Indian, and Pacific Oceans and the Mediterranean and Black Seas from latitudes of 40°N to 35°S

Shark, great hammerhead
Sphyrna mokarran

Description and biology

Hammerhead sharks acquired their name because their wide, flat heads resemble the head of a hammer. The great hammerhead shark's head is 25 percent the length of its body and flat in front. This strangely shaped head helps the shark find and kill its prey. Because its eyes are at each end of its head, the shark has a wide range of sight. As the shark swings its head above the ocean floor seeking prey, sense organs on the head detect the electrical impulses that stingrays, its favorite food, make. The shark then pins the ray down with its head and bites it. At the top of its food chain, the great hammerhead also eats many other types of prey, such as lobsters, squid, and small or young sharks.

The great hammerhead is the largest of the 10 hammerhead shark species. It can reach 20 feet (6 meters) long, although most are 10 to 13 feet (3 to 4 meters) long, and weighs from 500 to nearly 1,300 pounds (230 to 590 kilograms). Females are larger than males. Seventeen rows

The great hammerhead shark's strangely shaped head helps the creature find and kill its prey. © MARTIN STRMISKA/ALAMY.

of triangular, jagged teeth on either side of the top jaw, 16 or 17 teeth on either side of the lower jaw, and 1 to 3 teeth in the middle give this shark powerful biting power. The great hammerhead is dark brown to light gray or olive green, with a white underside. Its front dorsal (back) fin is very high and pointed, and tiny scales covering the skin help the animal slip smoothly through the water.

Great hammerhead sharks migrate through warm ocean waters worldwide, usually staying near the coast but sometimes venturing to the edge of the continental shelf. Female sharks have 20 to 40 offspring once every two years, giving birth to live young instead of producing eggs as most other fish species do. This species very rarely attacks humans, although it is considered potentially dangerous.

Habitat and current distribution

Great hammerhead sharks are found in the Atlantic, Indian, and Pacific Oceans and the Mediterranean and Black Seas from latitudes of 40°N to 35°S. The population size is unknown.

History and conservation measures

Twenty million years ago, the ancestor of today's hammerhead sharks roamed the oceans. A biologist (person who studies living organisms) first identified the great hammerhead species in 1837. Overfishing is the biggest threat to this shark. The Chinese use its large fins to make soup. Another threat is being caught by mistake by commercial fishing boats, because this species usually dies before it can be returned to the water.

Biologists lack good estimates of how many great hammerheads remain. Hammerhead fishing is poorly monitored, and this species is easily confused with other species of hammerheads. But it is estimated that the species' population has declined by 80 percent since about 1990. The great hammerhead shark is listed in Appendix II of the Convention on International Trade in Endangered Species of Wild Fauna and Flora (CITES; an international treaty to protect wildlife), indicating that its trade should be closely controlled to prevent its extinction.

No conservation bans exist for this species in particular, but several countries, such as the United States and Australia, now generally prohibit killing sharks for their fins. In 2014, however, the U.S. government decided not to list the great hammerhead shark as endangered. The government said that although the species may be in decline in some parts of its range, it is stable in others.

Sturgeon, Baltic
Acipenser sturio

PHYLUM: Chordata
CLASS: Actinopterygii
ORDER: Acipenseriformes
FAMILY: Acipenseridae
STATUS: Critically endangered, IUCN Endangered, ESA
RANGE: France, Republic of Georgia

Sturgeon, Baltic
Acipenser sturio

Description and biology

The Baltic sturgeon, also known as the European sturgeon, is a large, slow-moving fish that may grow to a length of almost 20 feet (6 meters) and weigh up to 2,200 pounds (998 kilograms). It has a shovel-shaped snout with four fleshy barbels (slender feelers) extending outward from between the tip of its snout and its mouth. Five rows of bony plates line its body.

Young Baltic sturgeons feed mainly on insect larvae, mollusks, and small fish, while adults eat small fish, worms, snails, and crustaceans (shellfish) such as crayfish. These sturgeons probe the bottom mud and sand of their water habitat in search of food. Their sensitive barbels detect prey, which they then pick up with their protruding lips.

Adult sturgeons spend most of their lives at sea. In early spring of each year, they enter the mouths of connected rivers to spawn (lay eggs).

Shown at the NABU-Nature Experience Center in Germany, young Baltic sturgeons, about 4 inches (10 centimeters) long, are among the 15,000 that were later released into the Oder River in fall 2014. They are part of a reintroduction effort. © PATRICK PLEUL/DPA/CORBIS.

These rivers are swift flowing, have gravel bottoms, and are 20 to 26 feet (6 to 8 meters) deep. After a female releases her eggs and a male fertilizes them with sperm, both return immediately to the sea. After hatching, the young sturgeons remain in the river or its estuary (coastal waters where a freshwater river empties into a saltwater sea or ocean) for two to three years. Baltic sturgeons grow more rapidly than other sturgeons.

Habitat and current distribution

Baltic sturgeons are found only in a small fraction of their former range. The fish is only known to exist in the Gironde, Dordogne, and Garonne Rivers in France and in the Rioni River in the Republic of Georgia. Biologists (people who study living organisms) estimate that the population declined more than 90 percent in the 20th century and that there are no more than 750 adult Baltic sturgeons in existence as of the 2010s. None of the populations is known to reproduce naturally in the wild; the population numbers depend on programs that breed and hatch the fish to restock the waterways.

Did You Know?

The sturgeon family, composed of 27 species, is a primitive family that has existed on Earth since the Paleozoic era (the division of geologic time occurring between 570 million and 240 million years ago). Present-day sturgeons are remarkably similar in appearance to their prehistoric ancestors. Instead of scales, these fish have rows of armorlike bony plates, called scutes, which partially cover their body.

Sturgeons are found only in the Northern Hemisphere in Europe, Asia, and North America. Worldwide, almost every species of sturgeon is endangered and 63 percent of all sturgeon species are critically endangered according to the International Union for Conservation of Nature and Natural Resources (IUCN). The demise of these fish began in the late 19th century, when humans began catching sturgeons solely to eat their eggs—a delicacy known as caviar. As a result, some species of this ancient fish family were brought to the edge of extinction in only 30 years.

Baltic sturgeons live in both marine (saltwater) and freshwater environments. While at sea, adults prefer to stay close to the coast at depths of up to 650 feet (198 meters).

History and conservation measures

Baltic sturgeons were once widespread on the coasts of most of Europe, including the coasts of the Atlantic Ocean and the Baltic, North, Mediterranean, and Black Seas. They were widely fished throughout Europe, and their eggs were commonly harvested for food.

While overfishing has been a problem, this fish has declined in number mainly because its spawning grounds have been damaged. In some cases, breeding rivers have been altered, such as widened or deepened, to make them more navigable for ships. In others, locks and dams have been built on rivers, preventing the sturgeons from reaching spawning grounds. Many of the rivers in the Baltic sturgeon's range are now polluted.

The Baltic sturgeon is protected by law in most countries throughout its range and by international treaties. Although it is not legal to fish this species, some get caught accidentally by fishing operations. Restocking programs were carried out in 1995 but as of 2012 only 3 to 5 percent of the restocked fish from that year had survived. Between 2007 and 2009 restocking programs released approximately 133,000 Baltic sturgeons into their habitat. The survival rate from these years is still not known. Restocking programs continue in Europe, particularly in France and Germany. Conservationists (people who work to manage and protect nature) hope the restocked populations will eventually breed naturally in the wild, but they have yet to determine if this is happening.

Sucker, shortnose
Chasmistes brevirostris

PHYLUM: Chordata
CLASS: Actinopterygii
ORDER: Cypriniformes
FAMILY: Catostomidae
STATUS: Endangered, IUCN
Endangered, ESA
RANGE: USA (California, Oregon)

Sucker, shortnose
Chasmistes brevirostris

Description and biology

Suckers are large fish that feed by siphoning food with their mouths from the bottom of their freshwater habitat. The shortnose sucker differs from other suckers in that its mouth does not run straight across the end of its head but is tilted at an angle. It feeds on zooplankton (microscopic aquatic animals), algae, and aquatic insects. The shortnose sucker can grow to a length of 25 inches (63.5 centimeters) and live as long as 33 years.

Female shortnose suckers spawn (lay eggs) in the spring in rivers, streams, or springs connected to their lake habitat. A single female can lay between 18,000 and 72,000 eggs during the spawning season.

Habitat and current distribution

Shortnose suckers prefer to inhabit freshwater lakes or reservoirs with cool water between 59°F and 77°F (15°C and 25°C). They migrate up

Dams prevent the shortnose sucker from reaching its spawning grounds. COURTESY OF THE U.S. FISH AND WILDLIFE SERVICE.

connected waterways to spawn. They are currently found primarily in Upper Klamath Lake and Gerber Reservoir in Oregon and in the Clear Lake Reservoir in California. Biologists (people who study living organisms) are not sure how many shortnose suckers exist but estimate that there are possibly more than 10,000 adults as of 2011.

History and conservation measures

The shortnose sucker was once common throughout the Upper Klamath River basin (region drained by the river and the streams that flow into it). This basin encompasses a drainage area of approximately 5.6 million acres (2.3 million hectares). In the 19th century the basin contained over 350,000 acres (141,600 hectares) of wetlands (areas where there is a lot of water in the soil, such as swamps or tidal flats) and floodplains, but 80 percent of these have been lost because of agricultural development, poor land management, and drought.

Over the years, these areas were drastically altered. Dams were built on rivers to supply water to communities and farms. Irrigation canals were also constructed to divert water to farms. Wetlands, marshes, and floodplains were drained to create land for houses and farms. These changes have destroyed about 75 percent of the shortnose sucker's former habitat, and broken up any remaining habitat into sections.

The draining of wetlands has also reduced the quality of water feeding the suckers' habitat. As water flows through wetlands into rivers and lakes, the wetlands act as a filter by capturing and neutralizing surface pollutants. Without them, the pollutants flow right through, eventually building to a point where they poison freshwater systems.

Dams have created reservoir habitats where the suckers can live, but they have also prevented the fish from reaching their spawning grounds. Biologists estimate that dams and other alterations to the shortnose suckers' habitat have reduced the fish's ability to reproduce by as much as 95 percent. Unless spawning areas are reestablished for the shortnose sucker, its survival is considered unlikely.

The U.S. Fish and Wildlife Service (USFWS) published a species recovery plan in 1993 and revised it in 2013. Its goal is to stop the decline of the shortnose sucker population by restoring spawning habitats and improving the water quality in the species' habitat. The USFWS estimates that, if its programs are successful, it will take 30 to 50 years for the species to be removed from the endangered list.

Totoaba

Totoaba macdonaldi (also *Cynoscion macdonaldi*)

PHYLUM: Chordata
CLASS: Actinopterygii
ORDER: Perciformes
FAMILY: Sciaenidae
STATUS: Critically endangered, IUCN
Endangered, ESA
RANGE: Mexico

Totoaba

Totoaba macdonaldi (also *Cynoscion macdonaldi*)

Description and biology

The totoaba (pronounced toe-TWAH-bah) is a large fish with a compressed body. It can grow to almost 6 feet (1.8 meters) long and weigh about 300 pounds (136 kilograms). It is silvery blue on the upper part of its body and dusky silver below. It feeds on a variety of prey, including fish, crabs, shrimp, and other crustaceans (shellfish).

The totoaba spends much of its life in the deeper waters of the Gulf of California (arm of the Pacific Ocean separating Baja California from the northwestern Mexican mainland). It spawns (lays eggs) in the shallow, brackish waters (mixture of freshwater and saltwater) where the Colorado River empties into the Gulf of California. Spawning takes place from mid-February until June. After hatching, young totoabas remain in the northern part of the gulf. After about two years, they migrate south to join the adult population. These fish grow rapidly, reaching a weight of 50 pounds (23 kilograms) after just 6 years. Biologists (people who study living organisms) believe totoabas may live up to 25 years.

Habitat and current distribution

The totoaba is unique to the Gulf of California. It was formerly found throughout most of the gulf, but is now found only in the northern end in water up to 75 feet (23 meters) deep. The totoaba migrates to the warmer and less salty waters near the mouth of the Colorado River to spawn. Biologists are unsure of the total number of totoabas in existence.

History and conservation measures

The totoaba, a tasty fish, was once hunted in great numbers for food and sport. In the early 1940s the amount of totoaba taken from the gulf

The totoaba, native to the Gulf of California in the eastern Pacific Ocean, is at risk because of overfishing and destruction of its habitat. © RICHARD HERRMANN/MINDEN PICTURES/CORBIS.

each year totaled about 5 million pounds (2,260 metric tons). By 1975 the yearly take had fallen to less than 128,000 pounds (58 metric tons).

The decline in the number of totoaba has been caused by overfishing and habitat destruction. Fishers captured totoabas primarily during their annual migrations. This diminished the number of fish that were able to reach their spawning grounds. In the northern section of the gulf, shrimp boats accidentally trapped and killed up to 90 percent of young totoabas in their shrimp nets. Dams built on the Colorado River decreased the amount of freshwater reaching the Gulf of California. The water in many spawning areas dried up, while the water in others became increasingly salty.

In 1975 the Mexican government declared a total ban on all fishing of the totoaba and created a reserve at the mouth of the Colorado River. The following year, the fish was placed on Appendix I of the Convention on International Trade in Endangered Species of Wild Fauna and Flora (CITES; an international treaty to protect wildlife). This banned all trade of the fish between nations that had signed the treaty. In 1979 the totoaba was listed as endangered under the U.S. Endangered Species Act. The Mexican government expanded the reserve zone in 1993 and improved its enforcement of legal protections for the totoaba and other endangered species in its habitat. Despite all of these actions, the totoaba continues to be threatened by illegal fishing and accidental catches.

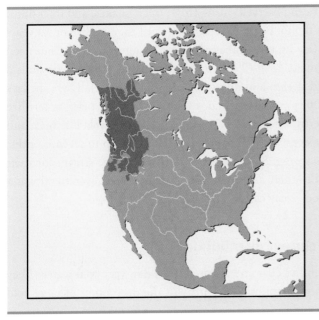

Trout, bull
Salvelinus confluentus

PHYLUM: Chordata
CLASS: Actinopterygii
ORDER: Salmoniformes
FAMILY: Salmonidae
STATUS: Vulnerable, IUCN
Threatened, ESA
RANGE: Canada, USA (Idaho, Montana, Nevada, Oregon, Washington)

Trout, bull
Salvelinus confluentus

Description and biology

The bull trout belongs to a subgroup of the salmon family called chars. Other char species are the lake trout, the Arctic char, and the Dolly Varden, which looks very similar to the bull trout and was once considered to be the same species. The adult bull trout typically weighs from 2.5 to 20 pounds (1.1 to 9 kilograms) and measures from 1 to 2 feet (0.3 to 0.6 meters) in length. Bull trout that live in streams and rivers tend to remain smaller, while those that live in lakes can grow larger, reaching weights of as much as 30 pounds (13.7 kilograms). Generally, bull trout are dark green to brown in color, with pale yellow and red spots and a white belly. There are many variations of physical characteristics within the species. The bull trout's name was inspired by its large head and jaws.

Young bull trout eat insects. As they mature they begin to hunt other fish species, especially mountain whitefish, sculpin, and other trout. Bull

657

trout have also been observed eating frogs, mice, snakes, and ducklings. Most bull trout do not begin to reproduce until they are five or six years old. Spawning (laying eggs) takes place in the autumn. Bull trout need cold waters of about 48°F (9°C) in order to spawn. The female finds a small, spring-fed stream and digs out a nest in the gravel. There she lays as many as 5,000 eggs. Next, a male bull trout releases sperm to fertilize the eggs. The fertilized eggs are then covered with gravel. The male and female leave the eggs, which incubate (develop) for up to seven months, hatching in the spring. Some bull trout remain in the stream for their whole lives, while others migrate to lakes and rivers and even to saltwater areas to find food. They can live to be about 20 years old.

Habitat and current distribution

Bull trout, like other char, are adapted for life in very cold water. They are found in snowy mountainous areas in the deep pools of large cold rivers and lakes and in coastal and mountain streams.

The bull trout was once found in river basins (regions drained by the river and the streams that flow into it) from Northern California to southeastern Alaska. In the United States, the bull trout currently exists in the Columbia and Snake River basins in Washington, Oregon, Montana, Idaho, and Nevada; Puget Sound and Olympic Peninsula in Washington; the Saint Mary River basin in Montana; and the Klamath River basin in Oregon. In Canada, the bull trout is currently found in rivers in British Columbia, western Alberta, southern Yukon, and central Northwest Territories.

Biologists (people who study living organisms) believe that the bull trout is no longer found in 50 percent of its former range. As of 2010, it was believed to be extinct in at least nine major rivers in Washington, Oregon, and California.

History and conservation measures

At one time the bull trout's range included large areas of the North American northwest, including the entire Columbia River basin from British Columbia, Canada, south to Washington and Oregon; the Jarbidge River in northern Nevada and southwestern Idaho; the Klamath River basin in Oregon; and the McCloud River in California. In the beginning of the 20th century, the bull trout experienced its first decline

Bull trout are adapted to live in cold waters. As such, climate change could be damaging to the fish if it causes waters to warm.
© RICHARD HERRMANN/ENCYCLOPEDIA/CORBIS.

in population in some areas where sportfishing was popular, when fishers began to stock new species of fish in streams and rivers. Because the bull trout ate other kinds of fish, including the new stock, fishers decided to try to eliminate the species from some streams to enhance their fishing.

Later, the bull trout faced the threats experienced by many species: logging; mining; urbanization; pollution; damming, dredging, or altering the course of rivers; oil and gas exploration; and, of course, overfishing. Climate change may also pose a serious threat, as it is warming the temperatures in the bull trout's habitat. The bull trout has very special needs because it is a cold-water species. Bull trout eggs will not hatch in waters with temperatures slightly warmer than required. Changes in water temperature cause severe declines in the population. Pollution, siltation (water choked with too much sediment and fine rock particles), and a degraded stream habitat have also been responsible for a reduction in the bull trout population. In addition, bull trout have bred with some of the introduced species of trout in their habitat. These matches have produced sterile (unable to reproduce) offspring.

There are many ongoing attempts throughout the bull trout's range to conserve stream habitats, not only for the bull trout but for other threatened species as well. Because there are several different types of bull trout—some migratory (traveling), some that remain in the stream in which they are born—threats to the species are varied, and each group needs separate actions to aid in its recovery. The species recovery plan of the U.S. Fish and Wildlife Service (USFWS) includes specific strategies for each of the large river basins where bull trout occur. In each recovery area, the USFWS aims to improve the bull trout's habitat and prevent negative effects from introduced fish species. The Canadian government has also instituted programs to protect the species, particularly by restricting fishing and educating fishers on ways to identify and protect the bull trout. Additional research into the species' biology and habitat is being conducted in both Canada and the United States.

In addition to the recovery efforts, the USFWS also began reintroduction efforts (efforts to introduce animals in captivity back into the wild) in 2009 to bring the bull trout back to the Clackamas River subbasin and the Willamette River in Oregon. The bull trout had not been seen in these water bodies since 1963, and there was not a way for the fish to return here without the efforts of humans. Conservationists (people who work to manage and protect nature) believe that reintroducing them here will aid in the species' recovery.

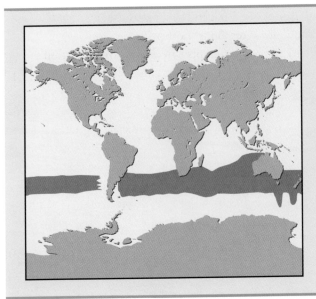

Tuna, southern bluefin
Thunnus maccoyii

PHYLUM: Chordata
CLASS: Actinopterygii
ORDER: Perciformes
FAMILY: Scombridae
STATUS: Critically endangered, IUCN
RANGE: Indian Ocean and southern Atlantic and Pacific Oceans

Tuna, southern bluefin
Thunnus maccoyii

Description and biology

A large fish, the southern bluefin tuna can weigh more than 440 pounds (200 kilograms) and can reach lengths of more than 6.5 feet (2 meters). The fish is dark blue on top with silvery-white sides and belly. Its first dorsal (on its back) fin is grayish yellow, its second dorsal red brown. Finlets, or small fins, lead from the second dorsal fin to its deeply forked tail. Faint, light-colored lines and rows of dots run along the fish.

The tuna's body has adapted to allow it to swim continuously and quickly through the ocean in search of food, moving up to 1.8 miles (3 kilometers) per hour. Its streamlined, torpedo-shaped body tapers in the front to a pointed snout. The fish's fins can be pulled into its body. Its body stays stiff as it swims, channeling energy to its tail. The tuna's large heart and the high oxygen-carrying capacity of its blood give the fish its speed and endurance. Because the fish can keep its body warmer than the surrounding water, it can live in varied temperatures. It prefers water

The southern bluefin tuna saw its population decimated by commercial fishing beginning in the mid-20th century. Despite efforts to limit the number that can be caught, the species remains at risk. © ROLAND SEITRE/MINDEN PICTURES/CORBIS.

at 64–68°F (18–20°C), but can withstand temperatures from 37–86°F (3–30°C).

Bluefin tuna eat many types of ocean animals, including fish, shellfish, and octopus. Southern bluefin tuna spawn (lay eggs) each year between September and April. Eggs hatch in 2 to 3 days. The fish reach maturity at 8 to 12 years, and may live up to 40 years.

Habitat and current distribution

This species is found in the southern Atlantic and Pacific Oceans and throughout the Indian Ocean. It spawns in the Indian Ocean off the west coast of Australia. Young tuna remain near Australia's western coast until age five, and then begin traveling in the open ocean. In 2009 there were an estimated 260,000 mature southern bluefin tuna.

History and conservation measures

Bluefin tuna have been eaten worldwide for thousands of years. Stone Age artists drew pictures of the fish on cave walls. Ancient Greek and Irish people put its image on coins. But now, overfishing threatens each of the three bluefin species. The southern bluefin is now critically endangered, the highest category of risk.

The southern bluefin population remained steady until the 1950s, when new fishing and fish-freezing techniques led fishers to catch more. At the same time, Japanese consumers began to prize the fish for its color, high fat content, and unique texture. Japanese diners eat about 90 percent of the southern bluefin caught. In 1969 about 60,850 tons (55,200 metric tons) of these fish were caught per year. Fishers caught young fish before they were mature enough to spawn, causing bluefin levels to decline. In 1991 fishers caught only 13,362 tons (12,122 metric tons). From 1973 to 2009 the species suffered an 85 percent population decline.

In 1994 Australia, New Zealand, and Japan created the Commission for the Conservation of Southern Bluefin Tuna (CCSBT). This group, which now includes other countries that fish for southern bluefin tuna, sets yearly fishing quotas for each country. Countries must monitor their fishing fleets and enforce the quotas. The International Union for Conservation of Nature and Natural Resources (IUCN) listed the southern bluefin as critically endangered in 1996.

Even so, overfishing of this species continues. At its current rate of decline, fewer than 500 mature southern bluefin tuna could remain by 2100. Some scientists and environmentalists think that the fish should be protected by the Convention on International Trade in Endangered Species of Wild Fauna and Flora (CITES; an international treaty to protect wildlife). Trade in CITES species is heavily regulated or banned. However in 2010 CITES member countries rejected a proposal to ban trade on the southern bluefin's close relative, the Atlantic bluefin.

Plants

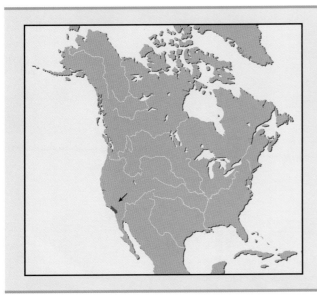

Barberry, Nevin's
Berberis nevinii

DIVISION: Tracheophyta
CLASS: Magnoliopsida
ORDER: Ranunculales
FAMILY: Berberidaceae
STATUS: Endangered, ESA
RANGE: USA (California)

Barberry, Nevin's

Berberis nevinii

Description and biology

Nevin's barberry is a large evergreen shrub with blue-green, spiny leaves; bright-red edible berries; and bright yellow flowers that bloom March through April. It is a rhizomatous plant (pronounced rye-ZHO-muh-tuss; a plant having an underground horizontal stem that puts out shoots above the ground and roots below) that measures from 3 to 12 feet (1 to 4 meters) in height. The leaves are pinnate, meaning they are arranged on opposite sides of the stemlike feathers. The flowers are clustered, with six petals in two rows. The tiny, juicy berries are about 0.3 inches (6 to 8 millimeters) long.

Nevin's barberry is a fire-adapted species within chaparral communities. Adult roots can survive wild fires and resprout.

Habitat and current distribution

Nevin's barberry is found primarily in sandy or gravelly soil and chaparral habitats at elevations between 1,400 and 1,700 feet (425 and

Nevin's barberry is native to California. © JOSHUA MC-CULLOUGH/GETTY IMAGES.

520 meters). It also occurs in a wide range of soil types and topographical areas.

The U.S. Fish and Wildlife Service (USFWS) estimates that there are 14 native populations of Nevin's barberry scattered throughout Los Angeles, San Bernardino, and Riverside Counties in California. The

Did You Know?

California chaparral is an ecological plant community made up of a variety of scruffy shrubs and bushes, most less than 10 feet (3 meters) tall, that are adapted to the dry summers and mild winters of Southern California. Some chaparral plants are: Manzanita, California lilac, Chamise, and Christmas holly. These chaparral plants typically have stiff, shiny leaves with a waxy covering that seals the moisture into the plants so they can survive the dry summer months. Chaparral bushes grow close to each other, forming large thickets across the slopes of hills.

As chaparral communities age, more and more dry wood and leaves build up on the ground under the brush and the area becomes particularly prone to fires. When a fire starts in chaparral country as a result of lightning or human carelessness, it will spread very quickly. The waxy substance that covers the leaves actually makes the fire burn hotter, and the older the chaparral thicket is when a fire starts, the more the fire will burn. Fires will tear across chaparral-covered hills, leaving a charred desertlike environment behind them.

This is actually good for the chaparral. Chaparral seedlings exist in a dormant (not active) state, sometimes for many years, and they are fireproof. When the fire burns off the older chaparral, it also burns off the protective coating of the seedlings in the ground. At the next rain, the seedlings will begin to sprout. (Some varieties of chaparral sprout from underground root systems that do not burn entirely in the fire.) Thus the fire both activates the seedlings and makes way for their growth, which would otherwise be crowded out by the older plants. The area is then repopulated with healthy young plants.

Conservationists (people who work to manage and protect nature) have realized over the years that fires serve a useful purpose in the life cycles of nature. But it is difficult for scientists to plan the frequency or strength of the fires. If there are too many fires in a chaparral area, the young plants may not have time to produce seedlings, and therefore the area will not repopulate. Too much fire prevention can eventually result in fires so hot they could destroy the seedlings or roots.

largest group is in the Vail Lake and Oak Mountain area near the foothills of the Peninsular Ranges in southwestern Riverside County. As of 2009 it was estimated that fewer than 200 individual plants were in existence in the wild.

History and conservation measures

The range of Nevin's barberry has always been limited to specific areas of Southern California. Scientists believe there never were more than 30 native populations scattered around Los Angeles, San Bernardino, and Riverside Counties, and possibly San Diego County.

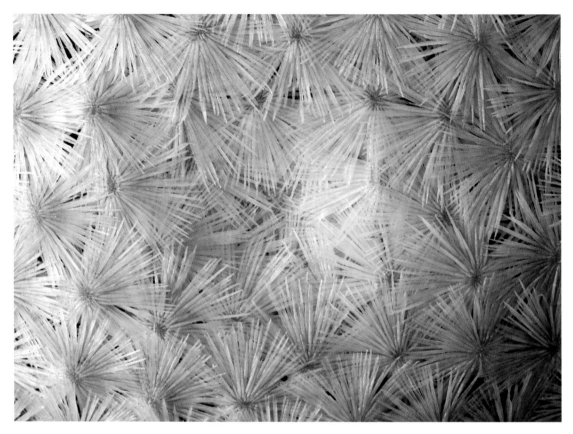

The golf ball cactus, found in a very small area of Querétaro, Mexico, has experienced a severe drop in population because of collectors removing the plants from their native habitat. © FERNANDO ARIAS/GETTY IMAGES.

Habitat and current distribution

Golf ball cacti grow on or between chalky limestone rocks. They are found in areas of desert scrub (land covered with stunted trees and shrubs), at high elevations. The cactus generally grows at elevations between 5,900 and 6,725 feet (1,800 and 2,050 meters) above sea level.

Wild golf ball cacti are found only in Querétaro, a state in north-central Mexico. Its total range is less than 0.4 square miles (1 square kilometer).

History and conservation measures

The golf ball cactus is critically endangered because of its restricted range and because of illegal collecting. Its attractive flowers are prized by ornamental gardeners. The population of wild golf ball cactus is believed to have decreased by 95 percent over the period from around 1993 to 2013. A commercial cactus nursery near its wild range has stripped and almost eliminated the area of wild plants. Local amateur collectors have also reduced its numbers.

Mexico has made the collection of the golf ball cactus illegal, and the species has been listed as protected by the Convention on International Trade in Endangered Species of Wild Fauna and Flora (CITES; an international treaty to protect wildlife). This listing bans international trade of the cactus. Illegal trade of the species still occurs, however, because the ban is not well enforced in certain countries that are the destinations for this trade.

Central Mexico's Cadereyta Regional Botanical Garden is working to conserve the golf ball cactus by studying its numbers and propagating it (helping it to multiply).

Cactus, Tamaulipas living rock
Ariocarpus agavoides

DIVISION: Tracheophyta
CLASS: Magnoliopsida
ORDER: Caryophyllales
FAMILY: Cactaceae
STATUS: Endangered, IUCN
RANGE: Mexico

Cactus, Tamaulipas living rock
Ariocarpus agavoides

Description and biology

Like all cactus plants, the Tamaulipas living rock cactus is a succulent (a plant that has thick, fleshy, water-storing leaves or stems). It measures only 2 to 3 inches (5.1 to 7.6 centimeters) across and is usually less than 2 inches (5 centimeters) tall. A stout stem grows up from the center of the plant. At the top of the stem is a rosette, or spreading cluster of fleshy, rough, gray-green, leaflike appendages. These measure about 1.6 inches (4.1 centimeters) long.

Flowers arise from these appendages, blooming in November and December. The flowers, which open at night, are rose pink to magenta (bright purplish red) in color. They are funnel shaped and measure 1.6 to 2 inches (4.1 to 5.1 centimeters) long. The fruits of this cactus are

The Tamaulipas living rock cactus is found only in northeastern Mexico. COURTESY OF DORNENWOLF.

brownish-red club-shaped berries that measure almost 1 inch (2.5 centimeters) long.

Habitat and current distribution

This species of cactus is found only in northeastern Mexico in very dry shrubland among chalky rocks. Its habitat covers an area of only about 154 square miles (400 square kilometers) in the states of Tamaulipas and San Luis Potosí. It is found mainly at an elevation of approximately 3,900 feet (1,190 meters). Biologists (people who study living organisms)

Did You Know?

Although most species of plants are pollinated by birds and insects, members of the Cactaceae family are pollinated predominantly by bats. One of the reasons for this is that bats are more prevalent than pollinating birds and insects in areas inhabited by cacti. Another reason is that most cacti open their flowers at dusk and hold them open during the night, a time when bats are most active. In order to attract the bats, the large pale flowers of cacti usually give off a melon-like or rotting odor, and visiting bats are rewarded with large quantities of nectar. The pollen produced by cactus flowers is also higher in protein than that of plants pollinated by birds or insects. In this way, the cactus supplies the nutritional needs of the bats, ensuring that they will return to help pollinate the plant in the future. The lesser long-nosed bat and the Mexican long-tongued bat frequently pollinate the cacti in Mexico and the American Southwest, but nectar-eating bats can be found in tropical and subtropical regions worldwide.

believe there are several thousand mature plants in existence in six isolated populations.

History and conservation measures

The Tamaulipas living rock cactus population has been reduced in number and continues to be threatened by collectors. It is highly prized by cactus enthusiasts because of its unusual shape. Urban expansion, rubbish dumping, and soil erosion have also contributed to the decline of this plant species.

This cactus is protected by international treaties and Mexican law, but illegal collection and trade continue. Only two of the populations of this species occur in protected areas. Conservationists (people who work to manage and protect nature) believe that to ensure the survival of the Tamaulipas living rock cactus, legal protection of the species must continue to be enforced.

The International Union for Conservation of Nature and Natural Resources (IUCN) uplisted the Tamaulipas living rock cactus from vulnerable to endangered status in 2002 because of continuing declines in the population and a reduction in the range of the species.

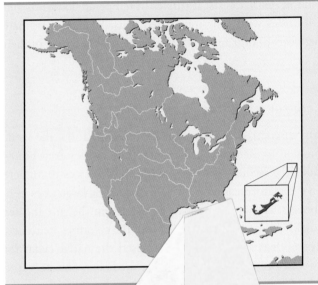

Cedar, Bermuda
Juniperus bermudiana

DIVISION: Tracheophyta
CLASS: Pinopsida
ORDER: Pinales
FAMILY: Cupressaceae
STATUS: Critically endangered, IUCN
RANGE: Bermuda

...rmuda

...udiana

...ogy

...da cedars, also known as Bermuda junipers,
...meters) tall, with a trunk measuring about
...diameter. However, where the trees are ex-
...in scarce soil, they are smaller. They have
...arrow strips and weathers to a gray color.
..., with small, leafy branchlets. The leaves
...ther. The trees produce dark blue seed
...ween September and December, and
...da cedars have a strong, sweet scent.
...prevents mildew and rot. Bermuda
...ars.

...nly occurring in) to Bermuda,
...tlantic Ocean. The tree once

covered its habitat in dense forests. It thrives in temperate lowlands and grows well on hillsides with limestone-based soils. Scientists estimate that there are between 10,000 and 25,000 adult Bermuda cedars in their natural habitat.

History and conservation measures

When Europeans discovered the island of Bermuda in 1609, the landscape was dominated by Bermuda cedar trees. The species grew abundantly throughout the islands, with an estimated 500 trees to an acre (0.4 hectares) in the many areas where it flourished. The large trees were useful as windbreaks, and protected early settlers from the sun and sea as well. They quickly became an essential part of the colonists' existence.

In the early 1600s colonists in Bermuda used the native cedar for building houses and ships; making furniture, medicine, and beer and wine; and as fuel. Soon after the first settlers arrived on the island, the

The Bermuda cedar population was drastically reduced by lumbering and disease in the mid-20th century. © NATURE'S IMAGES, INC./SCIENCE SOURCE.

forests showed signs of overexploitation, and early measures were taken to protect these trees. In 1627 export of cedar for shipbuilding was restricted. By 1878, 16 more acts to protect the species had been passed.

As settlers from all over the globe arrived on Bermuda, foreign species were introduced to the islands. Starting in 1943 the accidental introduction of two scale insects (the oystershell scale and the juniper scale), devastated the Bermuda cedars. Within a period of less than 10 years, 95 percent of the trees had been killed. An estimated 3.5 million trees were dead due to the infestation of these insects. A few stands in remote areas survived. Most surviving Bermuda cedars are now found in cemeteries, parks, and private gardens.

The government of Bermuda has led conservation efforts to save this species. In 1949 the Bermuda Board of Agriculture established a general reafforestation scheme, removing many of the dead cedar trees and replanting the cleared areas. The measures taken by the government helped in some recovery of the species in the wild. Extensive reforestation efforts that began in the 1980s helped the Bermuda cedar population recover to about 10 percent of its population before the insect infestation. The trees continue to do well in areas where invasive plants are managed so that they do not overwhelm the native trees.

The human population of the island, however, has grown and the tourist trade has caused extensive development. There are only small, isolated areas of natural habitat for the once dominant tree, and there are many newly introduced species with which the Bermuda cedar must compete. The Bermuda cedar is a popular tree for private gardens and does well in properties with large lawns.

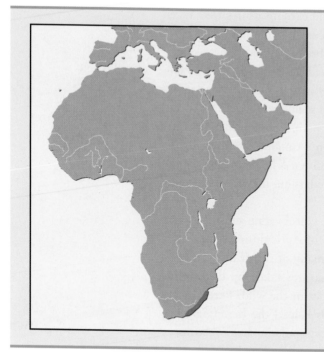

Cycad, Natal grass
Stangeria eriopus

DIVISION: Tracheophyta
CLASS: Cycadopsida
ORDER: Cycadales
FAMILY: Zamiaceae
STATUS: Vulnerable, IUCN
RANGE: Mozambique, South Africa

Cycad, Natal grass
Stangeria eriopus

Description and biology

The Natal grass cycad is a fernlike perennial (a plant that lives, grows, flowers, and produces seeds for three or more consecutive years). It grows to about 12 inches (30 centimeters) above the ground. Its underground stem may branch into several new stems. Up to four leaves grow from each of these growing points.

The plant's leaves measure from 1.5 to 6.5 feet (0.5 to 2 meters) long. Each leaf contains numerous leaflets that measure 4 to 16 inches (10 to 41 centimeters) long. The size and shape of the leaflets vary depending on the habitat. The leaflets of plants growing in open grassland are erect and compact, and have smooth margins or edges. Those of plants growing in forested habitats are taller and have serrated or saw-toothed margins.

The Natal grass cycad is dioecious (pronounced die-EE-shus). This means that one cycad will have male cones while another will have female cones. The male cones, which give off pollen, are 4 to 6 inches (10 to 15 centimeters) long and 1 to 2 inches (2.5 to 5 centimeters) in diameter. Female cones, which bear seeds after having been pollinated, are 7 to 8 inches (18 to 20 centimeters) long and 3 to 4 inches (8 to 10 centimeters) in diameter. Female cones bear as many as 100 seeds.

Habitat and current distribution

This species of cycad is unique to the eastern coastal areas of South Africa and the southernmost part of Mozambique. It is found both in coastal grasslands (where it grows in full sun) and in inland evergreen forests within 31 miles (50 kilometers) of the ocean (where it grows in semi-shade). Those plants growing in full sun produce more cones than those growing in the shade. The Natal grass cycad can live in areas from 33 to 2,460 feet (10 to 750 meters) above sea level.

Botanists (scientists who study plants) are unsure of the total number of plants currently in existence, but they estimated that there were more than 100,000 in the wild as of 2009.

History and conservation measures

The Natal grass cycad was first identified in 1853. Since then, it has been popular with collectors and in botanical gardens worldwide. The primary threat to this species today is over-collecting for magical and medicinal purposes.

Some native people in the cycad's range steep the plant in hot water to create a liquid extract or tea. They then sprinkle the liquid extract around their homes, believing it helps ward off lightning and evil spirits. They also give the liquid to infants suffering from congestion. Chemical

Did You Know?

Cycads are ancient seed plants that resemble palms or ferns, although they are not closely related to either. They have existed on Earth for almost 300 million years, predating the dinosaurs. In fact, dinosaurs probably ate cycads. Although cycads have outlasted the dinosaurs, they are not as common as they once were. Cycads were most abundant during the Jurassic period, also called the "Age of Cycads," which occurred 213 million to 144 million years ago. At that time, they grew over Earth from the Arctic to the Antarctic, making up 20 percent of the world's flora (plants). The approximately 300 species of cycads known to exist in the early 21st century are limited to tropical and subtropical regions of Earth.

The Natal grass cycad, native to coastal South Africa and Mozambique, has seen its population diminished by plant collectors and loss of habitat.
© BLICKWINKEL/ALAMY.

studies of the Natal grass cycad, however, have not found any medicinal properties.

Habitat destruction is also a threat to the cycad, as land is cleared for agricultural purposes. Natural vegetation (plant life) areas have been replaced with fields of sugarcane in KwaZulu-Natal Province and with pineapple plantations in Eastern Cape Province in South Africa.

The Natal grass cycad is protected by international treaties. In all South African provinces, it is listed as a specially protected plant. At least five protected areas are home to the Natal grass cycad, including natural reserves in the Lebombo Mountains and the Dwesa-Cwebe coast. In order to meet the increasing demand for the plant as an herbal remedy, attempts are being made to breed the cycad artificially on a large scale.

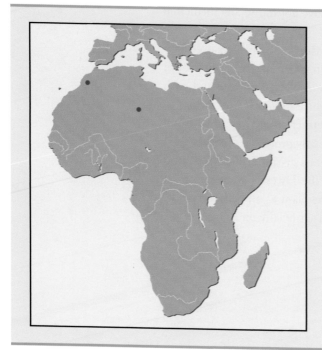

Cypress, Saharan
Cupressus dupreziana

DIVISION: Tracheophyta
CLASS: Pinopsida
ORDER: Pinales
FAMILY: Cupressaceae
STATUS: Endangered, IUCN
RANGE: Algeria, Morocco

Cypress, Saharan
Cupressus dupreziana

Description and biology

Cypresses are resinous (containing a substance used in varnishes and lacquers) evergreens that have fragrant, durable wood. The true cypresses, of the genus (a group with similar characteristics) *Cupressus*, are found in southern Europe, the Far East, western North America, and other warm regions.

A true cypress, the Saharan cypress is covered in reddish-brown bark containing many deep cracks. It can grow to a height of 66 feet (20 meters) and a diameter of 13 feet (4 meters). It has upward-curving branches with flattened branchlets that grow in two opposite rows. Its dense foliage consists of small green leaves measuring 0.04 to 0.06 inches (0.1 to 0.15 centimeters) long. The tree's small cones are yellow or gray brown. Some Saharan cypresses are more than 2,000 years old.

A Saharan cypress stands in the Tassili n'Ajjer National Park in Algeria, where it is threatened by climate change, tourist and animal traffic, fire, and grazing. © PICHUGIN DMITRY/SHUTTERSTOCK.COM.

Habitat and current distribution

In Algeria, the Saharan cypress can be found atop mountains and in deep valleys and gorges where the average annual rainfall is only 1.2 inches (3 centimeters) per year. In Morocco, the tree is found in dry to semidry Mediterranean climates with periods of drought and snow on steep mountain slopes between 3,280 and 6,560 feet (1,000 and 2,000 meters).

The tree grows in 46 locations in Algeria, where there are only 233 trees of this species in existence. There is only one population in one

Did You Know?

Between 5,000 and 10,000 years ago, the Sahara Desert was fertile and experienced frequent monsoon (heavy) rains. In the 1930s scientists exploring caves on the Tassili Plateau in the central Sahara (where remaining Saharan cypresses now stand) discovered pictographs (rock paintings) that depicted grasslands, forests, and rivers. Inhabiting these lush landscapes were crocodiles, elephants, giraffes, hippopotamuses, and rhinoceroses. In some caves, the scientists discovered 16 layers of drawings, indicating that humans—both hunters and herders—had inhabited the region for thousands of years. Around 5,000 years ago, Earth's tilt shifted slightly in its orbit around the sun, a natural process that can result in changes in climate. This caused rains in North Africa to cease and as the region began to dry up, humans left and the Sahara began to look like the desert it is today.

location left in Morocco. The number of trees in that location was estimated to be 6,650 in a 1998 survey.

History and conservation measures

Over thousands of years, humans have cut down many cypresses for their long-lasting timber. Today, the cypress is a symbol of immortality for many people.

Saharan cypresses are endangered because they do not reproduce very quickly, and humans have cut them down faster than they can reproduce. Most of the surviving trees are just over 100 years old. Grazing animals have also destroyed many cypress seedlings before they have had a chance to root and grow.

The trees in Algeria occur within the Tassili n'Ajjer National Park, a World Heritage Site. The population has continued to decline despite this designation because the number of staff and programs in place are not enough to protect the trees and their habitat. In Morocco, fences have been placed around the trees' area. Replantings have not been entirely successful, but the species is cultivated in botanical gardens in Europe and the United States.

The population of Saharan cypress found in Morocco is considered to be a distinct variety from the Algerian population. Both varieties are considered to be critically endangered by the International Union for Conservation of Nature and Natural Resources (IUCN). Because of the larger population size and greater range of the species as a whole, however, the Saharan cypress has been assigned endangered status.

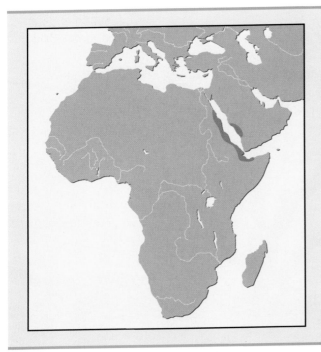

Dragon tree, Gabal Elba
Dracaena ombet

DIVISION: Tracheophyta
CLASS: Magnoliopsida
ORDER: Asparagales
FAMILY: Asparagaceae
STATUS: Endangered, IUCN
RANGE: Djibouti, Egypt, Eritrea, Ethiopia, Saudi Arabia, Somalia, Sudan

Dragon tree, Gabal Elba
Dracaena ombet

Description and biology

Dragon trees are famous in ancient myth, their genus (a group with similar characteristics) name coming from the Greek word for "female dragon." Most members of this particular species are found in the Gabal Elba area of Egypt, giving the trees their name. This short tree can live for more than 70 years and reaches a height of about 16 feet (5 meters). Its forked branches spread out to around 8 feet (2.5 meters) in diameter. The tree has stiff, sword-shaped leaves that gather raindrops, giving the tree most of its water. The tree produces 12-inch (30-centimeter) upright clusters of pink flowers and orange fruits. Nomadic peoples and animals sometimes consume its fruit. Botanists (scientists who study plants) think that the tree's seeds may be spread mainly by ravens that eat the fruits.

The Gabal Elba dragon tree, native to northeastern Africa and the Arabian Peninsula, has seen its numbers decline because of overcutting, drought, and disease. © ISTOCK.COM/MTCURADO.

All dragon trees live in semidesert regions; however, whereas most of the Gabal Elba area receives less than 2 inches (5 centimeters) of rain yearly, these particular trees enjoy a moister climate. They grow on mountains facing the sea, at altitudes of about 2,000 feet (600 meters). This sea air wraps the mountain slopes in mist and clouds, bringing 16 inches (40 centimeters) of rain a year.

Habitat and current distribution

The largest population of this tree occurs in Egypt's Gabal Elba Mountains, but smaller populations are found in the neighboring countries of Djibouti, Eritrea, Ethiopia, Saudi Arabia, Somalia, and Sudan. The total number of trees is unknown. The regions where it grows are remote and often dangerous because of fighting among various groups of people. In one part of the Gabal Elba region, researchers counted 353 trees, but only 161 were alive. In Sudan they counted 61 trees, most of which were healthy. Surveys are planned in other areas where the tree occurs.

History and conservation measures

The blood-red sap of the dragon trees native to the Canary Islands off the coast of Africa inspired the name of this type of tree. According to Greek myth, after Hercules slew a 100-headed dragon, these trees sprang up where the creature's blood soaked into the earth, so the trees' sap is red. Ancient peoples used the sap as dye and in traditional medicine (health practices used by specific cultures since before the time of modern medicine).

The biggest threat to this species has been drought, which was especially severe from 1960 to 1980. When conservationists (people who work to manage and protect nature) surveyed trees in portions of the Gabal Elba region in 2007, they found that only 27 percent of the trees were healthy and only 1 percent were newer-growth specimens. A 2014 study published in *Oryx,* a conservation journal, characterizes the tree as critically endangered in this portion of its range. In Sudan, however, most trees are healthy, and many are newer-growth trees.

Besides depriving Gabal Elba dragon trees of moisture, droughts have indirectly led to other threats to the species. Droughts have affected areas where nomads have roamed in the past, so the nomads have moved to the regions where the trees grow. The nomads' goats eat the tree's seedlings, so few new trees grow. People also supplement their incomes by making medicine and rope from the trees. Another issue for the dragon trees in the Gabal Elba area is the rapid spread of an invasive species, the mesquite tree. (Invasive species come from a different ecosystem. They spread or multiply, causing harm when they are introduced into a new environment.) These drought-resistant, fast-growing mesquite trees compete with the Gabal Elba dragon tree for space and for underground water.

Botanists are counting trees across this species' range and studying their health and age. As the botanists travel through the regions where the trees grow, they educate local communities about the species' importance. Other conservation projects, such as building enclosures for young trees, have also been proposed.

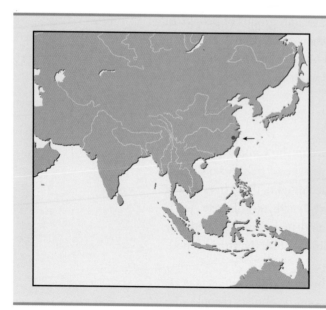

Fir, Baishan
Abies beshanzuensis

DIVISION: Tracheophyta
CLASS: Pinopsida
ORDER: Pinales
FAMILY: Pinaceae
STATUS: Critically endangered, IUCN
RANGE: China

Fir, Baishan

Abies beshanzuensis

Description and biology

The Baishan fir is an evergreen tree with spreading, whorled (or spiraled) branches. Its bark is grayish yellow. The tree can grow to a height of 56 feet (17 meters). Annual shoots (new stem and leaf growth) are smooth and pale yellow or gray yellow in color. The leaves on the tree measure 0.4 to 1.7 inches (1 to 4.3 centimeters) long and 0.1 to 0.14 inches (0.25 to 0.36 centimeters) wide. Its cones are pale brown or brownish yellow when mature. They measure 2.8 to 4.7 inches (7.1 to 11.9 centimeters) long and 1.4 to 1.6 inches (3.6 to 4.1 centimeters) wide. The cones ripen or open and shed their seeds in November.

Habitat and current distribution

Baishan firs are found only in southeastern China. They inhabit the sunny forest slopes of Baishanzu Mountain in southern Zhejiang

Province. They grow at an elevation of 4,920 to 5,575 feet (1,500 to 1,700 meters), where the climate is marked by warm summers and cool, moist winters.

As of the early 2010s, botanists (scientists who study plants) knew of only three living specimens of these firs in the wild.

History and conservation measures

The remaining Baishan firs are growing in an area where local farmers are constantly employing slash-and-burn agriculture. In this process, farmers cut down and burn all trees and vegetation (plant life) in a forest to create cleared land. Although this technique opens up the land quickly, it robs the soil of essential nutrients. The land does not stay fertile for very long. Thus, farmers must continually clear new land in order to grow crops.

Baishan firs have suffered as a result of this farming method. Most have been either cut down or burned. Those that remain cannot reproduce very well because the surrounding soil is not fertile enough. Some of the last remaining trees were also killed by flooding and landslides. Scientists fear that temperature and rainfall changes caused by global warming will be a significant threat to the species.

The three remaining Baishan firs are in a protected area within the Fengyangshan-Baishanzu National Nature Reserve in Zhejiang Province. A program is also underway to cultivate seedlings and replant them in the species' original habitat.

Goldenrod, Short's
Solidago shortii

DIVISION: Tracheophyta
CLASS: Magnoliopsida
ORDER: Asterales
FAMILY: Asteraceae
STATUS: Endangered, ESA
RANGE: USA (Indiana, Kentucky)

Goldenrod, Short's
Solidago shortii

Description and biology

Short's goldenrod is an herb that grows to 24 to 30 inches (61 to 76 centimeters) high. It is classified as a perennial (a plant that lives, grows, flowers, and produces seeds for three or more consecutive years). During the growing season, its underground stem may produce as many as six other separate stems that will create new plants.

The plant's leaves grow along the stem alternately (each leaf is attached to the stem on the side opposite to that of the leaf growing immediately above and below it). The leaves are narrow, measuring 2 to 4 inches (5 to 10 centimeters) long and 0.2 to 0.6 inches (0.5 to 1.5 centimeters) wide. Those leaves growing near the middle of the stem are larger than those growing toward each end.

The goldenrod's yellow flowers, which grow in clusters of 10 or more, bloom from mid-August to early November. Seeds are released

Short's goldenrod is an extremely rare plant, found only in Indiana and Kentucky. © ANNA YU/ALAMY.

Did You Know?

Short's goldenrod was originally found in 1840 by Charles Short, a Kentucky physician and botanist (a scientist who studies plants). His discovery was new to science, and in 1842 the plant was given the scientific name *Solidago shortii* in his honor. Short found the goldenrod on Rock Island, a rocky promontory (a ridge of land jutting out into a body of water) in the Kentucky portion of the Falls of the Ohio. The promontory was destroyed in the 1920s due to construction of a dam and locks in that part of the Ohio River, and Short's goldenrod has not existed there since.

from late September to late November. Botanists (scientists who study plants) believe sweat bees and other insects pollinate the plant when they seek out the flowers' nectar.

Habitat and current distribution

Throughout the 20th century botanists believed that this species of goldenrod was unique to Kentucky, where it can be found in the Blue Licks Battlefield State Resort Park. Early in the 21st century Short's goldenrod was discovered in Indiana, within the Blue River watershed in Crawford, Harrison, and Washington Counties.

Short's goldenrod inhabits cedar glades, pastures, and open areas in oak and hickory forests.

History and conservation measures

Short's goldenrod was first identified in 1842 at a site near the Ohio River in Jefferson County, Kentucky. All plants at that site were later destroyed when it flooded as a result of dam construction.

The primary threat to Short's goldenrod is the loss of its habitat due to human activities and fire (both human-made and natural). Over-collection by scientists is another threat to the species' survival in the wild.

Blue Licks Battlefield State Resort Park has been designated a nature reserve to protect Short's goldenrod. About 12 other sites in Kentucky are also home to the rare plant, including private lands and the Buffalo Trace Preserve, which is run by the Nature Conservancy of Kentucky. To ensure the survival of this plant species, conservationists (people who work to manage and protect nature) believe it is necessary that private landowners cooperate with conservation measures.

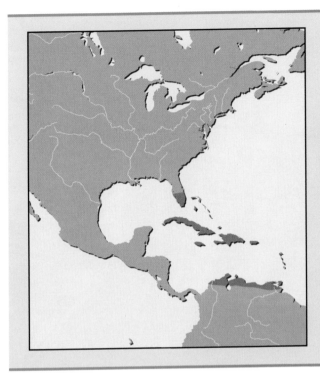

Mahogany, American
Swietenia mahagoni

DIVISION: Tracheophyta
CLASS: Magnoliopsida
ORDER: Sapindales
FAMILY: Meliaceae
STATUS: Endangered, IUCN
RANGE: Anguilla, Antigua and Barbuda, Bahamas, Barbados, Cayman Islands, Colombia, Cuba, Dominica, Dominican Republic, Grenada, Guadeloupe, Jamaica, Martinique, Montserrat, Saint Barthélemy, Saint Kitts and Nevis, Saint Lucia, Saint Martin, Saint Vincent and the Grenadines, Trinidad and Tobago, Turks and Caicos Islands, USA (Florida), Venezuela

Mahogany, American
Swietenia mahagoni

Description and biology

The American mahogany, also called the West Indian or Cuban mahogany, is a fast-growing semi-evergreen tree. It grows to a height of about 40 to 60 feet (12.2 to 18.2 meters) and spreads out to a width of about the same measure. Its bark is smooth and gray in its early years and becomes darker and browner as the tree ages. An older tree has flaky, ridged bark. The 4- to 8-inch (10.2- to 20.5-centimeter) leaves come in clusters, with 4 to 8 leaflets of about 0.25 inches (0.65 centimeters) in length. The oval leaves are dark green on top and reddish brown underneath. They have sharp tips and a smooth surface.

The American mahogany tree has small 3- to 6-inch (7.6- to 15-centimeter) green or white flowers that are barely noticeable to a casual

An American mahogany tree towers over Florida's Everglades. It is also native to the Caribbean Islands. © BLICK-WINKEL/ALAMY.

observer. The flowers are unisexual (either male or female, but not both, as some flowers are). They are pollinated by insects. In the fall or the winter, one flower will develop into a fruit, a large, woody, 2- to 5-inch (5- to 12-centimeter) pod. When the pods are mature (in 8 to

10 months), they release flat, brown seeds. This cycle usually takes place on an annual basis in trees that are 10 to 15 years old.

Habitat and current distribution

The American mahogany occurs in subtropical dry or wet forests at altitudes ranging from sea level to about 2,625 feet (800 meters). The species does best in rich, moist soil, but it is currently found most frequently in dry, stony areas. American mahogany trees are usually found scattered, with only one or two trees on a 1-acre (0.4-hectare) section of the forest.

The American mahogany is native to Cuba, Haiti, Jamaica, the Dominican Republic, the Bahamas, and southern Florida. The species, though, has been cultivated by humans for many years; in some cases it is difficult for scientists to determine which populations are native to an area. The species has been introduced to Puerto Rico, the Virgin Islands, the Lesser Antilles, and elsewhere in the Caribbean.

History and conservation measures

The American mahogany tree has long been prized for its durable, deep red, straight-grained wood, which has been used to make fine furniture for centuries. It was first used during the reign of King George I of England, from 1714 to 1727. Europe imported its mahogany from Jamaica, Cuba, and Honduras. By 1774 American mahogany had become scarce because of its popularity in furniture making. By the late 1800s the species was nearly eliminated from Cuba, and it was in decline elsewhere.

Few stands of American mahogany now exist in the wild because of the overexploitation of the species for the furniture industry and because of the development of the lands that the tree favors. The species is much more likely to be found planted in someone's yard or along a city street than in its natural habitat. Where it does grow wild, the species has undergone dramatic changes. Trees are likely to be much smaller and more like bushes, with many branches.

Although human use is by far the biggest threat to the species, American mahogany is also damaged by insects. The Cuban leaf beetle and the mahogany webworm eat its leaves; both pests can be controlled without the use of insecticides. In Florida, the Sri Lanka weevil has been found in many plants, including the American mahogany trees.

Since 1992 the trade of American mahogany has been restricted under the Convention on International Trade in Endangered Species of Wild Fauna and Flora (CITES), an international treaty to protect wildlife. It has an Appendix II listing under CITES, which means that an exporter of this wood must receive a permit from the government. Trade in the species is now often in salvaged wood.

Orchid, eastern prairie fringed
Platanthera leucophaea

DIVISION: Tracheophyta
CLASS: Magnoliopsida
ORDER: Asparagales
FAMILY: Orchidaceae
STATUS: Threatened, ESA
RANGE: Canada, USA (Illinois, Iowa, Maine, Michigan, Missouri, New York, Ohio, Wisconsin)

Orchid, eastern prairie fringed
Platanthera leucophaea

Description and biology

The eastern prairie fringed orchid is considered one of the most beautiful plants in North America. It is classified as a perennial (a plant that lives, grows, flowers, and produces seeds for three or more consecutive years). After lying dormant all winter, the plant finally sends up leaves and a flower spike in June. Depending on the amount of moisture that has fallen during the season, this stout orchid can grow to a height of almost 40 inches (102 centimeters).

The orchid's stem is angled and leafy. The silver-green leaves grow along the stem alternately (each leaf is attached to the stem on the side opposite to that of the leaf growing immediately above and below it). They measure 3 to 8 inches (7.6 to 20 centimeters) long and 1 to 2 inches (2.5 to 5 centimeters) wide. The two lowermost leaves on the stem are larger than the rest.

The eastern prairie fringed orchid is considered a threatened species because of loss of habitat, the effects of pesticides, and removal by plant collectors. © CLINT FARLINGER/ALAMY.

Some 10 to 40 white flowers grow off the stem. These showy flowers have a deeply fringed three-part lower lip, which gives the plant its common name. At night, the flowers release a scent to attract nocturnal (active at night) hawkmoths to help pollinate the plant.

Eastern prairie fringed orchids can be long-lived. Individual plants have been known to survive more than 30 years.

Habitat and current distribution

The eastern prairie fringed orchid is found in the Canadian provinces of Nova Scotia and Ontario and in eight U.S. states. The plant is considered rare in its Canadian range. In the United States, the species was once widespread throughout the northern Midwest, as well as Maine, New Jersey, Oklahoma, and Virginia. By the end of the 20th century, botanists (scientists who study plants) knew of only 59 populations left in existence. Most of the populations—usually with fewer than 50 plants each—are in Wisconsin, Illinois, Michigan, and Ohio.

The eastern prairie fringed orchid commonly grows in full sunlight on the rich, moist, and sandy soils of open prairies. It also grows on sedge (a grassy plant growing in wet areas) mats in open bogs, areas of wet spongy ground composed of decaying plant matter.

History and conservation measures

The main reason for the decline of this orchid species is habitat destruction. The fertile, moist soil in which the plant grows is prized by farmers, and much of its prairie land habitat has been converted into farmland. This process continues to pose a threat to some surviving orchid populations.

The U.S. Fish and Wildlife Service (USFWS) began a species recovery plan in September 1999 to protect the eastern prairie fringed orchid. The service's programs aim to protect the plant's habitat, increase the size and numbers of populations, and conduct research into the species. As of 2013, sections of the orchid's natural habitat had been restored successfully in northeastern Illinois, where the USFWS has begun to spread seed capsules. It is hoped that these seeds will grow to adult plants and will improve the eastern prairie fringed orchid's chances for survival in the wild.

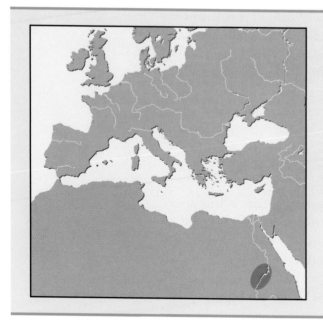

Palm, Argun
Medemia argun

DIVISION: Tracheophyta
CLASS: Liliopsida
ORDER: Arecales
FAMILY: Palmae
STATUS: Critically endangered, IUCN
RANGE: Egypt, Sudan

Palm, Argun
Medemia argun

Description and biology

The Argun palm can grow to a height of up to 39 feet (11.8 meters). Its bare trunk sprouts no branches but is topped by a crown of leaves. These fan-shaped leaves measure up to 4.4 feet (1.3 meters) long. Each compound leaf (called a frond) is composed of numerous stiff, sword-shaped leaflets, which measure 0.4 to 1.6 inches (1 to 4 centimeters) wide. These leaflets grow opposite each other on either side of the leaf's stalk or rachis (pronounced RAY-kiss). The palm produces purple, oval fruits that are about 1.6 inches (4 centimeters) long by 1.2 inches (3 centimeters) wide.

This palm is dioecious (pronounced die-EE-shus). This means that one Argun palm will have male flowers (which give off pollen) while another will have female flowers (which receive the pollen). The male flowers are small with three spreading petals. They are attached to the palm by dense spikes that measure 6 to 11 inches (15 to 28 centimeters)

The Argun palm is native to Egypt and Sudan. © HAITHAM IBRAHIM / ROYAL BOTANIC GARDENS, KEW / PALMWEB.

in length. The female flowers are rounded and measure approximately 0.2 inches (0.5 centimeters) across. They are attached to stout stalks 0.4 inches (1 centimeter) long that protrude from similar spikes.

Habitat and current distribution

The Argun palm has been found only in a few sites in Egypt and Sudan, in oases (fertile areas in a desert) of the Nubian Desert. As of 2014, there were only 31 individual palms in Egypt.

The Argun palm grows in groves on river banks and in oases or wadis (stream beds or valleys that are usually dry except during the rainy season).

History and conservation measures

In ancient Egypt, the Argun palm was widespread and was placed as an offering in tombs. By the mid-20th century the palm was thought to be extinct. Then in the early 1960s, botanists (scientists who study plants) found one adult tree and a few young ones in the uninhabited Dungul Oasis, which is 140 miles (225 kilometers) southwest of the Egyptian city of Aswan. Soon, a few other sites were discovered in Egypt, and a small population was found in the desert in northern Sudan in 1995.

In the early 2010s the Argun palm was among the most threatened of any palm species in the world. Since its rediscovery it has been cut down by native people in its range who use its leaves to make mats. Much of its natural habitat also has been destroyed by irrigation projects along the Nile River that feed water to farms. The oases that are home to the palms are threatened by human activities such as hunting and mining. Global climate change may also be a great challenge for the palm and its habitat because it is likely to reduce rainfall in the area.

Conservation programs, full legal protection, and cooperation between Egypt and Sudan are necessary to protect the Nubian Desert oases and prevent the extinction of the Argun palm. In Dungul Oasis, the number of palms increased from 8 to 36 trees by 1998. However, by 2007, there were only 25 palms. The population has continued to decrease since then.

Palm, carossier
Attalea crassispatha

DIVISION: Tracheophyta
CLASS: Liliopsida
ORDER: Arecales
FAMILY: Palmae
STATUS: Critically endangered, IUCN
RANGE: Haiti

Palm, carossier
Attalea crassispatha

Description and biology

The carossier palm, or *petit coco* (little coconut), is a tall, solitary palm that grows to a height of 65 feet (20 meters). Its smooth gray trunk measures up to 13.8 inches (35 centimeters) in diameter. It has a crown of 15 to 19 arching leaves that measure up to 17.5 feet (5.3 meters) long. Each compound leaf (called a frond) is composed of numerous smooth-edged leaflets. These leaflets grow opposite each other at regular spaces on either side of the leaf's stalk, or rachis (pronounced RAY-kiss).

This palm produces fruits that resemble tiny coconuts (hence the palm's common name on Haiti). Each fruit consists of a fibrous, hard shell surrounding a small, white, hollow kernel that is edible. The fruits are egg-shaped and taper to a sharp point. They measure 1.25 to

1.75 inches (3.18 to 4.45 centimeters) in length. When mature (ripe), they are reddish in color.

Habitat and current distribution

The carossier palm is found only on Haiti's southwestern peninsula, an area once dominated by tropical scrub vegetation (plant life such as stunted trees or shrubs). It is found on four areas of the Cavaillon and Côtes-de-Fer watersheds. As of 2014, only 25 to 30 individual plants survived on Haiti.

This palm prefers to grow in full sunlight at or near sea level up to 1,475 feet (450 meters).

History and conservation measures

The carossier palm was first described in 1689 by a French priest and naturalist (someone who observes nature to find its laws). He wrote that the palm was abundant in southwestern Haiti. By the 1920s, when botanists (scientists who study plants) first began to study the plant, it had begun to disappear and was considered a rarity. Botanists are deeply interested in the carossier palm because it is the only one of its genus (a group with similar characteristics), *Attalea*, that grows in the Caribbean.

Because of Haiti's growing human population and poor economy, many of the island's natural resources have been depleted. The carossier palm has been crowded out of its habitat by farming, and its edible seeds have been collected by local people. Since the carossier palm is not currently growing in any protected areas, the outlook for its future is grim.

A nongovernmental organization in Haiti started a program in the early 21st century to research the species' distribution, ecology, and conservation status. The Fairchild Tropical Botanic Garden in Coral Gables, Florida, also maintains a collection of these palms for conservation purposes.

Pine, bigcone pinyon
Pinus maximartinezii

DIVISION: Tracheophyta
CLASS: Pinopsida
ORDER: Pinales
FAMILY: Pinaceae
STATUS: Endangered, IUCN
RANGE: Mexico

Pine, bigcone pinyon
Pinus maximartinezii

Description and biology

The bigcone pinyon pine, or Martínez pinyon, is a small, bushy tree with a short trunk that is often contorted. It has widely spreading branches. They are spaced irregularly along the trunk and form an open, rounded crown. The tree normally grows to a height between 16.5 and 33 feet (5 and 10 meters), although some have grown as high as 49 feet (15 meters). Its trunk measures up to 19.5 inches (50 centimeters) in diameter.

The bark of the bigcone pinyon pine is dark brown in color and is broken into square plates measuring almost 4 inches (10 centimeters) in diameter. The needles usually grow in clusters of five. They are slender and flexible and measure 3.1 to 4 inches (8 to 10 centimeters) long. The

Pine, whitebark
Pinus albicaulis

DIVISION: Tracheophyta
CLASS: Pinopsida
ORDER: Pinales
FAMILY: Pinaceae
STATUS: Endangered, IUCN
Candidate, ESA
RANGE: Canada, USA (California, Idaho, Montana, Nevada, Oregon, Washington, Wyoming)

Pine, whitebark
Pinus albicaulis

Description and biology

Whitebark pine is a cone-bearing tree that lives on high mountains. Trees can live up to 1,000 years and may grow to 69 feet (21 meters), though many are much shorter, growing dense and twisted close to the ground. The trunk diameter can be as wide as 5 feet (1.5 meters). Other names for this tree include whitestem, alpine whitebark, white pine, and creeping pine.

The bark of the whitebark pine is actually pale gray. As the tree grows older its bark darkens and becomes scaly. The trees are evergreen, with short green to yellow-green needles 1 to 3 inches (2.5 to 7.6 centimeters) long. These needles are clustered in groups of five at the end of branches and remain on the tree from four to eight years.

The pinecones containing seeds are round or egg-shaped with thick scales, measuring around 2 to 3 inches (5 to 8 centimeters) long. They remain mostly closed, rather than spreading to release seeds. Two species in particular are able to open whitebark pinecones and carry the seeds away: red squirrels and a bird called Clark's nutcracker. A single Clark's nutcracker may hide up to 98,000 seeds in a year. Although the nutcracker eats some of the seeds, many of the seeds are abandoned and end up germinating into new trees. The nutcracker is therefore vital for the survival of the tree.

Habitat and current distribution

Whitebark pines are found in high elevation and high latitude areas, where the weather is windy and cold. It is very hardy and can grow in places where other pines cannot survive. Its range is western North

The whitebark pine, found in the alpine and subalpine regions of the western United States and Canada, is threatened by a disease known as white pine blister rust as well as infestation by the mountain pine beetle. © DE AGOSTINI PICTURE LIBRARY/GETTY IMAGES.

America, including British Columbia, Washington, Oregon, and Northern California, spreading through the Rocky Mountains to Alberta, Idaho, Montana, Wyoming, and Nevada.

History and conservation measures

The whitebark pine likely came to North America across the Bering land bridge, which once connected Russia and Alaska, 1.8 million years ago. Seeds were probably carried by Clark's nutcrackers.

The whitebark pine is a vital species in the areas where it flourishes. Its seeds have more calories per pound than butter or chocolate, and so are a high-energy food source for animals from Clark's nutcrackers to grizzly bears. This makes whitebark pine a keystone species—one that many other species depend on to survive. Its disappearance would cause drastic changes to its ecosystem (an ecological system including all of its living things and their environment).

Whitebark pine is also a foundation species, which means it can create a livable environment for other plants and animals. Whitebark pines are so sturdy that they are often the first plants to grow in harsh, high-altitude environments after avalanches or fires. They then provide shelter for other species, like firs and spruces. In addition, whitebark pines reduce springtime flooding by slowing snowmelt and soil erosion.

Because of the whitebark pine's ecological importance, threats to it are especially ecologically serious. A major danger to this species is white pine blister rust (WPBR), an exotic pathogen (disease-causing microorganism) that began infecting various whitebark pines in about 1925. WPBR kills around 35 percent of the trees, and as many as two-thirds are infected. Whitebark pine is also susceptible to the mountain pine beetle, which tunnels into the bark to lay eggs. This creates a fungus that can kill the tree.

Beetle infestations are worsened by climate change and warming temperatures. Climate change can also contribute to drought, wildfires, and habitat reduction, all of which threaten the long-term health of the trees. By some estimates, while individual trees will survive, whitebark pine forests may be gone in two or three generations, or around 150 years.

Pitcher plant, green
Sarracenia oreophila

DIVISION: Tracheophyta
CLASS: Magnoliopsida
ORDER: Ericales
FAMILY: Sarraceniaceae
STATUS: Critically endangered, IUCN
Endangered, ESA
RANGE: USA (Alabama, Georgia,
North Carolina)

Pitcher plant, green
Sarracenia oreophila

Description and biology

The green pitcher plant is classified as a perennial (a plant that lives, grows, flowers, and produces seeds for three or more consecutive years). It is insectivorous (pronounced in-sec-TIV-uh-res), meaning it depends on insects for food.

The plant's green or yellow-green leaves grow to a height of 8 to 29.5 inches (20 to 75 centimeters). Wider at the top than at the bottom, the leaves resemble pitchers or horn-shaped enclosures. The pitcher-shaped leaves usually contain a sweet-smelling liquid. Insects are drawn to the liquid or to the plant's bright coloration. Once the insect enters the leaf, it is prevented from escaping by bristles on the inside of the leaf surface. Eventually, the insect drowns in the liquid. It is then digested, or broken down, by enzymes (chemical compounds composed of proteins) and absorbed by the plant.

The green pitcher plant, native to the southern United States, is threatened by loss of its wetland habitat, the use of herbicides, the spread of invasive species, and removal by plant collectors. © RBFLORA/ALAMY.

The leaves and flower buds appear in early April. The leaves mature and yellow flowers bloom during late April and May. The pitcher-shaped leaves wither by late summer and are replaced by flat leaves that remain until the following spring.

Habitat and current distribution

The green pitcher plant is found in only a few areas in northeast Alabama. There is also one pitcher plant site in Georgia and two in North Carolina. The largest populations occupy the Cumberland Plateau region in Alabama. Botanists (scientists who study plants) estimate that about 30 green pitcher plant populations exist in the wild. The size of these populations varies from a single plant to more than 1,000 plants.

Green pitcher plants require very acidic soil in which to grow. They are found in a variety of habitats (mainly wetland areas). These include bogs (areas of wet spongy ground composed of decaying plant matter), woodland sites that have poor drainage in winter, and sloping stream banks.

History and conservation measures

The green pitcher plant was never common, but it was found over a wider range than it was in the mid-2010s. At one time, its range extended into Tennessee.

The decline of this plant is mainly due to the draining of its wetland (land where there is a lot of water in the soil) habitat. The green pitcher plant is further threatened by herbicide and fertilizer runoff (water that drains away, bringing substances with it) from farms in its range.

Collectors who prize the unusual-looking plant have also reduced its numbers in the wild. Collection of endangered or threatened plants without permission is banned in the United States.

The survival of the green pitcher plant can be ensured only if wetlands that form the base of its habitat are preserved. Scientists are also working on additional ways to preserve the plant. Its seeds are stored at the U.S. Department of Agriculture National Seed Technology Laboratory, and the Atlanta Botanical Garden is growing plants in hopes of reintroducing them to the wild in some areas.

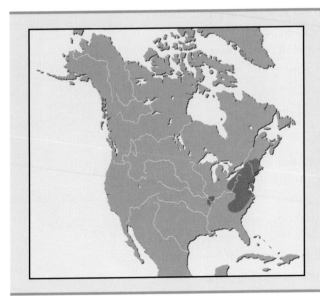

Pogonia, small whorled
Isotria medeoloides

DIVISION: Tracheophyta
CLASS: Magnoliopsida
ORDER: Asparagales
FAMILY: Orchidaceae
STATUS: Threatened, ESA
RANGE: Canada, eastern and mid-western USA

Pogonia, small whorled
Isotria medeoloides

Description and biology

The small whorled pogonia is considered one of the rarest orchids in eastern North America. It is a perennial (a plant that lives, grows, flowers, and produces seeds for three or more consecutive years). It has a waxy, pale green stem that grows 3.5 to 10 inches (8.9 to 25.4 centimeters) high. The stem is topped by five or six drooping, gray-green leaves arranged in a distinctive whorl, or spiral, from which the plant gets its common name. Each leaf measures 0.8 to 3.3 inches (2 to 8.4 centimeters) in length.

Growing above the leaves are one or two yellowish-green flowers that bloom in May and June and then die very quickly. The sepals (leaf-like external parts lying below the petals of the flowers) are green and narrow, measuring up to 1 inch (2.5 centimeters) in length.

Habitat and current distribution

The small whorled pogonia prefers open forests of deciduous (trees whose leaves fall off annually) hardwood trees such as beech, birch, and oak.

It grows best when there are breaks in the forest canopy (the uppermost layer of a forest) so that light shines through. The plant prefers acidic soil with many dead leaves covering the ground. It is often found on hills near small streams.

In the United States, the small whorled pogonia is found in Connecticut, Delaware, the District of Columbia, Georgia, Illinois, Maine, Massachusetts, Michigan, New Hampshire, New Jersey, New York, North Carolina, Ohio, Pennsylvania, Rhode Island, South Carolina, Tennessee, Vermont, Virginia, and West Virginia. The largest populations are in Maine and New Hampshire. In Canada, it is found only in the province of Ontario. As of 2008, botanists (scientists who study plants) found 150 groups of small whorled pogonias. Most of these groups contained fewer than 20 plants, but approximately 50 groups in New Hampshire contained more than 100 plants.

Did You Know?

In 1995 the New Hampshire chapter of the Nature Conservancy, a non-profit environmental organization, purchased 170 acres (68 hectares) at Mount Teneriffe, near the town of Milton, for use as a wildlife preserve. Biologists (people who study living organisms) consider this site to be one of the five most significant sites for the small whorled pogonia in the world. Besides providing a safe habitat for the plant, the preserve also provides a safe haven for a variety of birds and other rare plants, such as American ginseng. In addition to being open to the public, the preserve serves as a research area for university scientists and graduate students.

History and conservation measures

The small whorled pogonia has decreased in number because the forests in which it lives have been converted into land for housing or roads. In addition, reducing the plant's habitat crowds the deer and rabbits that eat this plant into the remaining forestland. Existing regulations do not protect this plant well enough, and in many states most small whorled pogonias grow on private land. Neither federal nor state endangered species listings require private landowners to preserve endangered species on their property. Government or conservation organizations must either buy the private land where the endangered species lives or persuade landowners to agree to protect the plants.

The status of the small whorled pogonia has improved since its 1982 listing as endangered, however. After botanists found new populations of the plant and some populations on private land became protected, the plant's listing was changed to threatened, which is less severe than endangered. Botanists have also discovered that when they create gaps in the forest canopy to let in more light where small whorled pogonias

Most small whorled pogonias grow on private land and therefore are not protected by the Endangered Species Act. COURTESY OF THE U.S. ARMY ENVIRONMENTAL COMMAND/FORT A.P. HILL ENVIRONMENTAL DIVISION.

grow, new plants appear and existing plants bloom better. Conservationists (people who work to manage and protect nature) are focusing on protecting existing populations of this species, increasing the number of protected populations. They are also experimenting further with habitats to find the best conditions for this plant to thrive.

Rhododendron, Chapman's
Rhododendron minus var. *chapmanii*

DIVISION: Tracheophyta
CLASS: Magnoliopsida
ORDER: Ericales
FAMILY: Ericaceae
STATUS: Endangered, ESA
RANGE: USA (Florida)

Rhododendron, Chapman's

Rhododendron minus var. *chapmanii*

Description and biology

Chapman's rhododendron is an evergreen shrub that grows 4 to 10 feet (1.2 to 3 meters) high. The bark on new shoots is reddish brown. As the plant ages, the bark turns gray and starts to peel. The rhododendron's leaves are oval-shaped, measuring 1.2 to 2.6 inches (3 to 6.6 centimeters) in length. They are green on top but reddish underneath because the surface is lined with flat red scales.

Chapman's rhododendron produces tight clusters of flowers that bloom in March and April. The flowers vary from pale to bright pink. Each flower has five petals measuring 1.2 to 1.4 inches (3 to 3.6 centimeters) long. The petals spread out in a funnel shape and are slightly unequal in size (the lowest being the largest).

Botanists (scientists who study plants) do not know how this plant reproduces in the wild but it does produce a great number of seeds. Plant

Chapman's rhododendrons live in a unique habitat—on gentle slopes between pine woods and forested swamps. © DAVID NOR-RIS/SCIENCE SOURCE.

nurseries have had great success growing the shrub from seed and also by using cuttings from the plant's stem or root.

Habitat and current distribution

Chapman's rhododendron needs a very specific type of habitat. It lives on gentle slopes between pine woods and forested swamps. The plant prefers acidic, sandy soil that does not flood. It does best with some shade and some sun. The species needs fires in its area in order to thrive. After a fire, Chapman's rhododendrons resprout and produce many blooms.

As of 2010, this species of rhododendron was found only in three separate areas in Florida. The largest area was in Liberty and Gadsden Counties, containing about 2,160 plants. Gulf County, the second-largest location, had about 1,000 plants. At the third location, Camp Blanding, a Florida National Guard base, only 31 plants existed.

History and conservation measures

When first listed as endangered in 1979, Chapman's rhododendron was considered its own species. Since then, botanists have reclassified it as a variety of the Piedmont rhododendron (*Rhododendron minus*). The Piedmont rhododendron is not endangered because there are many plants located throughout the southeastern United States. However, Chapman's rhododendron (*Rhododendron minus* var. *chapmanii*), being a variety with distinct characteristics and a unique habitat in north Florida, is endangered.

Much of this plant's habitat was destroyed by logging and by the clearing of areas to create pine plantations. In the early 2010s, two of the three areas where the plant occurs were protected from development. Camp Blanding and the Gulf Coast population were completely protected, the latter within a nature preserve. But the Liberty/Gadsden population, the largest, remained on private property owned by a timber company. Neither the U.S. Endangered Species Act nor Florida's Endangered and Threatened Species Act require private landowners to conserve endangered plants or animals. As a result, conservationists (people who work to manage and protect nature) must either buy land where endangered species live or persuade landowners to preserve these species and their habitats.

When Chapman's rhododendron was first listed, the collecting of wild specimens by plant nurseries was a threat but it is no longer a problem because nurseries now raise their own from seed.

Actions that could be taken in the future include buying land where the Liberty/Gadsden population occurs; resurveying all areas where the species is known to grow to accurately determine the number of plants; surveying other areas nearby to find potential new populations; studying how the Chapman's rhododendron reproduces in the wild; and establishing a seed bank.

Did You Know?

Chapman's rhododendron is an example of a plant that has adapted to the presence of wildfires, and even thrives where there are frequent blazes. Fire-adapted forests, which serve as the plant's native habitat, make up 95 percent of the historic coastal plain in the southeastern United States. Due to the large number of fire-starting lightning strikes in the area, fires were historically frequent here and the natural environment has become dependent on fire, which serves to clear out dead plant life and enrich the soil. However, as human populations grow in these areas, fires are suppressed to prevent damage to homes and other structures. In such areas, conservationists are seeking to balance the natural role of fire with the needs of human communities.

Rockcress, Braun's
Arabis perstellata

DIVISION: Tracheophyta
CLASS: Magnoliopsida
ORDER: Brassicales
FAMILY: Brassicaceae
STATUS: Endangered, ESA
RANGE: USA (Kentucky, Tennessee)

Rockcress, Braun's
Arabis perstellata

Description and biology

Braun's rockcress is a member of the mustard family. It is a perennial (a plant that lives, grows, flowers, and produces seeds for three or more consecutive years) that forms a low mat with gray foliage (leaves) and white-to-lavender flowers. There is downy hair on both its stem and its foliage. The plant's stem can grow to about 32 inches (80 centimeters) long.

The plant produces a new cluster of leaves at its base annually. New branches grow from the leaf cluster produced the prior year. Lower leaves range in size from 1.6 to 6 inches (4 to 15 centimeters). Upper leaves measure only about 1.4 inches (3.5 centimeters). The flowers have four tiny petals and four pale green sepals (the base of the flower petals). Braun's rockcress produces flowers from late March to early May and mature fruits in mid-May to early June. Its seeds are reddish brown and only about 0.04 inches (1 millimeter) long.

Habitat and current distribution

Braun's rockcress grows on moist, but not usually wet, rocky formations protruding from steep, wooded slopes. It also is found around the bases of trees. It prefers full or partial shade.

As of 2010, the plant had been found in 54 locations: 42 in Kentucky and 12 in Tennessee. At 31 of these locations, 50 or more plants were growing. In 2015 one more occurrence was reported in Kentucky.

History and conservation measures

Braun's rockcress, named after E. Lucy Braun, its discoverer, was listed as endangered by the U.S. Fish and Wildlife Service in 1995. At that point, biologists (people who study living organisms) had found the plant growing in 25 different places. The biggest threat to the plant is destruction of its natural habitat. People build homes and businesses, graze livestock, and harvest timber on the plant's habitat. In addition, nonnative weeds compete with the rockcress. Additionally, laws and regulations have failed to protect this species adequately. Most of these plants grow on private land, where landowners have no obligation to protect endangered species. To protect the plant, government or nonprofit groups must either buy land where the plant grows or persuade landowners to preserve the plant's habitat.

Protected spaces have been increasing. By 2010 a total of 10 populations of more than 50 healthy plants were growing on protected land, half of it state-owned and half private property where landowners have agreed to protect the species. The most severe continuing threat is competition from nonnative plants, especially the European garlic mustard and amur honeysuckle. Conservation actions planned include surveying the plants' range to find new populations, developing ways to control invasive nonnative plants, and continuing to try to protect plants located on private property.

Rosewood, Brazilian
Dalbergia nigra

DIVISION: Tracheophyta
CLASS: Magnoliopsida
ORDER: Fabales
FAMILY: Fabaceae
STATUS: Vulnerable, IUCN
RANGE: Brazil

Rosewood, Brazilian
Dalbergia nigra

Description and biology

The Brazilian rosewood is a tropical timber tree that grows to a height of 50 to 82 feet (15 to 25 meters). Because most of these trees have been logged, it is rare to find any with thick trunks. The remaining rosewoods have trunks measuring just 1 to 1.3 feet (0.3 to 0.4 meters) in diameter.

The tree's bark is thin, gray, and rough. Its branches are dark and roundish, and they grow in a slightly zigzag manner from the trunk. The compound leaves are divided into 12 to 18 leaflets, each one measuring up to 0.6 inches (1.5 centimeters) long and 0.3 inches (0.8 centimeters) wide.

The Brazilian rosewood flowers in August and September, and its fruits ripen from October to November. The pale, violet-scented flowers are about 0.35 inches (0.89 centimeters) long and are arranged in bunches on leafless shoots.

Habitat and current distribution

The Brazilian rosewood is found in the Atlantic coastal forests of Brazil in a range of climates from 98 to 5,575 feet (30 to 1,700 meters) in

A Brazilian rosewood towers over the rain forest at a nature reserve in eastern Brazil. © LUIZ CLAUDIO MARIGO/NATUREPL.COM.

elevation. The largest numbers of the tree are found in southern Bahia and Espírito Santo. It is most frequently found inhabiting rolling or mountainous terrain that has relatively fertile soil. Current population figures are not available.

History and conservation measures

The Brazilian rosewood is one of Brazil's finest woods. It is highly prized for its valuable heartwood, the central nonliving wood in the trunk of the tree. The heartwood is purplish black in color and is rather oily and fragrant—hence the common name of rosewood. The durable wood of the Brazilian rosewood has been used for decorative veneers, high-quality furniture, musical instruments, tools, and craft products.

Brazilian rosewoods grew in great numbers when European explorers first came to South America in the early 16th century. Once the Europeans realized the value of its wood, they began cutting down the rosewood and shipping it around the world. Other rosewoods were cut down simply to create plantations and farms. Still more were cleared to aid mining operations. This deforestation (large-scale removal of trees) continued for over 300 years, finally reaching its peak in the 20th century. At present, Brazilian rosewoods occupy just 5 percent of their former range.

Only a tiny portion of the remaining rosewood forests are protected in national parks and reserves. In 1992 the Brazilian rosewood was added to Appendix I of the Convention on International Trade in Endangered Species of Wild Fauna and Flora (CITES), an international treaty to protect wildlife. This act prohibits the trade of the tree between nations that have signed the treaty.

Brazilian rosewood was widely used in guitars and violin parts until the late 1960s. Now the wood may only be used if the tree was harvested and exported before 1992 or if it fell naturally. A number of valuable and collectible musical instruments made from Brazilian rosewood still exist, but musicians traveling with such instruments need special permits.

Despite these protective measures, the Brazilian rosewood remains threatened by those who cut it down illegally to sell for high prices.

Sequoia, giant
Sequoiadendron giganteum

DIVISION: Tracheophyta
CLASS: Pinopsida
ORDER: Pinales
FAMILY: Cupressaceae
STATUS: Endangered, IUCN
RANGE: USA (California)

Sequoia, giant
Sequoiadendron giganteum

Description and biology

"King Sequoia," as conservationist John Muir called this species, is the world's largest tree. The average giant sequoia is 150 to 280 feet (45 to 85 meters) tall and 16 to 23 feet (5 to 7 meters) in diameter, although some are much larger. One huge tree in Yosemite National Park even had a tunnel carved in it so that people could drive cars through it! Although this tree fell in 1969, today visitors to California's Calaveras Big Trees State Park can walk through a tunnel cut into another giant sequoia. Giant sequoias are evergreens (plants that keep green leaves all year). They have thick, reddish-brown, deeply ridged bark. Mature giant sequoias have no branches on the lower half of their trunks because of a lack of sunlight. On the top half, the branches form a rounded shape and sweep downward. The giant sequoia's leaves are small, flat, and prickly. Its reddish-brown cones are only about 3 inches (7.5 centimeters) long and 1.6 inches (4 centimeters) wide.

The giant sequoia population, once decimated by lumbering activity, is currently under threat by historical mismanagement of its habitat and competition from other species.
© NICKOLAY STANEV/SHUTTER-STOCK.COM.

Giant sequoias require deep, moist soil; a humid climate with autumn rains, winter snows, and dry summers; and an altitude of 5,000 to 7,000 feet (1,524 to 2,134 meters) above sea level. They can live to be older than 3,000 years old, resisting low-level forest fires, winds, and rot that kill other tree species.

Most giant sequoias do not make enough cones to reproduce until they are 150 to 200 years old. The trees produce both male and female cones. In spring, male cones release pollen to female cones, fertilizing them. The female cones then release about 200 seeds each. The cones must dry out in order to open up enough for the seeds to be released. Although beetles and squirrels that eat the green edges of the cones (which dislodges seeds and also speeds up their drying out) help to release the seeds, the most effective dispersal method is by low-level wildfires. The heat from a fire rises, drying out the cones and making them open up and release their seeds into the wind and onto the ground below.

Habitat and current distribution

The giant sequoia grows mainly on the western slopes of the Sierra Nevada, a rugged mountain range in central and Northern California and northern Nevada. The trees inhabit a strip of land 260 miles (420 kilometers) long and 15 miles (24 kilometers) wide. There are 68 groves of giant sequoia, some containing only a few trees and others containing more than 20,000. Most of the groves are in Sequoia and Kings Canyon National Parks, the Giant Sequoia National Monument, and Yosemite National Park.

History and conservation measures

Two hundred million years ago, the ancestors of giant sequoias dominated the landscape in North America and Europe. But at the end of the Cretaceous period (about 66 million years ago), other plant species became dominant. This species has grown in its current location for only about 2 million years. Pictures drawn by native peoples on rocks near the trees date as far back as 1350 BCE, but Europeans did not see sequoias until the mid-1800s. The U.S. government created Sequoia National Park in 1890 to save the trees there from being cut down; up until the 1950s, however, some sequoias elsewhere were chopped down, which reduced groves by about 25 percent. Giant sequoia wood is too brittle to be used for home building, but it was used to make fenceposts, shingles, and even pencils.

The giant sequoia is endangered because not enough new sequoias are growing to renew the population as old trees die. Other, faster-growing species of trees are replacing them instead. This is happening partly because fire-prevention methods have reduced the number of wildfires that naturally occur in sequoia groves. Low-level fires actually benefit the giant sequoia: they kill competitor trees, help dry out the sequoias' cones so their seeds can be released, and create favorable soil conditions for new sequoia seedlings. Therefore, the U.S. Forest Service and the National Park Service now ignite low-level, controlled fires in sequoia groves. Another threat to the giant sequoia is climate change. Drought and warm weather reduce the snowfall in the mountains, thus also reducing the moisture the trees need.

Organizations are working to preserve this much-loved species by studying the trees' ecosystems (ecological systems including all of their living things and the environment), their responses to fire, and possible ways they could adapt to climate change.

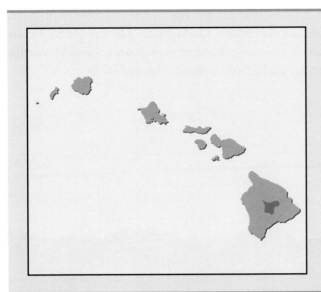

Silversword, Ka'u
Argyroxiphium kauense

DIVISION: Tracheophyta
CLASS: Magnoliopsida
ORDER: Asterales
FAMILY: Asteraceae
STATUS: Critically endangered, IUCN
Endangered, ESA
RANGE: USA (Hawaii)

Silversword, Ka'u
Argyroxiphium kauense

Description and biology

Ka'u (pronounced KAH-oo) silversword, also called Mauna Loa silversword, is a monocarpic plant (one that bears fruit and flowers only once and then dies) of the aster family. It grows to a height of up to 4.25 feet (1.29 meters) and has long flowering stems that grow from 3.3 to 6.5 feet (1 to 1.9 meters) long. The Ka'u silversword is a giant rosette (clustered) shrub with leaves covered with gray or silver hairs. The leaves are long and narrow, measuring about 8 to 16 inches in length and only about 0.2 inches (0.5 centimeters) in width.

When the Ka'u silversword grows, its rosette widens in diameter and its stem gets taller. This growth occurs for several years before the plant produces a flowering stalk, called an inflorescence. The inflorescence has many branches, and each branch has a flowering head made up of 3 to 11 ray flowers that are about 0.5 inches (1 centimeter) long. Each of the ray flowers contains 50 to 200 florets that are only about 0.2 inches (0.5 centimeters) long.

The flowers, which range in color from white or yellow to deep red, bloom in August and September. The fruits the plant produces are dry and black. Once the fruit sets, the plant dies. Scientists believe that flying insects, probably native bees, pollinate the species.

Ka'u silversword grows only near Hawaii's Mauna Loa volcano, where it is threatened by grazing animals and invasive plants. © IMAGEBROKER/ALAMY.

Habitat and current distribution

The Ka'u silversword grows in moist open forest areas or bogs (areas of wet spongy ground composed of decaying plant matter), generally at altitudes between 5,000 and 8,000 feet (1,525 and 2,440 meters). It also occurs in some dry areas in which smooth lava is covered by a shallow layer of soil. This species is found only on the slopes of Mauna Loa, a large volcanic mountain on the island of Hawaii. The Ka'u silversword populations inhabit a combined area of less than 10 acres (4 hectares). Botanists (scientists who study plants) believe that at one time there were thousands of the plants on Mauna Loa. In the early 21st century, there are fewer than 550 plants.

History and conservation measures

At one time the Ka'u silversword likely existed across the island of Hawaii, in a band stretching from the southwest of the island to the northeast slope of Mauna Loa. It also probably existed on the volcano Hualalai. It is interesting to note that the plant is endemic to (native to and occurring only in) a volcanic mountain and has survived its lava flows with a healthy population for many years.

In the early 21st century, because of its low population, the Ka'u silversword is extremely vulnerable to extinction. Browsing animals (animals that feed on tender shoots, twigs, and leaves) are a particular threat. Cows and feral animals (domestic animals that have become wild) such as pigs, goats, and mouflon sheep have greatly reduced its numbers and prevent it from recovery. The animals tend to eat older, more mature plants. Since the plant flowers only one time in its life, this browsing significantly reduces reproduction. With so few remaining plants, the gene pool (the number of units that pass on inherited traits) is quite low, which may weaken the species. Since there are only three surviving populations—and those three are located on a volcano—there is a strong risk that lava flow or fire could entirely wipe out the species. Pests, drought, disease, and the introduction of nonnative species also threaten the Ka'u silversword.

Protective fencing has been built around existing populations of the species since the 1970s to keep feral animals from browsing and trampling the plants. Controlling the ungulates (hooved animals) around the Ka'u silversword habitat is crucial to its survival. Research into the effects of nonnative plants and habitat requirements is ongoing.

To help reestablish the Ka'u silversword in Hawaii, a partnership was started in 1998 between government agencies and private entities. Conservation efforts include growing the plant at the Volcano Rare Plant Facility in Hawai'i Volcanoes National Park. Staff and volunteers then move large Ka'u silversword plants to their natural high-elevation habitat inside the park.

Torreya, Florida
Torreya taxifolia

DIVISION: Tracheophyta
CLASS: Pinopsida
ORDER: Pinales
FAMILY: Taxaceae
STATUS: Critically endangered, IUCN
           Endangered, ESA
RANGE: USA (Florida, Georgia)

Torreya, Florida
Torreya taxifolia

Description and biology

The Florida torreya (pronounced TORE-ee-uh) is a relatively small ever-green tree that usually grows to a height of 30 feet (9 meters). However, some torreyas grow as high as 65 feet (20 meters). Stiff, sharp-pointed needles grow along opposite sides of the branches, making them appear flattened. When crushed, the needles give off a strong resinous odor. Because of this, the tree is sometimes called the stinking cedar. It is also known as the Florida nutmeg tree.

The torreya is dioecious (pronounced die-EE-shus). This means that one torreya will have male cones, while another will have fe-male cones. Male cones give off pollen in March and April. Over the course of the summer, the pollinated female cones develop into dark green, oval-shaped fruits with one large seed 1 to 1.5 inches (2.5 to 3.8 centimeters) long. The seeds then drop off in the fall. The tree

The Florida torreya, native to Florida and Georgia, was heavily used for construction and fuel in the early 20th century, severely reducing its population. © ROB & ANN SIMPSON/VISUALS UNLIMITED, INC.

reaches maturity (and is thus able to give off pollen or seeds) after about 20 years.

Habitat and current distribution

Florida torreyas are found only in the Apalachicola River area in Gadsden, Liberty, and Jackson Counties in the panhandle of Florida and in an adjacent part of Decatur County, Georgia. The trees grow along the steep sides of ravines and on bluffs in the moist shade of pine and hardwood trees. Its habitat is only about 77 square miles (200 square kilometers). As of 2010, only 500 to 600 specimens remained; fewer than 10 were known to produce cones. Other individuals were stump sprouts (new growth from old stumps).

History and conservation measures

The range of the Florida torreya has not changed over the years, but the number of trees within that range has dropped significantly. One reason for this drop was that many sections within the range were cleared to create residential areas. This is no longer a threat, as the remaining habitat areas are not easily reached and are not suitable for development.

The main threat currently facing the Florida torreya is disease. Beginning in the 1950s, a fungal disease attacked and killed most of the trees in the area. The population declined from about 600,000 trees to only around 600. New trees resprouted from the old roots and stumps, but they also became infected and died before reaching maturity.

Scientists have attempted to replant trees in other areas, without success. Researchers continue to search for the cause of, and a cure for, the disease that is destroying the species. According to the International Union for Conservation of Nature and Natural Resources (IUCN), unless a solution can be found for the disease, the Florida torreya will become extinct in the wild.

Trillium, persistent
Trillium persistens

DIVISION: Tracheophyta
CLASS: Magnoliopsida
ORDER: Liliales
FAMILY: Melanthiaceae
STATUS: Endangered, ESA
RANGE: USA (Georgia, South Carolina)

Trillium, persistent
Trillium persistens

Description and biology

The persistent trillium is part of the lily order of plants. It is a rhizomatous plant (having an underground horizontal stem, or rhizome, that puts out shoots above the ground and roots below). A perennial (a plant that lives, grows, flowers, and produces seeds for three or more consecutive years), it is also herbaceous (pronounced ur-BAY-shuss), meaning its stems are soft, not woody, and its leaves and stem die each winter, though the underground parts of the plant remain alive. Persistent trilliums grow singly or in clusters of up to 10 plants. Each plant is 8 to 12 inches (20 to 30 centimeters) high.

In early spring, the plant produces a single white flower on an upright, slightly arching stalk. The flower turns pink as it ages. This flower has three petals, 0.8 to 1.4 inches (2 to 3.5 centimeters) long and 0.2 to 0.4 inches (0.5 to 1 centimeter) wide. It contains six stamens (male re-

The persistent trillium is a rare plant found in the Tallulah Gorge and surrounding region in Georgia and South Carolina. Human activity in the area is considered the plant's main threat. © JEFFREY LEPORE/SCIENCE SOURCE.

productive structures), each with a white filament (stalk) and a yellow anther (the pollen-producing top of the stamen). From a single point just below the flower sprout three leaves shaped like the heads of spears. In midsummer, the persistent trillium produces a tiny fruit.

For the first six years of its life, the persistent trillium has only one leaf and no flower. It matures in 7 to 10 years and can live for 30 years. The species is spread by ants, which collect the seeds, eat part of them, and leave the rest outside their nests, where they may take root. Persistent trilliums live on steep slopes in forests that contain a mix of deciduous trees (trees whose leaves fall off annually) and evergreen trees.

Habitat and current distribution

The persistent trillium grows only along the Tallulah-Tugaloo River system in northeastern Georgia and just across the South Carolina border. It has been found in Habersham, Rabun, and Stephens Counties in Georgia and Oconee County in South Carolina. The largest population occurs within Tallulah Gorge, a deep canyon made by the Tallulah River. The total population size is unknown because it is difficult to count plants on the remote, steep slopes where this species occurs. In 1985 botanists (scientists who study plants) found 20,028 persistent trillium stems. According to a 2011 U.S. Fish and Wildlife Service (USFWS) report on the plant, this number still represents the best estimate of the plant's population.

History and conservation measures

There are 48 other trillium species, and botanists identified the persistent trillium as its own species only in 1971. The USFWS listed the persistent trillium as endangered in 1978 because of its scarcity and because it faced possible threats from development and logging. Since then, the U.S. government and the Georgia state government have acquired much of the land where the persistent trillium grows, such as the land that now is called Tallulah Gorge State Park, and they protect the plant on their lands. Georgia Power, a utilities company that owns most of the rest of this plant's habitat, protects it as well.

In 2011 the USFWS decided, however, that the species should remain on the endangered list. The USFWS stated that it could not determine whether the population is increasing, stable, or decreasing because the plants are so hard to reach. One potential new threat is a beetle that destroys hemlocks, evergreens that form part of the forest where the persistent trillium is found. If hemlocks die, the species' environment could change, and plant competitors could appear. Kudzu, English ivy, and other nonnative, invasive plants could also threaten this species in the future. (Invasive plants come from a different ecosystem. They spread or multiply, causing harm when they are introduced into a new environment.)

Venus flytrap
Dionaea muscipula

DIVISION: Tracheophyta
CLASS: Magnoliopsida
ORDER: Caryophyllales
FAMILY: Droseraceae
STATUS: Vulnerable, IUCN
RANGE: USA (North Carolina, South Carolina)

Venus flytrap
Dionaea muscipula

Description and biology

The Venus flytrap is one of North America's most well-known carnivorous or insectivorous (in-sec-TIV-uh-res) plants. Insectivorous means "insect-eating," as the plant depends on insects for food (although it also preys on small animals). The Venus flytrap is classified as a perennial (a plant that lives, grows, flowers, and produces seeds for three or more consecutive years).

The plant can grow to a height of about 12 inches (30.5 centimeters). It has four to eight leaves, each measuring 0.8 to 4.7 inches (2 to 12 centimeters) in length. The leaves grow around the base of the plant, forming a rosette, or rounded cluster. The end of each leaf is divided into identical, semicircular halves that are connected or hinged at the midrib. The margins, or edges, of each half bear long, sharp spines.

The Venus flytrap's popularity as a plant that eats insects makes it a target for poachers, who have put its population in the wilds of its native North and South Carolina at risk. © DAVID HUNTLEY CREATIVE/SHUTTERSTOCK.COM.

The leaves secrete a sweet fluid, which attracts insects and small animals. When an insect lands on the leaf, it touches trigger hairs at the center of the leaf. When touched, these hairs cause the leaf to snap shut around the prey. The spines interlock and the prey cannot escape. The plant then releases digestive solutions to dissolve the prey's body. After the prey is fully digested, the leaf reopens.

Scientists are not certain how the Venus flytrap closes, since the plant has no nervous sytem and no muscles. One theory is that the closing is triggered by an electrical current that changes fluid pressure in the leaves.

The Venus flytrap has a flowering stem that rises above the rosette. At the top of the stem is a cluster of 4 to 10 small, white flowers. Flowering begins near the last week in May and is usually over before the middle of June.

Habitat and current distribution

This plant is found on the coastal plains of North Carolina and South Carolina. Its range extends for about 200 miles (320 kilometers) from Beaufort County in North Carolina to Charleston County in South Carolina. Botanists (scientists who study plants) are unsure of the total number of Venus flytraps currently in existence. However, they do know its numbers are declining. In North Carolina, flytraps once grew in 20 counties. As of 2013, that number had been reduced to 12.

The Venus flytrap prefers to inhabit open, sunny bogs (areas of wet, spongy ground composed of decaying plant matter). Because the soil in bogs is low in nitrogen, the plant derives that nutrient from the insects and small animals on which it feeds.

History and conservation measures

The Venus flytrap once existed in great numbers, but since the 1970s its populations have been small. The two main reasons for the plant's decline are habitat destruction and over-collection.

Fire plays an important role in the Venus flytrap's habitat. Frequent natural fires remove most of the low vegetation (plant life) in the plant's range. When these fires are put out quickly or even prevented, the flytrap faces competition from other plants and is often destroyed. Conservationists (people who work to manage and protect nature) in the Carolinas have staged controlled burns in parts of the flytrap's habitat to try to encourage the species.

Another habitat threat is the draining of wetland areas (areas where there is a lot of water in the soil, such as swamps) to create land suitable for housing or farming. Any permanent drop in the water level of a site can destroy any and all Venus flytraps inhabiting it.

Even though laws protect the Venus flytrap in both North Carolina and South Carolina, collectors treasure the plant, and it is still collected illegally from the wild. Until 2014 fines in North Carolina were $50 or less—too small to stop poachers (illegal collectors), since they can make thousands of dollars from flytrap sales. North Carolina does not keep records of poached plants, but in 2013 officials reported that thousands of plants were still being taken and that poaching occurred continuously through the spring and summer.

A 2014 law made poaching the flytraps a felony, a major crime punishable by 25 to 39 months in jail. It is hoped that this will slow poaching.

Flytraps thrive in greenhouses and can be easily grown, so they should not become extinct. But if poaching cannot be controlled, they may be wiped out in the wild.

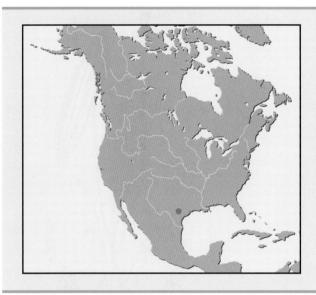

Wild rice, Texas
Zizania texana

DIVISION: Tracheophyta
CLASS: Magnoliopsida
ORDER: Poales
FAMILY: Poaceae
STATUS: Endangered, ESA
RANGE: USA (Texas)

Wild rice, Texas
Zizania texana

Description and biology

Texas wild rice is a coarse, aquatic grass with long, underwater stems. It is classified as a perennial (a plant that lives, grows, flowers, and produces seeds for three or more consecutive years). Its leaves are green, thin, flat, and very long. They measure up to 45 inches (114 centimeters) long and 0.25 to 1 inch (0.6 to 2.5 centimeters) wide. The lower part of the grass, with leaves, often floats on the water. This part of the plant can measure 3.5 feet (1.1 meters) long.

Flower stalks, when present, extend 12 to 35 inches (30.5 to 89 centimeters) above the surface of the water. The plant flowers and produces grainlike seeds at various times from April to November. The plant is related to the wild rice plants that people eat, but it is not used for human food.

Habitat and current distribution

This grass species is found only in a 2-mile (3.2-kilometer) length of the headwaters of the San Marcos River in central Texas.

Damming, dredging, sewage, and pollution have combined to severely impact the habitat of Texas wild rice. COURTESY OF THE USDA-NRCS PLANTS DATABASE/HITCHCOCK, A.S.

Texas wild rice forms large clumps that are firmly rooted in the gravel bottom near the middle of the river. It prefers clear, cool, fast-flowing springwater. An increase of silt (mineral particles) in the water, the disturbance of the river's bottom, and stagnant water will all kill the plant.

History and conservation measures

Texas wild rice was first identified in 1933. At the time, it was abundant in the headwaters of the San Marcos River, in nearby irrigation ditches, and for about 1,000 feet (305 meters) behind Spring Lake Dam (a dam on the San Marcos River that created Spring Lake). Within 30 years of its discovery, the plant had almost completely disappeared from Spring Lake. Its numbers were drastically reduced in other areas throughout its range. Today, Texas wild rice plants that flower are rarely seen.

The primary cause for the decline of this species has been the destruction of its habitat. The damming and dredging of the San Marcos River, an increase of sewage and chemical pollutants in the water, and human recreational activities such as boating and swimming have all played a role in damaging the plant's habitat.

Spring Lake and the San Marcos River are fed by the San Marcos Springs, a flow of groundwater into Spring Lake. Because of human population growth in the area and the higher demand for groundwater, the flow of water from the San Marcos Springs has been reduced. If the springs stop flowing, water levels of Spring Lake and the San Marcos River could drop and reduce the habitat of Texas wild rice.

The species was listed as endangered by the U.S. Fish and Wildlife Service (USFWS) in 1978. In order to save Texas wild rice, the USFWS recommends that a public education program focusing on the plight of the plant be established. In addition, all remaining Texas wild rice habitat must be protected. The USFWS also pots Texas wild rice plants and transfers them to the San Marcos Aquatic Resources Center and to safe locations elsewhere in the river. In the early 21st century, about 40 plants were kept at the San Marcos center and another 40 plants were kept at a fish hatchery in Uvalde, Texas.

Reptiles

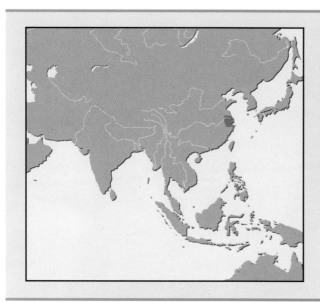

Alligator, Chinese
Alligator sinensis

PHYLUM: Chordata
CLASS: Reptilia
ORDER: Crocodylia
FAMILY: Alligatoridae
STATUS: Critically endangered, IUCN
Endangered, ESA
RANGE: China

Alligator, Chinese
Alligator sinensis

Description and biology

There are only two species of alligator: the Chinese alligator and the American alligator. An average Chinese alligator measures 6 to 6.5 feet (1.8 to 2 meters) long, about 3 feet (0.9 meters) shorter than the American species. The Chinese alligator is dark olive in color with yellowish spots. It has a large head with a short, broad snout that turns up slightly. The alligator feeds on snails, freshwater mussels, fish, insects, and small mammals.

The Chinese alligator spends much of its life in burrows that it digs in the banks of rivers, streams, and ponds. It hibernates (spends the winter in an inactive state) in a burrow from late October until early April. After emerging from hibernation, the alligator is active mainly during the day. In June, the beginning of the breeding season, the alligator becomes more nocturnal (active at night). After mating, a female Chinese alligator builds a mounded nest from dry leaves and grasses.

The endangered Chinese alligator is found at the lower reaches of the Yangtze (Chang) River and other parts of eastern China.
© DANIELE PIETROBELLI/SHUTTERSTOCK.COM.

She then lays 10 to 40 eggs between July and August. As the vegetation (plant material) that makes up the nest begins to rot, the temperature inside the nest rises and the eggs begin to incubate (develop). When they hatch about 70 days later, the young alligators measure just over 8 inches (20 centimeters) long and weigh about 1 ounce (28 grams).

Habitat and current distribution

As its name indicates, the Chinese alligator is found in China. It is restricted to the lower valley of the Yangtze (Chang) River in Anhui (Anhwei), Zhejiang (Chekiang), and Jiangsu (Kiangsu) Provinces. Biologists (people who study living organisms) estimate that fewer than 130 Chinese alligators now exist in the wild, and their population is declining. Most of these are found in Anhui Province. A large captive-breeding facility in Anhui holds another 10,000 alligators.

The Chinese alligator prefers to inhabit low beaches and dense stands of cane (type of plant) along the lower Yangtze River and its adjacent lakes and ponds.

History and conservation measures

The Chinese alligator once ranged more widely along the lower and middle Yangtze River basin (region drained by the river and the streams that flow into it), as far west as Hunan and Hubei Provinces. As the human population in China has soared, the alligator's habitat has dwindled. Most contact between the alligators and humans has proven fatal for the alligators: they are often killed for food or because they are feared.

Environmental factors have also endangered the Chinese alligator. A flash flood can quickly trap an alligator, and if it cannot reach an air pocket or the water's surface, it drowns. A drought can reduce its habitat, forcing the alligator to search for water and suitable nesting sites. Because most remaining Chinese alligators inhabit wetlands (areas where there is a lot of water in the soil, such as swamps) and ponds that are scattered widely apart, drought remains a serious threat.

The Chinese government has given the Chinese alligator legal protection. In addition, several conservation areas have been set aside for the alligator, including the Wuhu Alligator Sanctuary in Anhui Province. In 2007, six Chinese alligators raised in captivity were released into the wild at Chongming Island, which is located near the mouth of the Yangtze River. These alligators survived their first winter in hibernation and successfully bred. Fifteen hatchlings (newly hatched alligator young) were found at Chongming Island in 2008, a good sign for reintroduction efforts (efforts to introduce animals in captivity back into the wild).

Anole, Culebra Island giant
Anolis roosevelti

PHYLUM: Chordata
CLASS: Reptilia
ORDER: Squamata
FAMILY: Iguanidae
STATUS: Critically endangered, IUCN
Endangered, ESA
RANGE: British Virgin Islands, Puerto
Rico, U.S. Virgin Islands

Anole, Culebra Island giant
Anolis roosevelti

Description and biology

The Culebra (pronounced coo-LAY-bruh) Island giant anole (pro-nounced uh-NO-lee), also known as Roosevelt's giant anole, is a large lizard that dwells in tree canopies (the uppermost layers of forests). The main part of its body is brown gray. Its tail is yellow brown, and its belly is whitish. The anole's dewlap or throat fan (loose skin hanging from its neck) is gray, bordered by light yellow. The adult male of the species has a scalloped fin that runs along its tail. An average adult measures about 6.5 inches (16.5 centimeters) long. The tail adds another 6 to 7 inches (15 to 18 centimeters).

Scientists know almost nothing about the Culebra Island giant anole's daily habits, reproduction, or life history. They believe it acts the same way as another species of anole in Puerto Rico. Based on observations of that species, scientists think that the giant anole is found mostly in tree canopies at heights between 49 and 82 feet (15 and 25 meters). It probably has a varied diet consisting of many types of fruit and small animals.

Habitat and current distribution

The Culebra Island giant anole once inhabited Culebra and Vieques Islands (Puerto Rico), Tortola (British Virgin Islands), and Saint John (U.S. Virgin Islands). All of these islands lie east of the Puerto Rican mainland.

Scientists are unable to estimate the total number of Culebra Island giant anoles currently in existence. The species was last reported seen in the wild in 1978 and may be extinct.

History and conservation measures

The Culebra Island giant anole is a rare and critically endangered species. The most recent specimens of the giant anole were collected on Culebra Island in 1932. Casual searches for the lizard on the northern section of the island in 1991 were unsuccessful.

Exactly why the giant anole is so rare, or if it is now extinct, is unknown. Although much of the forest area on Culebra Island was cleared during the 20th century, patches of canopy forest (forest with tall, mature trees) remained until Hurricane Hugo struck the island in 1989. Suitable forest habitat no longer remains on Saint John. Canopy forest does remain on Tortola above 1,500 feet (457 meters) and probably also on Vieques. The clearing of forests by humans, introduced predators, and natural phenomena such as hurricanes have probably combined to reduce the number of giant anoles.

In 1982 the U.S. Fish and Wildlife Service approved a plan calling for the protection of the remaining giant anole habitat on Culebra Island. The plan also called for systematic searches of the island to locate

Did You Know?

The archipelago (island chain) of Culebra is made up of 24 tiny islands. It is located about 17 miles (27 kilometers) east of the main Puerto Rican island. As early as 1909, parts of Culebra were designated as wildlife reserves. But until 1976 some of the islands were used for gunnery and bombing practice by the U.S. Navy and Marine Corps.

The Culebra National Wildlife Refuge now protects about 2.4 square miles (6.1 square kilometers), almost a quarter of the archipelago's total land mass. The area hosts more than 50,000 seabirds of 13 species each year. Leatherback, hawksbill, and green sea turtles also nest on Culebra.

The Belalanda chameleon's already limited habitat in the wilds of Madagascar is under further threat by deforestation.
© PAUL SOUDERS/CORBIS.

Madagascar. For many years this was thought to be the only area in which Belalanda chameleons lived, but a third population was discovered in southern Madagascar in 2011.

Most of the mature trees in which the chameleon once thrived have been cut down by loggers. It survives in the nonnative species of trees that have been brought to Madagascar. It lives in the heights of the forest canopy (the uppermost layer of a forest) and has been sighted as high as 33 to 39 feet (10 to 12 meters) up in the trees.

The exact number of surviving Belalanda chameleons is unknown, but the population is thought to be very small and probably decreasing.

History and conservation measures

The indigenous forests in which the Belalanda originally lived have mostly been destroyed. The imported trees in which it now lives are also threatened, however, by loggers who cut them down for charcoal. The chameleons are also sometimes collected for export in the exotic pet trade, although this was officially banned in 1994.

The Belalanda chameleon's range has been placed within a protected area, and this may help protect the animal, but conservationists (people who work to manage and protect nature) believe that tighter restrictions on collection are needed. They have also suggested that surveys be conducted to determine the extent and number of the population.

The threat to the Belalanda chameleon is similar to threats facing many other reptile species in Madagascar. Many Madagascan species live nowhere else on Earth and, like the Belalanda chameleon, are threatened by the cutting down of forests and the destruction of other habitats.

According to the International Union for Conservation of Nature and Natural Resources (IUCN), about 40 percent of Madagascar's reptiles are threatened with extinction, and of these, the Belalanda chameleon is one of the most endangered. As of 2014, however, no extinctions in the wild had been documented for any of Madagascar's threatened reptile species, according to the IUCN. This suggests that new protected areas and the bans on collecting these animals for food or for pets may be helping.

Crocodile, American
Crocodylus acutus

PHYLUM: Chordata
CLASS: Reptilia
ORDER: Crocodilia
FAMILY: Crocodylidae
STATUS: Vulnerable, IUCN
Threatened, ESA (Florida)
Endangered, ESA (elsewhere)
RANGE: Belize, Colombia, Costa Rica,
Cuba, Dominican Republic, Ecuador, El
Salvador, Guatemala, Haiti, Honduras,
Jamaica, Mexico, Nicaragua, Panama,
Peru, USA (Florida), Venezuela

Crocodile, American
Crocodylus acutus

Description and biology

The American crocodile grows to an average length of 12 feet (3.6 meters), but is capable of reaching lengths between 15 and 20 feet (4.5 and 6 meters). It has a slender snout and a hump on its forehead between its eyes. Mature American crocodiles are dark brown to dark greenish brown in color. Young or juvenile crocodiles are light greenish brown with dark markings on their bodies and tails. Their undersides, or bellies, are pale. This species of crocodile feeds primarily on fish but also eats birds, crabs, small mammals, snakes, and turtles.

Once having mated, a female American crocodile will build a nest and lay between 20 and 60 eggs around the beginning of May. The nest can be either a hole dug in the sand on a beach or a mound built out of

The American crocodile is threatened by poaching and a loss of its habitat in the coastal areas of southern Florida, the Caribbean Islands, Mexico, Central America, and South America.. © ALL CANADA PHOTOS / ALAMY.

plant debris (leaves and other matter). These mounds vary in size: they can reach up to 15 feet (4.5 meters) in diameter and 2 feet (0.6 meters) in height. The female may use this same nest year after year. Once they hatch around the beginning of August, young crocodiles face a tough challenge. They are often preyed on by birds, crabs, raccoons, and even adult crocodiles. Very few survive to full adulthood.

Habitat and current distribution

The American crocodile is found in southern Florida, the southern coasts of Mexico, Central America, northern South America, and on the Caribbean islands of Cuba, Jamaica, and Hispaniola (divided between the Dominican Republic on the east and Haiti on the west). Biologists (people who study living organisms) estimate that there are about 2,000 crocodiles in Florida as of 2013, but they are unsure of the total world population.

American crocodiles prefer to inhabit shallow lakes, marshes, ponds, swamps, rivers, and creeks.

History and conservation measures

At one time, the American crocodile was abundant. But its numbers have been greatly reduced by the hunt for its valuable hide. The crocodile is protected in most of the 17 countries in which it exists, but this protection is not enforced. Illegal hunting continues in some areas. In recent decades, the development of cities and farms in the crocodile's range have robbed it of much of its habitat, causing a further drop in its numbers.

The hide of the American crocodile is still quite valuable. Crocodile ranches or farms have been established in five countries to breed crocodiles specifically to meet the demand for their hides. Conservationists (people who work to manage and protect nature) urge officials to monitor these farms to see that no wild American crocodiles are captured to build up captive populations.

The number of American crocodiles in Florida has increased significantly since the species was listed as endangered by the U.S. government in 1975. At that time, there were fewer than 500 of the crocodiles left in the state. All countries in the species range have programs to conserve the crocodile except for El Salvador and Haiti.

Crocodile, Orinoco
Crocodylus intermedius

PHYLUM: Chordata
CLASS: Reptilia
ORDER: Crocodilia
FAMILY: Crocodylidae
STATUS: Critically endangered, IUCN
Endangered, ESA
RANGE: Colombia, Venezuela

Crocodile, Orinoco
Crocodylus intermedius

Description and biology

The Orinoco (pronounced or-ee-NO-coe) crocodile is a very large crocodile that grows to an average length between 11 and 17 feet (3.4 and 5.2 meters). Some exceptionally large males of the species have been observed as being 23 feet (7 meters) long. The upper body of the crocodile is dark green to tan in color with dark markings. Its underside is lighter. It has a long nose and a narrow, slightly upturned snout. It feeds primarily on fish, small mammals, and birds.

After mating, a female Orinoco crocodile digs a hole in an exposed sandbar in a river in January or February (the dry season) and lays about 40 eggs. The eggs hatch about 70 days later, when the river begins to rise during the wet season. The female protects her young for one to three years.

The Orinoco crocodile is native to Colombia and Venezuela. © NAGEL PHOTOGRAPHY/SHUTTERSTOCK.COM.

Habitat and current distribution

This crocodile species is found only in the Orinoco River basin (area drained by the Orinoco River) in Colombia and Venezuela. It is considered almost extinct in Colombia and very rare in Venezuela. The largest population is found in the Cojedes river system of Venezuela, where scientists estimate there are about 350 adult Orinoco crocodiles. As of 2012, the total population in the entire range was estimated to be about 1,500.

The Orinoco crocodile prefers to inhabit wide and very deep parts of large rivers. During the wet season, when river currents are strong, the crocodile occupies lakes and pools.

History and conservation measures

Up until the 1930s the Orinoco crocodile was considered to be very common. Now it is one of the most critically endangered crocodiles in the Western Hemisphere. Its large, high-quality hide is valuable to hunters. From 1930 through the 1950s, hunters nearly wiped out the Orinoco crocodile population. The species has never recovered from the onslaught. The Orinoco crocodile is protected by the laws of both Colombia and Venezuela. However, the two countries have yet to successfully integrate their conservation programs.

Hunting remains a threat to the Orinoco crocodile. Humans in the region kill the crocodile for a number of reasons, including using its eggs and meat for food and its teeth for medicines. The crocodile now faces the added threat of habitat loss as human populations expand into its range.

Efforts to improve the plight of the Orinoco crocodile include hatching wild-caught eggs in captivity to allow young crocodiles to grow larger and stronger before their release in the wild. According to conservationists (people who work to manage and protect nature), Colombia especially needs to focus on improving its reintroduction programs, which are not as well developed as programs in Venezuela. National parks and wildlife refuges have been set up in Venezuela, but the areas lack strict protection and management. Local people in both countries continue to collect the eggs for food, collect young animals for sale as pets, and kill adult crocodiles for food. To be successful, it is critical that conservation efforts educate local communities about the Orinoco crocodile and involve them in the protection of this endangered species.

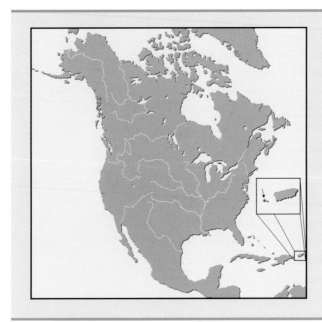

Gecko, Monito
Sphaerodactylus micropithecus

PHYLUM: Chordata
CLASS: Reptilia
ORDER: Squamata
FAMILY: Sphaerodactylidae
STATUS: Endangered, IUCN
Endangered, ESA
RANGE: Puerto Rico

Gecko, Monito
Sphaerodactylus micropithecus

Description and biology

The Monito gecko is a tiny lizard that grows to be about 1.5 inches (4 centimeters) long from tail to snout. It has a flattened body covered in mottled dark brown or gray scales. Its tail is tan. The Monito gecko has short limbs, each equipped with tiny suction cups for climbing around on cliffs. Its bulging eyes are protected by transparent scales. Monito geckos are quite vocal—they croak, bark, squeak, and make clicking noises.

Most geckos are nocturnal (active at night), but the Monito gecko is diurnal (active during the day). They eat an assortment of insects, including beetles, flies, crickets, and ants as well as spiders. Eating is generally done in groups. No studies have been done on their life cycles, so information is limited. Scientists believe that their mating season is from March to November. A Monito gecko in the wild probably lives from 4 to 10 years.

Habitat and current distribution

Monito geckos can be found only on the island of Monito, located 3 miles (4.8 kilometers) northwest of Mona Island in the Mona Passage midway between Puerto Rico and the Dominican Republic. Although wildlife biologists (people who study living organisms in the wild) do not know the total population of the Monito gecko, they estimate the number to be extremely small.

Monito Island has a total area of 39.5 acres (16 hectares) and is surrounded on all sides by 100- to 150-foot (30- to 45-meter) cliffs. The top of the island is flat and composed of limestone (a form of rock) covered in cacti, shrubs, and stunted trees that manage to grow through cracks in the limestone. When the island was surveyed for Monito geckos in 1982, they were found only in two small areas. The places where they were found, though, did not seem to differ from other parts of the island.

History and conservation measures

Although geckos of a different species on nearby Mona Island are abundant and well known, the Monito gecko was not discovered until 1974. At that time, scientists found one adult male and one egg on Monito Island. They hatched the egg in a laboratory and then released the animals on the island. Until 1982 no Monito geckos were found, even when the island was surveyed. Then 18 were found in 1982. By all indications, this has long been a very rare animal.

Black rats, introduced to Monito Island decades ago, are known to eat a variety of reptiles and are likely responsible for the very low population of the Monito gecko. The government of Puerto Rico conducted a program in the 1990s that eliminated black rats from Monito Island.

Because the population is so dangerously low, the entire area of Monito Island has been designated as critical habitat (area necessary for the protection and preservation of a species that has been listed under the Endangered Species Act). However, a critical habitat designation does not create a wildlife refuge or eliminate human activities in the area.

The U.S. Fish and Wildlife Service (USFWS) recommends a complete biological study of the Monito gecko, including surveys of the gecko population and additional research on the species' habitat preferences, to develop future recovery plans.

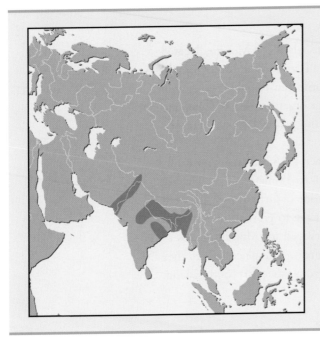

Gharial
Gavialis gangeticus

PHYLUM: Chordata
CLASS: Reptilia
ORDER: Crocodilia
FAMILY: Gavialidae
STATUS: Critically endangered, IUCN
Endangered, ESA
RANGE: Bangladesh, Bhutan, India,
Nepal, Pakistan

Gharial
Gavialis gangeticus

Description and biology

The gharial (GAIR-ee-uhl), also known as the gavial (GAY-vee-uhl), is a large crocodile. This reptile has an olive-green to gray-brown body above and cream-colored undersides. It has an average body (including tail) length of 13 to 20 feet (4 to 6 meters). Unlike other members of the crocodile family, the gharial has long, slender jaws with 106 to 110 sharp teeth. The shape of its jaws allows the gharial to move its head rapidly from side to side in the water to catch small fish, its primary food. Some larger gharials will eat mammals, but the creature is not dangerous to humans.

Mature males have a growth next to their nostrils that the people of northern India thought looked like an earthen pot known as a *ghara*. This is how the animal got the name *gharial*, which Europeans misheard

The gharial of India and Nepal has experienced an extreme drop in population since the mid-20th century because of changes to its habitat caused by water diversion and agriculture, its use in traditional medicine, and its vulnerability to fishing nets.
© MILKOVASA/SHUTTERSTOCK.COM.

as *gavial*. The animals make a buzzing noise with this growth during courtship.

Around the beginning of April, after having mated, the female gharial digs a hole in a sandbank and lays a clutch (a number of eggs produced at one time) of 30 to 50 oval-shaped eggs. The eggs hatch after 83 to 94 days. Since predators threaten the eggs and the young gharials, the mother guards the nest and protects the young for several months after they hatch.

Habitat and current distribution

The gharial prefers to inhabit high-banked rivers with clear, fast-flowing water and deep pools. It basks in the sun on sandbanks. The largest breeding population of gharials lives in India's Chambal River.

This reptile may be extinct in the neighboring lands of Bangladesh, Bhutan, and Pakistan. It is critically endangered in India and Nepal. Surveys dating from 2006 suggest that about 200 breeding adults and about 800 total gharials live in the wild. One gharial researcher, however, estimates that there may be 1,500 to 2,000 breeding-age adults.

History and conservation measures

The gharial was still quite common in many areas in its range at the beginning of the 20th century. Then, its numbers dropped quickly because people hunted it for its skin and ate its eggs. Biologists (people who study living organisms) estimate that the gharial population has decreased by 96 to 98 percent since 1946. Now, people seldom hunt the animal. The biggest threat to the gharial in the 21st century continues to be changes to its habitat. Dams and reservoirs built on the rivers where the reptile lives have destroyed the sandbanks and deep pools the animal needs. River waters have also been diverted to irrigate crops. Illegal fishing and sand mining, even in supposedly protected areas, also threaten the gharial, as does agriculture and livestock grazing on sandbanks where the animal basks. The reptile can also become entangled in fishing nets when people fish or illegally hunt turtles in the rivers. Pollutants in the water, too, have been known to kill gharials.

Efforts to save this critically endangered animal are ongoing. Most gharials live in a wildlife sanctuary in India, and Nepal also has a national park containing gharials. An Indian program to hatch gharial eggs in captivity and release the young animals into the wild failed, as the animals did not survive. The river was no longer a safe habitat for them. Biologists claim that identifying the hazards facing gharials in the wild is essential to saving this animal from extinction. Conservationists (people who work to manage and protect nature) believe that a plan needs to be developed that includes all countries in the gharial's current and historical range. They say that the plan must involve both government agencies and local people who live along the rivers inhabited by gharials.

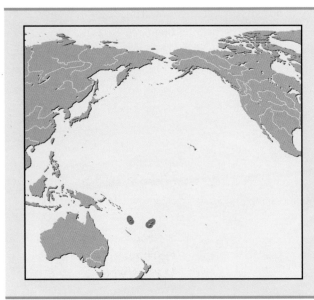

Iguana, Fiji banded
Brachylophus bulabula (also
Brachylophus fasciatus)

PHYLUM: Chordata
CLASS: Reptilia
ORDER: Squamata
FAMILY: Iguanidae
STATUS: Endangered, IUCN
Endangered, ESA
RANGE: Fiji, Vanuatu

Iguana, Fiji banded
Brachylophus bulabula (also *Brachylophus fasciatus*)

Description and biology

The Fiji banded iguana is so named because males of the species have pale, bluish-green bands covering their green bodies. Females are usually entirely green. The banded iguana's skin color changes in response to light, temperature, and the animal's mood. The male's banding is most obvious when courting a female or when fighting with another male.

Adult Fiji banded iguanas have a body length of about 7.5 inches (19 centimeters). Their tails measure two to three times their body length. Males are generally longer than females. These banded iguanas are primarily vegetarians, feeding on leaves, fruit, and flowers. They occasionally eat insects.

Male Fiji banded iguanas are territorial and aggressive. They fight among themselves to determine who is dominant, and only the dominant male mates with available females. A male's courtship behavior

The Fiji banded iguana faces threats to its population from predators, deforestation, and the introduction of invasive species to its habitat. © MATT GIBSON/SHUTTERSTOCK.COM.

includes head bobbing and a display of his banding and bright coloration. After mating with a dominant male, a female Fiji banded iguana digs a burrow, or hole, into which she lays about five eggs. She then covers the burrow with dirt and the eggs are left to incubate (develop).

Habitat and current distribution

The Fiji banded iguana exists on about 10 islands that are a part of the Fiji archipelago (chain of islands) in the southwest Pacific Ocean. The species range extends over an area under 1,540 square miles (4,000 square kilometers) in total. The largest populations of the species exist on the islands of Makogai and Makodroga. Biologists (people who study living organisms) estimated in 2012 that there were a total of about 6,000 iguanas left in these two islands. There is also a population of Fiji banded iguanas in the island nation of Vanuatu, west of Fiji, though they were introduced there in the 1960s and are not native.

This iguana prefers to inhabit dense, undisturbed forests in islands with wet weather at elevations of up to 1,640 feet (500 meters).

History and conservation measures

The biggest threat to the Fiji banded iguana has been the Indian mongoose, which was introduced to Fiji in 1883. The mongoose was imported to kill rats infesting agricultural fields, but the animal also killed large quantities of iguanas, snakes, and other reptiles. The largest populations of Fiji banded iguanas are located on two islands that are mongoose-free. The species is believed to be extinct in many of the 13 islands where the mongoose has been introduced. Black rats and cats are among the other predators that also threaten the Fiji banded iguana.

The clearing of its forest habitat is another reason why the Fiji banded iguana has declined or disappeared from many islands in its range. The species' natural island habitats continue to be damaged by forest burning, logging, mining, and agriculture. Biologists have found it difficult to monitor or study the Fiji banded iguana in the wild. The animal is hard to find because it is secretive by nature and its coloring provides excellent camouflage.

The banded iguana breeds well in captivity, and several zoos have breeding programs. If this animal becomes critically endangered in the near future, then captive-bred Fiji banded iguanas may be reintroduced into the wild. However, as of 2015, there was no conservation plan for this species, and the iguana was not known to exist in any of Fiji's protected forests.

Iguana, Grand Cayman blue
Cyclura lewisi

PHYLUM: Chordata
CLASS: Reptilia
ORDER: Squamata
FAMILY: Iguanidae
STATUS: Endangered, IUCN
Endangered, ESA
RANGE: Cayman Islands (Grand Cayman Island)

Iguana, Grand Cayman blue
Cyclura lewisi

Description and biology

The Grand Cayman blue iguana is the largest animal on its Caribbean island. This stocky reptile can reach more than 5 feet (1.5 meters) long (half of which is tail), and weigh up to 25 pounds (11 kilograms). Short spines run from its neck down its back and tail. At rest, males are blue gray, while females are olive green to pale blue. When excited or during breeding season, the reptiles become a brighter blue.

This iguana species prefers rocky, sunlit, open land near both dry forests and fruit farms. In such locales, the individuals move between warmer and colder areas in order to regulate their body temperature; they nest in soft soil when breeding. Grand Cayman blue iguanas eat fruit, leaves, and flowers and occasionally small animals, such as snails, slugs, and crabs. Adult iguanas have no natural predators, but young iguanas are preyed on by snakes.

Grand Cayman blue iguanas are solitary. Females bask in the sun, feed, and defend a small territory. Males bask, feed, and roam a little farther. In the spring, males fight each other to monopolize the territory of as many females as possible. Iguanas mate during the first two weeks of May. In June or July, the females dig a burrow, laying 1 to 22 eggs in

The Grand Cayman blue iguana has responded well to efforts to conserve and grow its population, including captive-breeding programs and the establishment of areas where it is protected. © FRONTPAGE/SHUTTERSTOCK.COM.

it, and cover it with leaves for protection and warmth. The eggs hatch anywhere from 60 to 100 days later, depending on the temperature. The young are green with dark bands. They fend for themselves from birth. The iguanas becomes sexually mature at age 3 and can live to age 50 in the wild. One captive Grand Cayman blue iguana lived to age 69.

Habitat and current distribution

The Grand Cayman blue iguana lives only on the eastern portion of Grand Cayman Island, the largest of the Cayman Islands in the Caribbean Sea. In 2002 only 10 to 25 iguanas remained in the wild. A successful conservation program increased the species' population to 750 by 2013.

History and conservation measures

Having survived for three million years, this species has been endangered since Europeans settled Grand Cayman Island in the late 17th century. When settlers began inhabiting the island's coastal areas, Grand Cayman blue iguanas lost habitat, moving inland. They were also killed by the cats and dogs the Europeans introduced to the island. The iguanas had not learned to fear these animals, leaving themselves vulnerable to attack. The 20th century brought a new threat: motor vehicles that often hit the slow-moving reptiles. More recently, the iguana's habitat has shrunk further as fruit farms have given way to pastureland for cattle.

This species was listed as critically endangered by the International Union for Conservation of Nature and Natural Resources (IUCN) in 1996. It appears on Appendix I of the Convention on International Trade in Endangered Species of Wild Fauna and Flora (CITES), which bans international trade in listed species. In 1990 the island's government began a conservation program for the almost-extinct species. Under the program, iguanas are bred in captivity, raised until they can survive in the wild, and released into three national parks. There, they have been breeding successfully in the wild. In 2012, because of this program's success, the IUCN downlisted the species to endangered. The program's goal is to have 1,000 iguanas living in the wild. As of 2014, conservationists (people who work to manage and protect nature) estimated that there were more than 850 in the wild.

The animal still faces the same threats that nearly resulted in its extinction, however: development, dogs, and cats. In addition, now that this species is no longer listed as critically endangered, potential donors to Grand Cayman blue iguana conservation programs may turn their attention to other animals that seem more at risk.

Lizard, blunt-nosed leopard
Gambelia sila (also *Gambelia silus*)

PHYLUM: Chordata
CLASS: Reptilia
ORDER: Squamata
FAMILY: Iguanidae
STATUS: Endangered, IUCN
Endangered, ESA
RANGE: USA (California)

Lizard, blunt-nosed leopard
Gambelia sila (also *Gambelia silus*)

Description and biology

As its name indicates, this lizard has a blunt nose and a leopard-like pattern on its body. To help regulate the lizard's body temperature, its color and pattern change throughout the day. For example, in the morning, when it is cool, dark spots and light sand-colored bars appear on the surface of the lizard's body; as the temperature rises during the day, the pattern fades to a lighter shade.

This lizard species also changes color during mating season. During courtship, the sides of males turn salmon or light pink. After having mated, females develop rusty-orange to red blotches on their sides that remain until they lay their eggs.

An average blunt-nosed leopard lizard has a body length of 3.5 to 5 inches (8.9 to 12.7 centimeters). Its tail can often reach a length of 8 inches (20 centimeters). If a predator such as a squirrel, skunk, shrike

The blunt-nosed leopard lizard species is found in south-central California. © RICHARD R. HANSEN/SCIENCE SOURCE.

(type of bird), or snake catches the lizard by its tail, the lizard can shed the tail and grow a new one. The blunt-nosed leopard lizard feeds on grasshoppers, caterpillars, flies, bees, and occasionally other young lizards. This species may also eat its own young.

The blunt-nosed leopard lizard spends its winter hibernating (spends the winter in an inactive state) in a deep burrow made by a rodent or other small animal. It emerges from hibernation around the beginning of April, and is then active only during the coolest hours of the day. Mating season takes place during May and June. A single male may defend a territory that includes several females. After mating, a female enters a burrow in June or July to lay a clutch (a number of eggs produced at one time) of two or three eggs. The eggs hatch in August.

Habitat and current distribution

Sometimes called the San Joaquin leopard lizard, this species is found only in parts of the San Joaquin Valley and adjacent foothills in south-

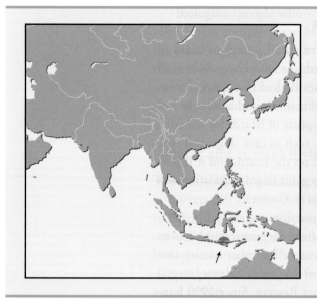

Monitor, Komodo Island
Varanus komodoensis

PHYLUM: Chordata
CLASS: Reptilia
ORDER: Squamata
FAMILY: Varanidae
STATUS: Vulnerable, IUCN
Endangered, ESA
RANGE: Indonesia

Monitor, Komodo Island
Varanus komodoensis

Description and biology

The Komodo Island monitor, also called the Komodo dragon or the ora by the people of Komodo, is the largest living lizard on Earth. An adult can measure up to 10 feet (3 meters) long and weigh 300 pounds (136 kilograms). Despite its size, it can move quickly on the ground and is an agile swimmer and climber. The monitor has a dark gray, stocky body and stout, powerful legs with sharply clawed feet. It has a large head and a long, forked tongue that it uses to "taste" the air, following the scent of its prey.

This species feeds on wild pigs, deer, water buffalo, dogs, goats, rats, snakes, birds, other monitors, and, if given the chance, humans. It attacks by ambushing its prey, lunging from the tall grass of its savanna (flat, tropical or subtropical grassland) habitat. The Komodo Island monitor has razor-sharp serrated teeth. One bite is often enough to subdue its prey. If the prey happens to escape, it usually will not live long.

The Komodo Island monitor, a giant lizard native to Indonesia, is considered endangered because of its low population of breeding females. © NATALI GLADO/SHUTTERSTOCK.COM.

The mouth of a monitor is filled with poisonous bacteria. The bite area becomes infected over the course of a few days, and the prey weakens until it can no longer flee. The monitor then moves in and devours the prey completely—nothing is left. The monitor's large tongue and foul mouth odor (caused by the bacteria present) may have inspired legends of fire-breathing dragons.

After mating, female Komodo Island monitors lay 15 to 30 eggs with smooth, leatherlike shells in a hole. They usually lay eggs several times between July and early September. The eggs hatch after about 34 weeks. For the first year of their lives, young monitors live in trees and feed on insects. When they have grown to a length of about 3 feet (0.9 meters), they move to the ground. This helps protect them from predators, including adult monitors.

Habitat and current distribution

The Komodo Island monitor is found on only five islands in eastern Indonesia. Four of the populations are on islands within Komodo National Park: Komodo, Rinca, Gili Motang, and Nusa Kode. Another population is found on the larger island of Flores. Biologists (people who study living organisms) estimate that the monitor's population is about 2,500 in the protected area of the national park and potentially up to 2,000 on Flores as of 2014.

Monitors prefer to inhabit dry savanna, woodland thickets, and forest fringes and clearings.

History and conservation measures

The Komodo Island monitor once occupied many Indonesian islands. It was first seen by European scientists in 1911. Since that time, its population has been drastically reduced—mainly by humans. The monitor has been hunted for sport, for collections, and for its hide. Although laws now limit commercial hunting, the monitor is still sometimes poisoned by villagers who believe it is a threat to children and domestic animals.

The overhunting of deer by humans in the monitor's range has reduced its available prey. Its habitat also has been reduced by the burning and clearing of woodland to create farmland and villages. Komodo National Park has the largest number of Komodo Island monitors, and it also has a large and growing number of human inhabitants in four settlements. People have lived on the islands of the national park for centuries, and human development has continued despite its current protected status as a conservation area.

Captive-breeding programs for the Komodo Island monitor have not had much success because the species does not reproduce well in captivity. Male and female monitors paired up in zoos and institutions will not necessarily mate and breed. Hatchlings born in captivity often die from diseases and infections.

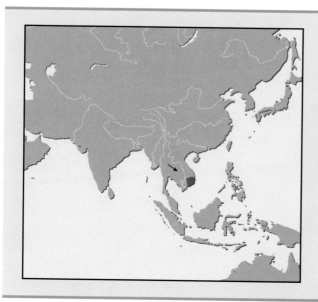

Pit viper, ruby-eyed green
Cryptelytrops rubeus

PHYLUM: Chordata
CLASS: Reptilia
ORDER: Squamata
FAMILY: Viperidae
STATUS: Vulnerable, IUCN
RANGE: Cambodia, Vietnam

Pit viper, ruby-eyed green
Cryptelytrops rubeus

Description and biology

The ruby-eyed green pit viper is a slender, grass-green snake with large, bright-red eyes and an orange-red tail. A white stripe runs along the bottom of its side. In males, this stripe may have a red-brown bottom edge. The underside of the snake is greenish yellow. The snake's triangular head looks large for its body size. Around the edge of the mouth, pale blue scales are scattered. The snake is about 24 inches (60 centimeters) long.

The ruby-eyed green pit viper lives in trees, where it blends in with the leaves, but it also hunts on the ground. All specimens have been found at night; like its close relative the large-eyed pit viper, it likely sleeps in trees during the day and hunts at night. Some individuals have been discovered near fast-moving streams. Biologists (people who study living organisms) believe the snake eats frogs and small mammals.

Pit vipers are so named because they have small pits on their heads, between the eye and the nostril on each side of the head. The pits sense

The ruby-eyed pit viper is found in the dense forests of Vietnam and Cambodia, which are threatened by the spread of rubber and cassava plantations. © OSCAR DOMINGUEZ/ALAMY.

heat and are used to locate warm-blooded prey. Pit vipers inject prey with venom through hollow fangs. No ruby-eyed green pit viper bites have been recorded in humans, but people bitten by the large-eyed pit viper, its close relative, have suffered severe pain, swelling, and cell death near the bite area. It is rarely fatal.

Like all pit vipers, this snake is ovoviviparous. This means that the eggs are not laid but stay inside the mother until they hatch.

Habitat and current distribution

The ruby-eyed green pit viper has been found in evergreen forests in the low hills of southern Vietnam and eastern Cambodia. Biologists believe its range spans about 7,556 square miles (19,570 square kilometers). No population estimates exist, but the species has been seen often in Cambodia, and biologists think it is common in Vietnam.

History and conservation measures

Since 2000 herpetologists (people who study reptiles and amphibians) have studied the genus (group with similar characteristics) of snakes called Asian green pit vipers more closely than before. They have identified several new snake species within this genus by closely examining the structure of the reptiles' bodies and conducting genetic analyses. In 2011 herpetologists identified the ruby-eyed green pit viper for the first time, describing its differences from the large-eyed pit viper (*Cryptelytrops macrops*), its close relative.

The International Union for Conservation of Nature and Natural Resources (IUCN) listed the newly discovered species as vulnerable in 2012. The IUCN took this action because the snake appears to live within a relatively small area and its habitat is threatened by deforestation (large-scale removal of trees). Most of the areas where this snake has been found are protected by the governments of Cambodia and Vietnam. Despite this legal protection, some of the snake's habitat in Cambodia has been converted to plantations where rubber and cassava (an edible root) are grown. Another threat is that people might take ruby-eyed green pit vipers from the wild. In southern Vietnam, green pit vipers are sometimes eaten or used as medicine. People might also kill the snake because it is venomous, and reptile collectors might desire it because of its beauty and rarity. The only conservation action the IUCN recommended when it listed the snake, however, was to survey plantations within the snake's known range to determine how well it survives threats to its habitat.

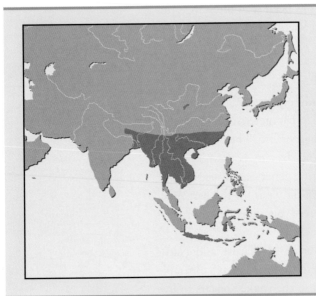

Python, Burmese
Python bivittatus

PHYLUM: Chordata
CLASS: Reptilia
ORDER: Squamata
FAMILY: Pythonidae
STATUS: Vulnerable, IUCN
RANGE: Bangladesh, Cambodia, China, India, Indonesia, Laos, Myanmar, Nepal, Thailand, Vietnam

Python, Burmese
Python bivittatus

Description and biology

The Burmese python is one of the world's largest snakes. Long and heavy bodied, it averages 10 feet (3 meters) in length but has been known to grow to over 20 feet (6 meters). It has dark-brown blotches that look like jigsaw puzzle pieces or the markings on a giraffe. The skin in between the blotches is tan. On its head is a dark wedge shape that looks like an arrowhead pointing toward the snout.

Burmese pythons will prey on birds and other reptiles but prefer small mammals such as rats. A large python will even prey on pigs and deer. Pythons have small heat pits on their heads that help them sense the body heat of prey. They are nonvenomous animals that kill by coiling around the prey animal and squeezing it to death. They are also good swimmers and climbers.

After mating in springtime, the female lays 35 to 100 eggs. She remains with the eggs throughout the 60-day incubation (development)

Did You Know?

The Burmese python is not in danger everywhere. Although it is listed as vulnerable over its native range, in other areas it is thriving as an invasive species (species from a different ecosystem that spread or multiply and cause harm when they are introduced into a new environment). This means that it is able to outcompete other species in environments other than its native range. A highly publicized example of this is its spread in the U.S. state of Florida, especially in the swampy area known as the Everglades. The snakes were introduced to the state as pets that then escaped or were released by their owners. Now, an estimated 30,000 to 50,000 pythons are thriving in the wild and preying on native wildlife in Florida despite efforts to remove them. Over 300 sightings have taken place each year in the state since 2008. The python is considered a threat to such endangered and threatened Florida species as Key Largo wood rats, round-tailed muskrats, and even alligators. The U.S. government has therefore banned further importation of these reptiles.

period, leaving them only to drink water. The snake warms the eggs by wrapping her body around them and controlling her body temperature by twitching her muscles. Upon hatching, the young pythons average around 21 inches (53 centimeters) in length. The mother does not take care of them after they hatch. Burmese pythons live from 15 to 25 years.

Habitat and current distribution

Burmese pythons are found in a variety of habitats but prefer wooded areas, and they like damp terrain. They are always found near water. This python is widespread in South and Southeast Asia. Biologists (people who study living organisms) have no estimate of the total number of Burmese pythons in the wild.

History and conservation measures

Taxonomists (biologists who classify species on the basis of their genes, characteristics, and behavior) formerly divided the *Python molurus* species into two subspecies: the Indian python (*Python molurus molurus*) and the Burmese python (*Python molurus bivittatus*). In 2009 it was determined that the Burmese python is a separate species: *Python bivittatus*, but the reptile is still sometimes referred to as *Python molurus bivitattus*.

Humans are a huge threat to the Burmese python because they hunt the snakes for their skin, to eat them, to use them in traditional medicine, and to sell in the pet trade. © IRINA OXILIXO DANILOVA/SHUTTERSTOCK.COM.

The International Union for Conservation of Nature and Natural Resources (IUCN) classifies the Burmese python as vulnerable, meaning it is likely to become endangered unless its circumstances improve. By 2009 the Burmese python population had declined by more than 90 percent in mainland China and by more than 80 percent in Vietnam. Conservationists (people who work to manage and protect nature) estimate that across the species' range its population declined by at least 30 percent from 2002 to 2012.

Hunting and habitat loss are the species' biggest threats. People hunt Burmese pythons to make leather out of their skin, for food, for use in traditional medicine (health practices used by specific cultures since before the time of modern medicine), and to sell in the pet trade. Habitat loss occurs when people convert land into farmland. This python is protected in Thailand and so is more common there. In China and Vietnam it is protected but still illegally hunted. Conservationists have called for increased enforcement of these protections to preserve this species outside Thailand.

Rattlesnake, Santa Catalina Island
Crotalus catalinensis

PHYLUM: Chordata
CLASS: Reptilia
ORDER: Squamata
FAMILY: Viperidae
STATUS: Critically endangered, IUCN
RANGE: Mexico (Santa Catalina Island)

Rattlesnake, Santa Catalina Island
Crotalus catalinensis

Description and biology

The Santa Catalina Island rattlesnake is a venomous, thin, short-bodied snake that can grow to 2 feet (0.6 meters) in length. Its head is triangular and clearly distinguished from its neck. Most of these snakes are light brown or reddish brown, with darker diamond-shaped markings. A few of the snakes are gray, with markings in a darker gray. The snake is mostly nocturnal (active at night), although in cool weather it may come out during the early morning. Scientists believe that it hides in burrows during the heat of the day.

The most distinctive feature of the Santa Catalina Island rattlesnake is that it does not have a rattle. Its tail has round scales, or "buttons," which in most rattlesnakes develop into a rattle. But the Santa Catalina

The Santa Catalina Island rattlesnake, which is found only on Mexico's Santa Catalina Island, is at risk largely because of people who hunt, collect, or kill the animal.
© MICHAEL NOLAN/ROBERT HARDING IMAGES.

Island rattlesnake sheds its buttons every time it sheds its skin, so the rattle never fully develops.

Scientists are unsure why the Santa Catalina Island rattlesnake has lost its rattle. The snakes are good climbers, and for a time scientists believed that it had lost its rattle because it needed to be silent to sneak up on birds in the shrubs and bushes. Further research has shown, however, that 70 percent of the snake's diet consists of the Catalina deer mouse, with the rest made up of small lizards. The deer mouse climbs into the bushes, too, so it still may be the case that the lack of a rattle helps the snake when sneaking up on prey. The snake has other adaptations common to tree hunters, including a more elongated body and longer teeth than most rattlesnakes have.

Not much is known about the Santa Catalina Island rattlesnake's life cycle. It is believed that it breeds in the spring and gives birth to live young in late summer.

Habitat and current distribution

The Santa Catalina Island rattlesnake is found only on Santa Catalina Island, a small, uninhabited island off the eastern coast of Baja California, in the Gulf of California, Mexico.

The rattlesnake mostly lives in the dry creek beds known as arroyos because these have abundant vegetation (plant life). But it sometimes may be found on the island's scrubby (covered with stunted trees and shrubs) hillsides and on open ground. It was once common on the island, but it is believed that its numbers are in decline.

History and conservation measures

The Santa Catalina Island rattlesnake is a close relative of the red diamond rattlesnake (*Crotalus ruber*). Red diamond rattlesnakes live on the Mexican mainland, a short trip across the water from Santa Catalina Island. Scientists believe some red diamond rattlesnakes may have floated across from the mainland on natural "rafts." Eventually, they evolved into a separate species, *Crotalus catalinensis*, the Santa Catalina Island rattlesnake.

Because it lives only on an island that is just 15.4 square miles (40 square kilometers) in size, the Santa Catalina Island rattlesnake is considered to be at risk. The main threat to the species is collection by humans. The snake is mostly quiet and easy to capture, and its rarity has made it valued as a pet.

Feral (once domesticated, now wild) cats that were introduced on the island also reduced rattlesnake numbers by lowering the Catalina deer mouse population, the snake's main food. The cats have now been removed. Human collection of the snakes continues, however. Conservationists (people who work to manage and protect nature) have suggested that greater regulation of such collection is needed to protect the Santa Catalina Island rattlesnake in the wild.

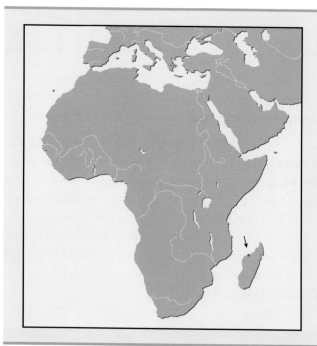

Tortoise, angulated
Astrochelys yniphora (also *Geochelone yniphora*)

PHYLUM: Chordata
CLASS: Reptilia
ORDER: Testudines
FAMILY: Testudinidae
STATUS: Critically endangered, IUCN
Endangered, ESA
RANGE: Madagascar

Tortoise, angulated
Astrochelys yniphora (also *Geochelone yniphora*)

Description and biology

The angulated tortoise, also known as the Madagascar tortoise or plow-share tortoise, is one of the rarest tortoises in the world. It can weigh up to 40 pounds (18 kilograms), and its rotund carapace (pronounced CARE-a-pace), or top shell, can be up to 17 inches (43 centimeters) long. Adult males are usually larger than adult females. Dark wedge-shaped markings appear across its light-brown carapace. The tortoise's characteristic feature is a hornlike protuberance, or projection, that juts out underneath its neck from its plastron, or ventral (bottom) shell. Angulated tortoises are herbivores (animals that eat mainly plants), feeding on leaves, grasses, and shoots.

Angulated tortoises mate between October and February. Males engage in duels, apparently over the right to mate with females. Females lay clutches (eggs produced at one time) of between one and six eggs in nests made in open areas of savanna (flat, tropical or subtropical grassland). When the eggs hatch around November, the hatchlings are completely independent.

Habitat and current distribution

Unique to Madagascar (an island off the southeastern coast of Africa), the angulated tortoise is found in a limited area around Baly Bay, in the northwestern part of the island. The tortoise prefers to inhabit a mixture of tropical deciduous forests (made up of trees whose leaves fall off annually) and grasslands. The habitat suitable for the angulated tortoise is between 27 and 35.5 square miles (70 and 92 square kilometers) in area.

Biologists (people who study living organisms) estimated as of 2008 that there may be as few as 400 angulated tortoises in the wild and that the species' population is decreasing.

The angulated tortoise, found in Madagascar, is considered threatened because of its small habitat. It is also targeted by international pet traders. © PETE OXFORD/MINDEN PICTURES/CORBIS.

History and conservation measures

Between the 17th and 20th centuries, angulated tortoises were hunted in great numbers for food. Madagascan law now protects the tortoise from such hunting, but serious threats remain. Predators, such as wild pigs, destroy the tortoises' nests. Much of the tortoises' habitat has been cleared and converted into farmland.

In 1986 the Durrell Wildlife Conservation Trust (then known as the Jersey Wildlife Preservation Trust) and the Department of Waters and Forests of Madagascar mounted a species recovery plan for the tortoise. The plan included breeding the tortoise in captivity, preserving its natural habitat, and educating local people about the threat facing the tortoise. As of 2015 the Durrell trust has released 100 angulated tortoises into the wild.

Despite legal protections for the tortoise, illegal smuggling is known to take place occasionally. These extremely rare tortoises are sometimes sold to collectors in exotic pet markets. Smugglers have even stolen angulated tortoises from captive-breeding programs.

Tortoise, desert
Gopherus agassizii

PHYLUM: Chordata
CLASS: Reptilia
ORDER: Testudines
FAMILY: Testudinidae
STATUS: Vulnerable, IUCN
Threatened, ESA
RANGE: Mexico, USA (Arizona, California, Nevada, Utah)

Tortoise, desert
Gopherus agassizii

Description and biology

The desert tortoise has an oblong, domed, brown carapace (CARE-a-pace), or top shell, that measures between 7.5 and 15 inches (19 and 38 centimeters) long. Its head is narrow and scaly, and its tail is short. The tortoise has armored front legs, which it uses for digging, and large, powerful rear legs. Males of the species are much larger than females.

The desert tortoise's diet consists primarily of plants that contain a high level of water. In its desert habitat, the tortoise drinks from depressions that it often scrapes out itself to catch rainwater. The desert tortoise is active mainly in the spring. In summer, it is active when rains provide moisture and food.

During courtship, males often hiss and butt females. After mating, a female desert tortoise lays two to seven hard-shelled eggs in early summer. She covers the eggs with only a thin layer of sand, allowing the sun's

The desert tortoise is native to the southwestern United States and Mexico. COURTESY OF THE NATIONAL PARK SERVICE/ BRAD SUTTON.

heat to incubate them (keep them warm until ready to hatch). The eggs hatch after three to four months. The young tortoises have soft shells that begin to harden after about five years. Only about 2 percent of the hatchlings survive to adulthood because the young are more vulnerable to disease and being killed and eaten by predators.

Desert tortoises do not reach sexual maturity until they are 15 to 20 years of age, but can live as long as 100 years.

Habitat and current distribution

Tortoises are difficult to find, since they spend 95 percent of their lives underground.

They live in sandy or rocky areas, where there is soil they can dig in to make a den. Their range includes the Mojave and Sonoran Deserts in the southwestern United States and northwestern Mexico. Although this range is wide, the tortoise population is scattered and isolated throughout it. Biologists (people who study living organisms) believe the total desert tortoise population to be only around 100,000 as of 2013. Populations have dropped by as much as 90 percent. In the 1950s there were often 200 tortoises per square mile (2.5 square kilometers) in their range; now that number has dropped to only 5 to 60 adults.

To the north and west of the Grand Canyon, desert tortoises inhabit valleys and tracts where creosote bushes (evergreen resinous desert shrubs) and yucca plants grow. To the south and east of the Grand Canyon, isolated populations of tortoises inhabit steep, rocky slopes of mountain ranges where paloverde trees (small, bushy trees with sharp spines and green trunks) and various cacti grow. Biologists are unsure of the tortoise's habitat in Mexico.

History and conservation measures

The desert tortoise was once found at lower elevations throughout the Mojave and Sonoran Deserts. Since 1950, however, the species' numbers have declined in most areas. Many factors have led to this decline. Their habitat has been lost or destroyed as farms and cities have been built, roads have been constructed, mining explorations have been undertaken, and toxic and radioactive waste dumps have been created. Livestock from nearby ranches and farms have trampled their food sources, and off-road vehicles have further disturbed what remains of the animal's fragile habitat.

Tortoises have also been illegally hunted, sometimes for food but especially as pets. The pet market can be especially dangerous for these animals because tortoises live a long time; people often tire of them or precede them in death. The now-domesticated tortoises are then released into the wild, where they compete with wild tortoises, and frequently spread disease. For a time, Nevada pet owners who wanted to rid themselves of their tortoises could take them to the Desert Tortoise Conservation Center in Las Vegas, but that was shut down in 2014 when its federal funding ran out. Some of the tortoises being kept there were euthanized (put to death) because they were too unhealthy to survive a move or would spread disease if they were put in contact with healthy turtles. Now conservationists (people who work to manage and protect nature) encourage pet tortoise owners to have their tortoises sterilized (unable to reproduce) so that no tortoise offspring will be released into the wild.

The desert tortoise is California's official state reptile. At present, there are two reserves in California providing protected habitats for the tortoise: the Desert Tortoise Natural Area near California City and the Chuckwalla Bench Area of Critical Environmental Concern, which lies between the Salton Sea and the Arizona border. A small reserve in Utah provides another protected habitat for a few desert tortoises.

A federal plan to save the desert tortoise was developed in 1995; a new version was released in 2011. The plan recommended research on populations and protection of habitat. However, the plans have not been fully implemented, in part because people often want to use tortoise habitat for recreational purposes or even, in some cases, solar and wind energy installations. Setting aside land for the tortoises can therefore be politically difficult to achieve.

Tortoise, Galápagos giant
Chelonoidis nigra (also *Geochelone nigra*)

PHYLUM: Chordata
CLASS: Reptilia
ORDER: Testudines
FAMILY: Testudinidae
STATUS: Vulnerable, IUCN
Endangered, ESA
RANGE: Ecuador (Galápagos Islands)

Tortoise, Galápagos giant
Chelonoidis nigra (also *Geochelone nigra*)

Description and biology

The Galápagos giant tortoise can weigh more than 700 pounds (318 kilograms). There are 12 subspecies of the tortoise, although some of the subspecies have gone extinct. In certain subspecies, the tortoise's top shell, or carapace (pronounced CARE-a-pace), is high and dome shaped. In others, the carapace is high only in front. This type of carapace—called a saddleback—flares out at the bottom. The length of a Galápagos giant tortoise varies depending on its gender and the shape of its carapace. The tortoise itself can reach lengths of almost 4 feet (1.2 meters).

Galápagos giant tortoises reach sexual maturity between 20 and 25 years of age in captivity, and potentially as late as 40 years of age in the wild. Breeding usually peaks between February and June—the rainy season. After mating, a female Galápagos giant tortoise migrates to a dry lowland area to lay her eggs. Sometime in June, she lays between 8 and 17 (depending on the subspecies) tennis-ball-shaped eggs in a nest she has dug out in the ground. She then covers the nest and returns to the highlands. The eggs incubate (develop) for three to eight months, depending on the surrounding air temperature, before hatching. The nest's temperature also determines the offspring's gender: warmer temperatures produce more females; cooler temperatures produce more males. Between November and April, the eggs hatch, and the young tortoises begin to dig their way out of the nest. At birth, they weigh about 0.1 pounds (50 grams).

Galápagos giant tortoises, which can live for as long as 150 years, are herbivores (animals that eat mainly plants). The species is the largest herbivore on the Galápagos Islands and maintains pathways through

The Galápagos giant tortoise saw its population drastically reduced by hunters and predators for several centuries until it became a protected species in 1970. © MICHAEL NOLAN/ROBERT HARDING WORLD IMAGERY/CORBIS.

the brush. It keeps vegetation (plant life) from getting too thick, allowing light to reach plants on the ground. The tortoise has a keen sense of smell, and it will smell all its food before eating it. It can survive for a long period without food or water, living on fat stored in its tissues.

Habitat and current distribution

The Galápagos giant tortoise is found only on the Galápagos Islands, a province of Ecuador lying about 600 miles (965 kilometers) west of the mainland. The animal inhabits the islands of Española, Isabela, Pinzón, San Cristóbal, Santa Cruz, and Santiago. Biologists (people who study living organisms) estimate that about 10,000 to 15,000 Galápagos giant tortoises currently exist.

This tortoise is found in various areas on these islands, from sea level to the highest elevations. During the dry season, the tortoise migrates to higher altitudes to find food and water. Most larger Galápagos giant tortoises are found in the higher altitudes.

History and conservation measures

Humans have been a major threat to the Galápagos giant tortoise. When Spanish bishop Tomás de Berlanga and his shipmates became the first Europeans to discover the Galápagos Islands on their way to Peru in the 1530s, they found so many giant tortoises there that they named the islands the *Galápagos*, which is Spanish for "giant tortoise." Biologists estimate that 250,000 tortoises inhabited the islands when Berlanga and his fellows arrived.

In the 19th century, whalers and explorers who visited the islands slaughtered thousands of Galápagos giant tortoises for their meat and fat. One tortoise could provide hundreds of pounds of meat. To have fresh meat during their voyages, these men sometimes took live tortoises onboard their ships and stored them in the holds—sometimes for more than a year—before slaughtering them.

The Galápagos giant tortoise is currently threatened by animals introduced by humans into its habitat. Dogs and pigs prey on tortoise eggs and young tortoises. Goats compete with the tortoises for food. Burros trample or roll in tortoise nesting areas, often damaging eggs. In addition, the tortoises' slow growth rate and late sexual maturity makes them particularly vulnerable to extinction.

In 1959 the Ecuadoran government declared all uninhabited areas of the Galápagos Islands to be a national park. This act prevents any island species from being hunted, captured, or disturbed. The Charles Darwin Research Station on Santa Cruz Island launched a program to control the predator population. Furthermore, new hybrids (genetic mixtures) of subspecies previously thought to be extinct have been found across the Galápagos, and captive-breeding programs continue to release tortoises into the wild. Although this conservation effort has been mostly successful, the outlook for the survival of the Galápagos giant tortoise remains uncertain.

Turtle, bog
Glyptemys muhlenbergii (also *Clemmys muhlenbergii*)

PHYLUM: Chordata
CLASS: Reptilia
ORDER: Testudines
FAMILY: Emydidae
STATUS: Critically endangered, IUCN Threatened, ESA
RANGE: USA (Connecticut, Delaware, Georgia, Maryland, Massachusetts, New Jersey, New York, North Carolina, Pennsylvania, South Carolina, Tennessee, Virginia)

Turtle, bog
Glyptemys muhlenbergii (also *Clemmys muhlenbergii*)

Description and biology

The bog turtle is only about 4 inches (10 centimeters) long, making it one of the smallest turtles in North America. On each side of a bog turtle's head there is a bright yellow, orange, or red patch, making the turtles easy to identify. Their shells range in color from mahogany to black.

Female bog turtles are slightly smaller than males. They lay two or three (but sometimes up to five) eggs once a year during June or July. The eggs are left to hatch on their own. When they hatch, the baby turtles are around 1 inch (2.5 centimeters) long.

Bog turtles are semiaquatic (living part-time in the water, part-time on land) and eat insects, snails, worms, seeds, and dead animals, as well as fruits and grasses. They are preyed on by raccoons, foxes, and dogs.

The bog turtle, native to the eastern United States, has seen its numbers dwindle due to the pet trade, disease, destruction of its wetland habitat, and other human activity. © PURE-STOCK/ALAMY.

Bog turtles hibernate (spend the winter in an inactive state) underwater during the winter, burrowing deeply into the mud. They are active in late spring and summer. In hot weather they spend much of their time dug into the mud. They are believed to live for up to 40 years.

Habitat and current distribution

Bog turtles live in marshes and other swampy habitats or near small streams. Despite their name, they do not only live in bogs (areas of wet spongy ground composed of decaying plant matter). They prefer environments that provide a variety of wet and dry conditions so they can more easily regulate their body temperature.

Bog turtles are found from New York to western Massachusetts and south to Maryland. The turtles are also found in the Appalachian Mountains from Virginia to Georgia. The northern turtles are separated from the southern turtles by a stretch of land of about 250 miles (400 kilometers) between northeastern Maryland and southern Virginia.

Most bog turtle populations are isolated, or separate, from one another. There are generally a maximum of 40 adults in each group. In the north, populations declined by 50 percent between 1977 and 1997, with around 360 bog turtle populations remaining. In the south, a 1980s survey found around 96 sites. Estimates from 1997 for the northern part of the bog turtle's range (New York and Massachusetts south to Maryland) suggested a population there of no more than 12,700 turtles, and possibly even fewer than 3,275. The population in the southern part of the range is unknown.

History and conservation measures

The main threat to bog turtles is habitat destruction. They often live on land with a high potential for agriculture. Farmers have been draining bog turtle habitat for centuries—and continue to do so.

Scientists also fear that global warming may damage the bog turtles' delicate habitats. The turtles are also endangered by the pet trade; they are much in demand because of their small size and dramatic coloring.

The bog turtle was protected under the Endangered Species Act in the United States in 1997. The International Union for Conservation of Nature and Natural Resources (IUCN) listed the species as critically endangered in 2013. Some bog turtle sites are in protected areas. Private owners of sites are encouraged to manage the turtles carefully. Conservationists (people who work to manage and protect nature) avoid revealing the sites where bog turtles are found to the public because of the danger of illegal collecting.

Turtle, Central American river
Dermatemys mawii

PHYLUM: Chordata
CLASS: Reptilia
ORDER: Testudines
FAMILY: Dermatemydidae
STATUS: Critically endangered, IUCN
Endangered, ESA
RANGE: Belize, Guatemala, Mexico

Turtle, Central American river
Dermatemys mawii

Description and biology

The Central American river turtle is the largest freshwater turtle in its range. An average adult measures 24 inches (61 centimeters) long and weighs almost 50 pounds (23 kilograms). The turtle is a uniform dark gray on most of its upper body and shell, while its undersides are a lighter shade of gray. Adult males have a yellow patch in the shape of a triangle on the top of their heads, which is not present on females. The turtle has webbed feet for swimming and is able to remain underwater for long periods without surfacing for air. Its feet, however, force it to move awkwardly on solid objects and land. Because of this, the Central American river turtle does not climb up on logs or riverbanks to bask in the sun like other freshwater turtles do but it will occasionally float on the water's surface to warm itself in the sun.

The Central American river turtle, native to Belize, Guatemala, and Mexico, saw its population decimated by hunters and trappers. Its webbed feet help it swim. © RAUL & LEAH GONZALEZ.

This species of turtle is primarily nocturnal (active at night), remaining inactive during the day until twilight. It feeds on aquatic plants and fallen leaves and fruit. Otters are its main predators.

During the wet season from September through November, the rivers in the Central American river turtle's habitat swell with water. The higher water allows the female of the species to access more protected areas farther from the flow of the river. These secluded areas are where she chooses to build her nest. After having mated, a female Central American river turtle digs a hole in sand, clay, or mud within a few feet of the water's edge. She then lays a clutch (a number of eggs produced at one time) of 6 to 20 hard-shelled eggs and buries them. Little else is known about the eggs and the young once they hatch.

Habitat and current distribution

Central American river turtles inhabit large, open rivers and permanent lakes. Although they prefer clear freshwater, the turtles are sometimes found in brackish water (a mixture of freshwater and saltwater). The turtle is found only in the coastal lowlands of the western Caribbean. Its range extends from the Mexican state of Veracruz southeast through Guatemala and Belize. The turtle is not found on Mexico's Yucatán Peninsula.

Biologists (people who study living organisms) are unable to estimate the total number of Central American river turtles currently in existence; however, they know the species' population is declining. In the 1970s harvesters would capture 1,000 to 2,000 turtles per lake. By 1990 it was difficult to find harvests of even 5 turtles in one place, and the only healthy populations as of 2006 were those located far from civilization.

History and conservation measures

The main threat to the Central American river turtle is hunting by humans. The turtle is very easy to catch, and both its meat and eggs are valued by people living in its range. In the southern Mexican state of Chiapas, newly built roads have opened up formerly remote areas, giving hunters greater access to turtle populations. Although large populations of the turtle remain in Belize, it is hunted in great numbers. The International Union for Conservation of Nature and Natural Resources (IUCN) predicts that its reduction in Mexico will also encourage smuggling of the species from Belize, threatening populations there. The IUCN uplisted the Central American river turtle from endangered to critically endangered in 2006 because of its ongoing population collapse.

Restrictions on the hunting of the turtles exist, but they are poorly enforced. In 2005 a conservation area was established in Laguna La Popotera (located in the Mexican state of Veracruz), specifically as a preserve for these turtles. In addition, zoos are trying to establish viable captive populations of the species.

Programs to farm the Central American river turtle as a food source are also being studied. The IUCN has suggested that it is unlikely the turtle will survive in the wild unless such farms can be established to meet the huge demand for its meat.

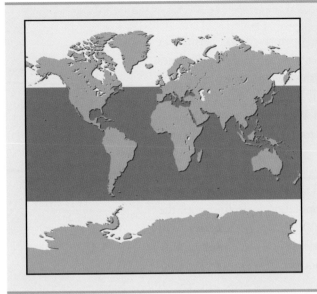

Turtle, green sea
Chelonia mydas

PHYLUM: Chordata
CLASS: Reptilia
ORDER: Testudines
FAMILY: Cheloniidae
STATUS: Endangered, IUCN
Endangered, ESA (breed-
ing grounds in Florida and
Mexico)
Threatened, ESA (elsewhere
in its range)
RANGE: Coastal waters of more than
140 countries; Oceanic

Turtle, green sea
Chelonia mydas

Description and biology

The green sea turtle is the largest of the hard-shelled sea turtles. An average adult weighs 300 to 350 pounds (136 to 159 kilograms) and has a top shell, or carapace (CARE-a-pace), length of about 40 inches (102 centimeters). The large, heart-shaped carapace varies in color from dark greenish brown to olive brown. The turtle's head is small, and it has large, flipper-shaped front legs. It feeds mainly on sea grasses and algae.

Green sea turtles build nests on beaches at various times during the year depending on their location. Mating usually occurs in the water within 0.5 miles (0.8 kilometers) of the nesting beach. After mating, the female crawls slowly up on the beach at night, being very sensitive to light, sound, and other disturbances. Using her rear flippers to dig a hole, she lays her eggs, covers them with sand, and then returns to the ocean. The average clutch (a number of eggs produced at one time) size is 110 eggs, and a female may lay between 3 and 7 clutches a season. The eggs incubate (develop) for a period of 52 to 61 days. Upon hatching, the young turtles race for the water but are often preyed on by birds. In the water, they are preyed on by fish.

Habitat and current distribution

The green sea turtle ranges widely, having been observed as far south as northern Chile and as far north as the English Channel. However, it mainly nests in tropical and subtropical regions. Biologists (people who study living organisms) believe there are about 150 nesting sites worldwide. Only about 10 to 15 of these sites support large populations (2,000 or more nesting females per year). The largest sites are found on Ascension Island in the southern Atlantic, between Brazil and Africa; Costa Rica; the Pacific coast of Mexico; Florida; the northeastern coast of Oman; the island of Europa, between Madagascar and Mozambique;

The green sea turtle is threatened by several types of human activity, including the demand for its eggs and adult animals, habitat damage, fishing, pollution, boat traffic, and other dangers. © SCUBAZOO/SCIENCE SOURCE.

Tromelin Island, located east of Madagascar; Pakistan; and western Australia.

Biologists estimate that there are 85,000 to 95,000 nesting female green sea turtles. These can be counted when they come ashore to nest. But because males do not leave the water, it is difficult to obtain accurate population totals for the species as a whole.

History and conservation measures

Green sea turtles have had declining numbers for hundreds of years. They have always been hunted for food. In modern times, this hunting has increased with advancements in fishing technology and increases in human populations in tropical areas. Turtle eggs are collected for food; young turtles are killed and stuffed for souvenirs; and adults are hunted for their meat (for food), for their skins (for leather goods), and for their oil (for cosmetics).

Like other sea turtles, the green sea turtle faces the threat of loss of nesting habitat. Beachfront development has decreased suitable nesting habitat for the turtle throughout its range. Even development nearby to nesting beaches has hurt the turtle: increased shoreside lighting at night interferes with a female's ability to lay eggs. Another serious threat to the green sea turtle is fibropapillomatosis (pronounced FYE-bro-PAP-uh-loh-muh-TOE-sis). This disease causes tumors on the turtle's skin and internal organs that can grow to the size of a grapefruit. The tumors harm the turtle's ability to feed, swim, and escape predators. The disease affects all sea turtles, but green sea turtles seem to suffer the most.

Green sea turtles are often caught in shrimp nets and drown. A tool called a turtle excluder device is often used to prevent this. The device allows small sea animals such as shrimp to enter the net but prevents larger sea animals such as turtles from entering.

In the United States, most nesting areas are protected, and research is being conducted on the turtle disease described earlier. Because green sea turtles range across such a wide area, international cooperation is needed to conserve the species and its habitat. Agreements on how best to do that have not yet been reached.

In 2015 two U.S. agencies, the National Oceanic and Atmospheric Administration and the Fish and Wildlife Service, proposed revising the green sea turtle's Endangered Species Act status. The revisions would divide the world population of green sea turtles into 11 distinct regions and give each region's population its own status. The population at the Florida and Mexico breeding grounds would be changed from endangered to the less severe threatened because nesting populations have greatly increased. On the other hand, the agencies also proposed uplisting the Mediterranean Sea, central West Pacific, and central South Pacific turtle populations from threatened to endangered. These populations are more in danger of becoming extinct for reasons such as declining populations, poor conservation efforts, or too many threats to the species' survival.

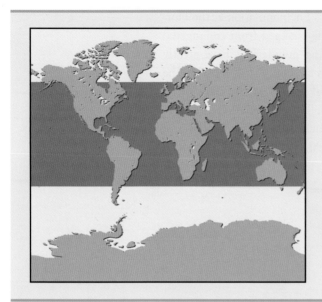

Turtle, leatherback sea
Dermochelys coriacea

PHYLUM:	Chordata
CLASS:	Reptilia
ORDER:	Testudines
FAMILY:	Dermochelyidae
STATUS:	Vulnerable, IUCN Endangered, ESA
RANGE:	Globally oceanic, except for polar latitudes

Turtle, leatherback sea
Dermochelys coriacea

Description and biology

The leatherback is the largest sea turtle in the world. An average adult can measure up to 5 feet (1.5 meters) long and weigh between 800 and 1,000 pounds (363 and 454 kilograms). Other marine turtles have hard, bony-plated top shells, or carapaces (pronounced CARE-a-paces). The dark-brown to black carapace of the leatherback sea turtle is made of seven raised ridges that are somewhat soft and rubbery. Its front flippers are exceptionally long and powerful. When extended, they may span over 8 feet (2.4 meters). The turtle's head and neck are dark brown or black with white or yellowish blotches.

Powerful swimmers, leatherbacks spend most of their lives at sea. They have special physical adaptations—including a thick layer of insulating fat—that allows them to stay underwater for long periods of time. Having relatively weak jaws, the turtles feed almost entirely on jellyfish, often consuming twice their weight each day.

A leatherback sea turtle is seen nesting on a beach. She is preparing to lay dozens of eggs. © FRANS LANTING/LATITUDE/CORBIS.

Female leatherback sea turtles lay their eggs at different times of the year, depending on their location. Those that build nests at North Atlantic sites lay their eggs between April and July. Those at eastern Pacific sites lay theirs between November and January. After mating with a male offshore, a female leatherback crawls up on a sandy, undisturbed beach at night and digs a shallow body pit with all four limbs. She then digs out a nest cavity about 3.3 feet (1 meter) deep with her hind limbs. She lays a clutch (a number of eggs produced at one time) of about 100 round, white-shelled eggs in the nest, covers them with sand, and then returns to the ocean.

After 56 to 65 days, the eggs hatch and the young leatherbacks, measuring 2 to 2.5 inches (5 to 6.4 centimeters) long, emerge from the nest and crawl toward the ocean. Very few survive to adulthood. Pigs, lizards, and other predators (including humans) prey on the eggs. Before they even reach the ocean, young leatherbacks are preyed on by birds and small mammals. In the water, both young and adult leatherbacks are preyed on by sharks.

Habitat and current distribution

Leatherback sea turtles are among the widest ranging of sea animals, inhabiting waters from the tropics to the subarctic. They migrate vast distances to and from nesting sites. Female leatherbacks prefer to nest on relatively undisturbed beaches that have a heavy surf and deep water immediately offshore. These sites are usually located on tropical beaches in the Atlantic, Indian, and Pacific Oceans. Sometimes the turtles gather in temperate (mild) waters where jellyfish are more abundant.

Because males do not come ashore, it is almost impossible for biologists (people who study living organisms) to estimate how many currently exist. But because females do, biologists are able to count them. In the 1980s and 1990s, it was estimated that about 100,000 nesting females existed around the world. A 2000 survey showed more than an 80 percent decline in nesting in the Pacific populations of the species. While Pacific populations continue to decline, more extensive surveys in the early 21st century indicate that the global population is larger than earlier estimates suggested, and in some areas the population is even growing. One such area is the North Atlantic, where the number of adult leatherback sea turtles is estimated to be between 34,000 and 94,000.

History and conservation measures

In the 1960s biologists believed the leatherback sea turtle was on the verge of extinction. The turtle's population has since increased in certain regions and declined in others. It faces many threats, including the loss of its coastal nesting habitats, entrapment in fishing nets, poaching (illegal hunting) of turtles and their eggs, and poisoning or choking from swallowing plastic trash that's been littered in the ocean. Conservation efforts have aimed to address many of these issues and have been successful where they have been implemented.

By far the greatest threat to leatherback sea turtles comes from fishing operations. Turtles (and other large sea animals) are often caught in shrimp-fishing nets or longline fishing operations (fishing with a line up to several miles long with a series of baited hooks along its length) and drown. It is estimated that 50,000 leatherback sea turtles or more are trapped by longline fisheries each year, and many of them die. In the early 21st century, the U.S. government closed a large area in the Pacific Ocean to the U.S. longline fishery in order to protect leatherbacks from being caught unintentionally.

Meanwhile, shrimp fisheries have also incorporated protections; many nets now have turtle excluder devices, or TEDs, built into them. A TED is a grid of bars with an opening at either the top or the bottom. This grid is fitted into the neck of a shrimp net. Small sea animals, such as shrimp, pass easily through the bars into the bag end of the net. Large sea animals, such as turtles, strike the bars and are thrown back out through the opening. TEDs safely remove about 97 percent of the turtles that become trapped in the shrimp nets. Shrimpers complain, however, that TEDs also allow some shrimp to escape and thus reduce their catches. In the United States, fisheries are required to use shrimp nets with TEDs, but many other countries in the leatherback sea turtle's range do not have such a requirement.

The second-largest threat to leatherback sea turtles, according to the International Union for Conservation of Nature and Natural Resources (IUCN), is poaching of the species and its eggs for food or for other uses. This is especially a problem among the Pacific populations of leatherbacks, and the species' eggs are especially prized in Malaysia. International trade of all sea turtle products is forbidden under the Convention on International Trade in Endangered Species of Wild Fauna and Flora (CITES; an international treaty to protect wildlife), but some nations still allow the use of leatherback sea turtle meat, oil, and eggs.

The leatherback sea turtle's habitat is in jeopardy as well. Many areas that were once leatherback nesting sites have been converted into living areas for humans or developed into tourist areas. Other nesting sites have been destroyed as off-road vehicles and the development of nearby land have caused beach erosion. Conservation efforts seek to set aside critical habitat for leatherbacks at their nesting beaches by creating refuges and protected areas. As a result of these efforts, leatherback nests in Florida increased from 27 to 641 between 1989 and 2014. There has also been an increase in nests on islands in the Caribbean Sea.

Plastic trash in the ocean, such as clear sandwich bags, is a grave concern because leatherbacks cannot distinguish between jellyfish and clear plastic. Examinations have found many turtles with plastic in their stomachs. Biologists do not know how much plastic it takes to kill a leatherback sea turtle, but no amount is beneficial, and the oceans are becoming more polluted with plastics every day.

In 2010 the IUCN downlisted the species from critically endangered to vulnerable, but this was largely because new data became available about population numbers that had not been taken into account in the previous assessment. Conservation efforts have also been successful in improving the turtle's status, especially in the northwestern Atlantic Ocean. Largely because of their success in that region, scientists estimate that by 2025 the leatherback sea turtle may no longer be threatened globally. However, turtle populations in other regions, especially the eastern and western regions of the Pacific Ocean, may still be threatened because their populations continue to decline there and conservation measures have yet to be put in place.

Viper, meadow
Vipera ursinii

PHYLUM: Chordata
CLASS: Reptilia
ORDER: Squamata
FAMILY: Viperidae
STATUS: Vulnerable, IUCN
RANGE: Albania, Bosnia and Herzegovina, Croatia, France, Greece, Hungary, Italy, Macedonia, Montenegro, Romania, Serbia

Viper, meadow
Vipera ursinii

Description and biology

The meadow viper, also called Orsini's viper, is Europe's smallest viper. It is a venomous (poisonous) snake. Adults average about 16 to 18 inches (40 to 45.7 centimeters) long, although they can reach lengths up to 2 feet (0.6 meters) in length. Females are usually larger than males. The snake's color ranges from light gray to brown, and it has a zigzag pattern down the center of its back in a darker gray or brown color, outlined in black.

The meadow viper preys on insects, especially grasshoppers, as well as small mammals and lizards. Its hollow fangs inject poison into its prey; the poison will usually kill the prey quickly. The snake's fangs can be used in self-defense as well, although its venom is not strong and it poses little threat to humans.

Meadow vipers mate in April and May, and in August or September, females give birth to live young (rather than laying eggs). They usually give birth to 4 to 8 offspring at one time, though they may have as many as 15.

Habitat and current distribution

Until 2005 taxonomists (biologists who classify species on the basis of their genes, characteristics, and behavior) recognized *Vipera ursinii* as a species that ranged from western Europe to central Asia. However, in 2005 this range was broken up into various separate species. *Vipera ursinii* now describes only those meadow vipers ranging from France in the west to Romania in the east. When the International Union for Conservation of Nature and Natural Resources (IUCN) updated its listing of this species in 2009, the meadow viper's new range was taken into account, and its status was downlisted from endangered to vulnerable based on these changes.

The meadow viper, native to central Europe, is at risk as agricultural development shrinks and fragments its habitat. © FABIO PUPIN/ENCYCLOPEDIA/CORBIS.

Meadow vipers currently exist throughout Europe but in fragmented populations that are isolated from each other. It is extinct in Austria and Bulgaria and thought to be extinct in Moldova. In Hungary it is close to extinction.

There are five subspecies of meadow viper in Europe. Two of these subspecies are found in lowland meadows, while the other three exist in southern-facing mountain pastures at elevations between 4,600 and 8,000 feet (1,400 and 2,440 meters). The lowland subspecies are most often found in steppe (large, semiarid, grass-covered plains found in southeastern Europe and Asia) or semi-steppe environments. Each of the different subspecies of meadow viper has its own range, and in some areas meadow vipers remain relatively abundant, though still threatened.

One of the lowland subspecies, the endangered Hungarian meadow viper, *Vipera ursinii rakosiensis*, now occurs only in the Great Hungarian Plain between the Danube and Tisza Rivers and in the Fertő-Hanság National Park in the northwestern part of Hungary. Its range is less than 1,930 square miles (5,000 square kilometers), and it exists in five locations at most. The other lowland subspecies, *Vipera ursinii moldavica*, native to Romania and Moldova, is even rarer.

The three mountain subspecies of meadow viper inhabit alpine (above the tree line of high mountains) areas of southeastern France and central Italy, mountainous areas in the Balkans in southeastern Europe, and the Pindos mountains of Greece.

History and conservation measures

Throughout Europe, the meadow viper has been endangered by the loss and fragmentation (breaking up of habitat into smaller areas that no longer border each other) of its habitat due to agriculture, road building, and livestock practices. Habitat loss has had a more devastating effect on the two lowland subspecies because they are located in areas that humans are more likely to use for agriculture or development.

The Hungarian subspecies of meadow viper once ranged throughout suitable habitats in Hungary, the easternmost part of Austria, Transylvania (central Romania), and northern Bulgaria. The range of this subspecies has been greatly fragmented by human-related habitat disturbance. Croatia has had protective measures for the meadow viper in place since 1965.

Because the Hungarian subspecies is close to extinction, the Council of Europe Convention on the Conservation of European Wildlife and Natural Habitats Standing Committee recommended that the government of Hungary: 1) establish protected meadow habitats in the range of the existing meadow viper populations; 2) open up surrounding habitats where the species once occurred; and 3) prohibit the burning of farmland in Hungary.

Scientists believe that the Hungarian subspecies of meadow viper, because of its very low population and the isolation of the various remaining groups, is experiencing what is called inbreeding depression. This occurs in a small, closed population in which all individuals eventually become related to one another by descent. Over time, this will cause a loss of genetic diversity, a lowering of the number of genes that can be passed on to the next generation. The effects of inbreeding depression build up over time, most seriously affecting the reproductive health of the animals, thus making them even more vulnerable to extinction.

One way to increase the genetic diversity among the Hungarian meadow vipers is to begin a captive-breeding program using genetically screened vipers. In 2004 the Viper Conservation and Breeding Centre was established in Hungary. Its breeding program has been extremely successful. In 2004 there were only about 500 Hungarian meadow vipers in existence; that number had quadrupled by 2014 thanks to captive breeding.

Although their populations are very small, the meadow vipers that inhabit mountainous areas are more secluded from human activities and thus more protected. These populations are, however, threatened by the construction of ski facilities and climate change, which could alter the conditions of their habitat.

These small snakes have also been illegally captured for trade as pets. Pollution is dangerous to the animals as well, as it reduces the crickets that make up an important part of their diet. To ensure the survival of the meadow viper, conservationists (people who work to manage and protect nature) recommend protecting and managing the viper's habitat wherever the species occurs.

Critical Thinking Questions

1. Why might conservationists specializing in trying to protect a specific animal species have mixed feelings about that animal becoming downlisted (given a less endangered status) under the Endangered Species Act (ESA) or the Red List of the International Union for Conservation of Nature and Natural Resources (IUCN)?

2. Describe three reasons why it is important that species not become extinct. Consider possible effects on other species and on humans.

3. Some species face a greater risk of endangerment than others. What are some characteristics of species and their particular habitats that can lead to greater risks of extinction?

4. What are four effects that increased carbon dioxide emissions can have on the planet's climate and weather patterns? What are some of the impacts on living organisms?

5. Scientists have extracted DNA from the bodies of extinct animals such as the woolly mammoth and are exploring possible ways to use this DNA to create new animals, a process known as "de-extincting." Do you think this scientific pursuit is a good idea? Why or why not? Does your answer depend on which species would be "de-extincted"?

6. In 2012 the United States spent $1.7 billion to conserve endangered species. Do you think this investment is worthwhile? Why or why not? Is it too much or too little? (For comparison, consider that in 2015, the lowest state budget was $4.3 billion and the U.S. military budget was approximately $600 billion.)

7. Some conservation groups focus on a small number of endangered species that people find appealing. These "flagship species" include

tigers, leopards, elephants, chimpanzees, gorillas, giant pandas, polar bears, dolphins, sea turtles, and whales. What characteristics do these animals have that might account for their public appeal? Does focusing on these animals help or hurt other endangered species that might not be as appealing?

8. Traditional practices or customary behaviors in a culture can contribute to the endangerment of species. What are some practices that do so? Think about practices in developed countries, such as the United States, and in less-developed countries.

9. What are three ways that nonnative species can be introduced into an environment? What effects can nonnative species have on native species?

10. What are some actions that you and other students could take that would help preserve endangered species?

Classroom Projects and Activities

1. Investigate a Species

Research an endangered species in your state and write a report about it. First describe the animal's appearance, social behavior, food sources, reproduction, and raising of its young. Then discuss where it lives, what its total population is, and why it is endangered. Detail conservation efforts undertaken to save it, if any. Mention interesting facts about the animal and its behavior. Include pictures of the animal and links to websites discussing the animal or videos showing it.

2. Impersonate a Conservationist

Pick an important biologist or conservationist such as Charles Darwin, Jane Goodall, Jeff Corwin, Steve Irwin, Dian Fossey, Jacques Cousteau, John Muir, or Henry David Thoreau. Research this person's life and his or her work with animals and plants. Then, either:

1. Perform a 5–10 minute monologue for your class in the character of this person. Tell stories of "your" life and conservation work. Dress up as the character if you like.

2. Present a 5–10 minute play dramatizing events from the person's life, with you and classmates acting the roles.

3. Immerse Yourself in an Issue

It can be difficult to balance people's needs and wants with the needs of animals. Consider this situation: A conservation group applies to have a bird listed as endangered. The bird's habitat includes areas where natural oil and gas are found, as well as land used for grazing livestock. Divide into groups of six, each person taking a role representing a specific point of view, then debate whether the bird should be listed. The roles are:

1. A representative of a conservation group.
2. The head of an oil and gas company that plans to drill for oil and gas on land within the bird's habitat.
3. A rancher who grazes cattle on land within the bird's habitat.
4. A local birdwatcher who enjoys observing this bird in its habitat.
5. The governor of the state where the bird is found.
6. The government official who must make the decision whether to list the bird. (This person asks questions, makes a decision at the end of the debate, and explains why she or he made that decision.)

Once the debate is done, look up the case of the greater sage grouse online. How did the decision that was made balance these different interests?

4. Invent an Animal

Invent a new animal species—a mammal, bird, amphibian, or reptile that lives on land or in the sea. Write a description and draw a picture of the animal. Describe what it looks like; its habitat (air, land, water, climate) and how it has adapted to this environment; what it eats and how it protects itself against predators; its social behavior, reproduction, and care of its young. Is the animal endangered? If so, why?

5. Invite Others to Save a Species

In a small group, choose an animal or plant from *U•X•L Endangered Species, 3rd Edition*, that is not well known. Brainstorm and write down ideas for an advertising campaign educating people about this species and the need to preserve it. Create a slogan, think about which facts and issues you would emphasize, and discuss what kind of pictures you would choose to present. Consider ways to use social media, such as Facebook, Instagram, and Snapchat, in your campaign. For inspiration, look up World Wildlife Fund's campaigns online.

6. Inspire Awareness

Create a YouTube video for other students about an endangered species topic. You could focus on one of the reasons for endangerment (habitat loss, overexploitation, invasive species, climate change), a specific species, or ways people can help save endangered species.

7. Imagine Saving the Day

Create a comic book about endangerment of species. One option: create a superhero who tries to fight endangerment, villains who put species at risk, and animals to be rescued.

8. Examine the Five Deciding Factors

Some species are listed as endangered or threatened by the International Union for Conservation of Nature and Natural Resources (IUCN), but not under the Endangered Species Act (ESA). Examples include the addax, axolotl, European mink, Ganges River dolphin, giant sequoia, and Grand Cayman blue iguana. Look up the five factors for listing a species under the Endangered Species Act. Pick and research one of the six species listed above focusing on why it is at risk. Use *U•X•L Endangered Species, 3rd Edition*; the IUCN site; and at least two other sites as sources. Then, using the 5 factors, write an argument that this animal should— or should not—be listed under the ESA.

9. Explore Ecotourism: Pros and Cons

Ecotourism is a form of tourism in which people travel to natural areas to view wildlife and other aspects of the natural environment. It has some positive aspects, but also some negative ones. Research ecotourism and list the benefits and possible disadvantages of this practice. Describe some factors that should be considered in order for ecotourism to be done in a responsible way.

10. Evaluate Common and Endangered Animals

Many endangered animals resemble similar animals that are not endangered. In the United States, for example, the American bullfrog, black bear, whitetail deer, gray squirrel, and common garter snake are not at risk, but other species of bullfrog, bear, deer, squirrel, and garter snake are endangered or threatened under the Endangered Species Act. Pick one of the animals above, and on the U.S. Fish and Wildlife Service Endangered Species website, find the similar species that are endangered. Compare and contrast the common and endangered animals. Look at geographic ranges, adaptations, habitats, value to or relationship with humans, predators and prey, and other differences. Then, in a small group, discuss your findings with students who chose other animals. Do the endangered species share characteristics in common?

11. Expand Focus

Biologist Colin Stevenson argues that conservationists' focus is often too narrow. In a March 6, 2015, interview with the BBC, a British news service, he said, "The traditional approach is to . . . study the animal, tell people about the declining numbers and the threats, and then call for people to stop doing the things causing the threats. But this approach doesn't work. The real problem is usually that the people in these areas have nothing and are just trying to survive." Choose the gharial, the giant catfish, the okapi, the dama gazelle, the markhor, or the carossier palm (a plant) and research the reasons for endangerment. In a small group, discuss how Stevenson's statement applies (or does not apply) to your species' situation.

Where to Learn More

Books

Corwin, Jeff. *100 Heartbeats: The Race to Save Earth's Most Endangered Species.* New York: Rodale, 2009. Television host and biologist Corwin interweaves personal stories of animal encounters with serious discussions of why animals face danger from humans. The book includes powerful sections on global warming and pollution.

Danson, Ted, and Michael D'Orso. *Oceana: Our Endangered Oceans and What We Can Do to Save Them.* New York: Rodale, 2011. Actor Danson traces his journey as an environmental activist, describes how actions such as deep-sea drilling and overfishing endanger the ocean and its inhabitants, and offers suggestions for reclaiming the seas. Illustrated with helpful charts and graphics.

Garbutt, Nick. *100 Animals to See Before They Die.* Buckinghamshire, UK: Bradt Travel Guides, 2007. Published by a travel company, this book profiles 100 endangered species, listed by regions where they live. Each entry offers photos, a distribution map, and a discussion of reasons for endangerment, conservation efforts, and how travelers can visit the region.

Goodall, Jane. *Hope for Animals and Their World.* New York: Hachette, 2009. Renowned chimpanzee researcher and conservationist Goodall traces ways that dedicated conservationists have worked and are working to save specific species of endangered animals.

Hoare, Ben. *DK Eyewitness: Endangered Animals.* London: DK, 2010. This guide for students aged 8 to 12 discusses why species become endangered, profiles threatened animals, and describes efforts to save species in danger. Numerous photos, pictures, charts, and graphs enliven the book.

Hoose, Phillip. *The Race to Save the Lord God Bird.* New York: Farrar, Straus, and Giroux, 2014. Using extensive archival research, Hoose traces the late-19th-century decline of the legendary ivory-billed woodpecker, a victim of habitat loss and eager hunters, and chronicles conservationists' desperate efforts to save the species.

IUCN Red List. *Species on the Edge of Survival.* London: HarperCollins UK, 2012. The International Union for Conservation of Nature and Natural

Resources (IUCN), which issues the official *Red List of Threatened Species*, describes 365 species on its list. Entries include reasons for endangerment, location maps, and photographs.

Kolbert, Elizabeth. *The Sixth Extinction: An Unnatural History*. New York: Henry Holt, 2014. Science writer Kolbert won the Pulitzer Prize for this book, which argues that humans' consumption of fossil fuels has led to a sixth period of widespread species extinctions paralleling the first five naturally caused extinction periods.

Mackay, Richard. *The Atlas of Endangered Species*, 3rd ed. Berkeley: University of California Press, 2008. A resource suitable for young adults and older readers, this atlas provides vital information on ecosystems, identifying wildlife, the importance of biodiversity, the transplanting of plants and animals across continents, and more. Also included in its 128 pages are case studies illustrating the major threats to biodiversity and the measures being taken to conserve the species.

McGavin, George. *Endangered: Wildlife on the Brink of Extinction*. Buffalo, NY: Firefly, 2006. This volume aimed at young adults explains that after five great extinction periods caused by natural events, human disregard for the environment is causing a sixth period of extinction. It describes endangered species and includes more than 400 photographs.

Montgomery, Sy. *Kakapo Rescue: Saving the World's Strangest Parrot*. New York: Houghton Mifflin Harcourt, 2010. Author Montgomery traveled to New Zealand to accompany biologists trying to save a critically endangered parrot species. It is part of the publisher's "Scientists in the Field" series, which includes books on many different animals, often endangered.

Neme, Laurel A. *Animal Investigators: How the World's First Wildlife Forensics Lab Is Solving Crimes and Saving Endangered Species*. New York: Simon & Schuster, 2009. Neme profiles a laboratory at the U.S. Fish and Wildlife Service where scientists use the bodies of animals to investigate wildlife crimes and curb trafficking in endangered species.

Pobst, Sandra. *National Geographic Investigates: Animals on the Edge*. Washington, DC: National Geographic, 2008. This short book for students ages 10 to 14 describes threats to animal species, outlines conservation efforts and what young people can do to help, and discusses formerly endangered animals now off the endangered species list.

Rogers, Kara. *The Quiet Extinction: Stories of North America's Rare and Endangered Plants*. Tucson: University of Arizona Press, 2015. Science writer Rogers explores why thousands of North American plants face possible extinction, why their survival is important, and how conservationists are working to save them.

Sartore, Joel. *Rare: Portraits of America's Endangered Species*. Washington, DC: National Geographic, 2010. National Geographic photographer Sartore presents haunting photographs of endangered animals and plants. The book is organized according to the size of the populations remaining of the photographed species, counting down to those on the edge of extinction.

Scardina, Julie, and Jeff Flocken. *Wildlife Heroes: 40 Leading Conservationists and the Animals They Are Committed to Saving.* Philadelphia: Running Press, 2012. This volume profiles 40 conservationists and the animal each works to save. Often in the conservationists' own words, entries reveal the backgrounds and experiences of these activists and describe the animals that are the focus of their efforts.

Turner, Pamela. *A Life in the Wild: George Schaller's Struggle to Save the Last Great Beasts.* New York: Farrar, Straus, and Giroux, 2008. Written for readers ages 10 to 14, this biography of noted biologist and conservationist Schaller explores his early life and his work studying gorillas and lions in Africa and tigers in India, among others. It richly describes the joys and challenges of studying endangered species in remote regions.

Watt, Simon. *The Ugly Animals: We Can't All Be Pandas.* Gloucestershire, UK: The History Press, 2014. Biologist and TV presenter Watt founded the Ugly Animal Preservation Society to humorously introduce endangered animals that are often ignored. His book features photographs and descriptions of animals such as the dromedary jumping-slug.

Periodicals

Endangered Species and Wetlands Report
P.O. Box 5393
Takoma Park, MD 20913
http://www.eswr.com/

Endangered Species Bulletin
U.S. Fish and Wildlife Service
Endangered Species
5275 Leesburg Pike
Falls Church, VA 22041
http://www.fws.gov/endangered/news/bulletin.html

World Wildlife
World Wildlife Fund
1250 24th St. NW
Washington, DC 20037
http://www.worldwildlife.org/magazine

Websites

Bagheera: An Education Website about Endangered Species and the Efforts to Save Them
www.bagheera.com/

BirdLife International
http://www.birdlife.org/

Convention on International Trade in Endangered Species of Flora and Fauna
www.cites.org

Defenders of Wildlife: Endangered Species Act 101
www.defenders.org/endangered-species-act/endangered-species-act

Defenders of Wildlife Kids' Planet: Especies Fact Sheets
www.kidsplanet.org/factsheets/map.html

Ecology: Ecology Global Network
www.ecology.com/

International Union for Conservation of Nature and Natural Resources
(IUCN) Red List of Threatened Species
www.iucn.org/about/work/programmes/species/our_work/the_iucn_red
_list

International Wild Cat Conservation Directory—Big Cats Wild Cats: Endangered Wild Cats
http://bigcatswildcats.com/endangered-wild-cats

Kids Discover Spotlight: Endangered Species
www.kidsdiscover.com/spotlight/endangered-species

National Geographic Education: Endangered Species
http://education.nationalgeographic.com/topics/endangered-species/

National Oceanic and Atmospheric Administration (NOAA) Fisheries: Endangered and Threatened Marine Species
www.nmfs.noaa.gov/pr/species/esa

Species in Pieces (online interactive exhibition)
http://species-in-pieces.com

University of Michigan: Animal Diversity Web
http://animaldiversity.org

U.S. Department of Agriculture: Threatened and Endangered Plants
http://plants.usda.gov/threat.html

U.S. Fish and Wildlife Service: Endangered Species
www.fws.gov/Endangered/index.html

Wildscreen Arkive
www.arkive.org

World Wildlife Fund: Wildfinder
www.worldwildlife.org/pages/wildfinder

The Xerces Society for Invertebrate Conservation: Endangered Species
www.xerces.org/endangered-species

Young People's Trust for the Environment: Endangered Animals of the World
https://ypte.org.uk/factsheets/endangered-animals-of-the-world/you-can
-help-too

Zoological Society of London: EDGE (Evolutionarily Distinct and Globally
Endangered) of Existence
www.edgeofexistence.org

Other Sources

Selected Organizations

*[Note: The following is an annotated compilation of organizations and advocacy
groups relevant to the topics found in U•X•L Endangered Species, 3rd Edition.
Although the list is comprehensive, it is by no means exhaustive and is intended to
serve as a starting point for assembling further information. Gale, a part of Cengage
Learning, is not responsible for the accuracy of the addresses or the contents of the
websites, nor does it endorse any of the organizations listed.]*

African Wildlife Foundation
Ngong Road, Karen
P.O. Box 310, 00502
Nairobi, Kenya
Phone: +254 (0) 711 630 000
Fax: +254 20 2765030

U.S. office:
1400 Sixteenth St. NW, Suite 120
Washington, DC 20036
Phone: (202) 939-3333
Fax: (202) 939-3332
Email: africanwildlife@awf.org
Website: www.awf.org
The African Wildlife Foundation is an organization that works to craft and
deliver creative solutions for the long-term well-being of Africa's remarkable
species and habitats. It also maintains offices in the Democratic Republic of
the Congo, South Sudan, Tanzania, the United Kingdom, and Zambia.

Australian Marine Conservation Society
P.O. Box 5815
West End Queensland 4101
Phone: +61 07-3846-6777
Email: amcs@amcs.org.au
Website: http://www.marineconservation.org.au/
The Australian Marine Conservation Society is the only nonprofit Austra-
lian organization focused exclusively on protecting ocean wildlife and hab-
itats. It creates large marine national parks, promotes sustainable fishing,
and protects threatened ocean animals such as sharks, seals, and whales. Its
programs also combat climate change and reduce ocean pollution.

Australian Wildlife Conservancy
P.O. Box 8070 Subiaco East
Western Australia 6008
Phone: +61 8-9380-9633

Email: info@australianwildlife.org

Website: http://www.australianwildlife.org/

Organized because Australia's animals face a particularly high extinction and endangerment rate, this nonprofit is Australia's largest private owner of conservation land, protecting endangered wildlife in 23 sanctuaries spanning more than 3.15 million hectares (7.78 million acres).

Bat Conservation International

P.O. Box 162603

Austin, TX 78716

Phone: (512) 327 9721

Website: www.batcon.org

Bat Conservation International works worldwide to save, conserve, and protect the 1,300 species of bats and their ecosystems, including 77 endangered species. Its approaches include preventing extinctions, protecting areas with large bat populations, addressing major threats to species, and sponsoring research.

Canadian Wildlife Federation

Ottawa—Head Office

c/o Customer Service

350 Michael Cowpland Dr.

Kanata, Ontario K2M 2W1

Phone: (800) 563-9453

Website: http://www.cwf-fcf.org/en/

This nonprofit's mission is to conserve and inspire the conservation of Canada's wildlife and habitats for the use and enjoyment of all. Its Endangered Species Program is the biggest nongovernmental source of funding to recover Canadian species at risk. The organization also produces TV programs, magazines, and books about species and sponsors programs encouraging people to experience nature firsthand.

Center for Biological Diversity

P.O. Box 710

Tucson, AZ 85702-0710

Phone: (520) 623-5252

Fax: (520) 623-9797

Email: center@biologicaldiversity.org

Website: www.biologicaldiversity.org

The Center for Biological Diversity is a nonprofit conservation organization dedicated to protecting biological diversity through science, law, policy advocacy, and creative media. By filing petitions and lawsuits, the Center has obtained endangered species status for more than 500 species.

Center for Plant Conservation, Inc.

P.O. Box 299

St. Louis, MO 63166-0299

Phone: (314) 577-9450

Fax: (314) 577-9465

Email: cpc@mobot.org
Website: www.centerforplantconservation.org/welcome.asp
The Center for Plant Conservation, Inc., is a national network of 39
botanical gardens and arboreta dedicated to the conservation and study of
rare and endangered U.S. plants.

Defenders of Wildlife
1130 17th St. NW
Washington, DC 20036
Phone: (202) 682-9400
Email: defenders@mail.defenders.org
Website: www.defenders.org
Defenders of Wildlife is a nonprofit organization that works to protect
and restore native species, habitats, ecosystems, and overall biological
diversity in North America.

Earth Island Institute
2150 Allston Way, Suite 460
Berkeley, CA 94704-1375
Phone: (510) 859-9100
Fax: (510) 859-9091
Website: www.earthisland.org/index.php
Earth Island Institute sponsors many environmental groups such as the
International Marine Mammal Project, the Urban Bird Foundation, and
Generation Waking Up, which involves young people in creating a sus-
tainable world. It also funds young conservationists and wetland conserva-
tion projects.

Earthjustice
500 California St., Suite 500
San Francisco, CA 94111
Phone: (800) 584-6460
Fax: (415) 217-2040
Email: info@earthjustice.org
Website: http://earthjustice.org
Founded in 1971 as Sierra Club Legal Defense Fund, Earthjustice is a
nonprofit law firm dedicated to protecting nature by working through the
courts. Earthjustice has played a leading role in developing environmental
law in the courtrooms and also in Washington, D.C., where it helps shape
policies and legislation.

Endangered Species Coalition
P.O. Box 65195
Washington, DC 20035
Phone: (240) 353-2765
Website: www.endangered.org
This nonprofit coalition of conservation, scientific, education, religious,
sporting, outdoor recreation, business, and community organizations
works to preserve and improve the Endangered Species Act. Its goals are to

end human-caused extinction of species in the United States, to safeguard animal and plant habitats, and to help endangered populations recover.

Endangered Species International (Headquarters)
2112 Hayes St.
San Francisco, CA 94117
Email: info@endangeredspeciesinternational.org
Website: www.endangeredspeciesinternational.org
This nonprofit focuses on species in the gravest danger of extinction, including those the media often ignores. It conducts scientific research about conservation, uses this research in projects worldwide, and builds relationships between governments, communities, and businesses.

Environmental Defense Fund
1875 Connecticut Ave. NW, Suite 600
Washington, DC 20009
Phone: (800) 684-3322
Website: www.edf.org
One of the world's largest environmental organizations, Environmental Defense Fund addresses Earth's most pressing environmental problems in the areas of climate, oceans, ecosystems, and health. It partners with businesses to craft solutions that help the planet while benefiting people economically.

Environmental Investigation Agency (EIA)
P.O. Box 53343
Washington, DC 20009
Phone: (202) 483-6621
Fax: (202) 986-8626
Email: info@eia-global.org
Website: http://eia-global.org
Environmental Investigation Agency is an international campaigning organization formed in 1989 that is committed to investigating and exposing environmental crime, often working undercover. One of the group's efforts is protecting endangered species by investigating illegal poaching and smuggling.

Fauna and Flora International
Jupiter House, 4th Floor
Station Road
Cambridge, CB1 2JD, United Kingdom
Phone: (202) 375-7766
Email: info@fauna-flora.org
Website: http://www.fauna-flora.org/
Founded in 1903, this British organization attempts to conserve threatened species and ecosystems worldwide, choosing sustainable, science-based solutions that take into account human needs. Its projects often focus on developing countries. It secures endangered species' habitats, monitors species' survival, and raises local awareness about species' impor-

tance. The group also works with businesses, partners with local organizations, and publishes a major conservation journal.

Foundation for Australia's Most Endangered Species, Ltd. (FAME)
P.O. Box 482
Mitcham, SA 5062 Australia
Phone +61 8-8374-1744
Email: fame@fame.org.au
Website: http://fame.org.au/
FAME is the only Australian organization completely focused on saving the more than 300 endangered species in that country. It works with other organizations, wildlife authorities, and private landowners and raises funds from individuals for specific projects, such as saving the mountain pygmy possum and the Tasmanian devil.

International Union for Conservation of Nature and Natural Resources (IUCN)
Rue Mauverney 28
1196 Gland, Switzerland
Phone: +41 (22) 999-0000
Fax: +41 (22) 999-0002

U.S. office:
1630 Connecticut Ave. NW, 3rd Floor
Washington, DC 20009
Phone: (202) 387-4826
Fax: (202) 387-4823
Website: www.iucn.org
An international independent body that promotes scientifically based action for the conservation of nature and for sustainable development. The Global Species Programme and the Species Survival Commission (SSC) of the IUCN publish a Red List online that describes threatened species of mammals, birds, reptiles, amphibians, fish, invertebrates, plants, and fungi.

National Audubon Society
225 Varick St.
New York, NY 10014
Phone: (212) 979-3000
Website: www.audubon.org
Audubon is a national network comprised of nearly 500 local chapters that are dedicated to the conservation and restoration of natural resources and focused on birds and their habitat. The group's work includes restoring habitats, operating nature centers and bird sanctuaries, and encouraging governmental policies that safeguard birds.

National Wildlife Federation
11100 Wildlife Center Dr.
Reston, VA 20190

Phone: (800)-822-9919

Website: www.nwf.org

This group works to protect U.S. wildlife and habitat for future genera-tions, concentrating on safeguarding wildlife and ecosystems in an era of climate change. It lobbies for environmentally sound policies and educates the public about conservation.

Nature Conservancy

4245 North Fairfax Dr., Suite 100

Arlington, VA 22203-1606

Phone: (703) 841-5300

Website: www.nature.org

The Nature Conservancy is an international nonprofit organization com-mitted to preserving biological diversity by protecting natural lands and the life they harbor.

Oceana

1350 Connecticut Ave. NW, 5th Floor

Washington, DC 20036

Phone: (202) 833-3900

Fax: (202) 833-2070

Email: info@oceana.org

Website: http://oceana.org

Oceana, the world's largest international advocacy group focused solely on ocean conservation, promotes policies that preserve the ocean's marine life. Fighting overfishing and ocean pollution, members advocate for science-based fishery management and restoring the world's oceans.

Wild Aid

744 Montgomery St., Suite 300

San Francisco, CA 94111

Phone: (415) 834-3174

Fax: (415) 834-1759

Website: www.wildaid.org

The goal of Wild Aid is to end the illegal wildlife trade by persuading consumers not to buy products made from illegally caught animals and by strengthening enforcement against capturing these animals. Its slogan is "When the buying stops, the killing can too."

Wildlife Conservation Network

209 Mississippi St.

San Francisco, CA 94107

Phone: (415) 202-6380

Fax (415) 202-6381

Website: http://wildnet.org

Wildlife Conservation Network is a nonprofit that protects endangered species in 24 countries by supporting independent conservationists with innovative approaches that focus on work with local communities. The group trains these activists and brings them together with donors.

Wildlife Conservation Society
2300 Southern Blvd.
Bronx, New York 10460
Phone: (718) 220-5100
Website: www.wcs.org
Founded in 1895 to protect the American bison, the nonprofit Wildlife Conservation Society works to save wildlife and wild places worldwide, managing more than 500 conservation projects. It is the parent organization of the four major zoos and the aquarium in New York City.

Wildlife Preservation Canada
RR#5, 5420 Highway 6 North
Guelph, ON N1H 6J2
Phone: (800) 956-6608
Website: http://wildlifepreservation.ca/
This organization provides direct intervention with specific Canadian animals in grave danger of extinction. Its programs include captive breeding and release, reintroduction of species, nest protection, and other interventions. The organization focuses on preserving specific species, not just protecting their habitats; it relies on well-designed scientific research and hands-on work.

World Wildlife Fund, International (also called World Wide Fund for Nature)
Av. du Mont-Blanc
1196 Gland, Switzerland
Phone: +41 22 364 9111
Website: http://wwf.panda.org/

U.S. office:
1250 24th St. NW
Washington, DC 20037-1193
Phone: (202) 293-4800
Website: http://www.worldwildlife.org/
World Wildlife Fund works to address global threats to wildlife and habitats. The group focuses on six areas: fighting climate change, feeding the world sustainably, conserving forests, protecting freshwater habitats, influencing policy worldwide, and supporting healthy oceans. Local offices exist in many countries, including Australia, Brazil, Canada, Chile, China, Fiji, France, Greece, India, Italy, Japan, Kenya, Malaysia, Mexico, Philippines, Peru, Romania, Russia, South Africa, Tanzania, Thailand, Turkey, United Arab Emirates, and the United States.

The Xerces Society for Invertebrate Conservation
628 NE Broadway, Suite 200
Portland OR 97232
Phone: (855) 232-6639
Fax: (503) 233-6794
Email: info@xerces.org
Website: www.xerces.org

The Xerces Society for Invertebrate Conservation is dedicated to protecting and conserving invertebrates, animals such as butterflies and insects that are often ignored by other conservation groups. It advocates for policies protecting these animals, conducts research, and trains farmers and the public about invertebrate conservation.

Young People's Trust for the Environment
Suite 29, Yeovil Innovation Centre
Barracks Close, Copse Road
Yeovil, Somerset, UK BA22 8RN
Phone: +44 01935 385962
Website: https://ypte.org.uk
This British organization's goal is to help young people understand environmental issues, including wildlife endangerment, climate change, and threats to the ocean and rain forest. Its site includes educational materials, videos, and links.

Movies, Documentaries, and TV Miniseries
Arctic Tale (movie, National Geographic, 2007)
Born to Be Wild (movie, 2011)
Death of the Oceans (documentary, BBC, 2010)
EARTH: A New Wild (National Geographic series, 2015)
Frozen Planet (miniseries, BBC, 2011)
Last Lions (movie, National Geographic, 2011)
Life (miniseries, BBC, 2009)
Racing Extinction (documentary, 2015)

Apps
Endangered Species Finder (Android)
GeoEndangered (Apple)
Project Noah (Apple)
Species on the Edge (Apple)
Survival (game, free, Apple and Android)
WWF Together (Apple, Android, Kindle Fire)

General Index

B

C

D

F

H

(M)

S

Sage grouse, greater, *2:* 441

Sage grouse, Gunnison, *2:* **441–43,** 442 (ill.)

Saharan cypress, *3:* **684–86,** 685 (ill.)

Saiga, *1:* **225–27,** 226 (ill.)

Saiga tatarica, 1: **225–27,** 226 (ill.)

Saiga tatarica mongolica, 1: 227

Saimiri oerstedii, 1: **168–70,** 169 (ill.)

Saimiri oerstedii citrinellus, 1: 170

Saimiri oerstedii oerstedii, 1: 169–70

Saint Barthélemy

    mahogany, American, *3:* **695–98,** 696 (ill.)

Saint Kitts and Nevis

    mahogany, American, *3:* **695–98,** 696 (ill.)

    plover, piping, *2:* **428–30,** 429 (ill.)

Saint Lucia

    mahogany, American, *3:* **695–98,** 696 (ill.)

    thrasher, white-breasted, *2:* **457–59,** 458 (ill.)

Saint Martin

    mahogany, American, *3:* **695–98,** 696 (ill.)

Saint Pierre and Miquelon

    eagle, bald, *2:* **332–35,** 333 (ill.)

    plover, piping, *2:* **428–30,** 429 (ill.)

Saint Vincent and the Grenadines

    mahogany, American, *3:* **695–98,** 696 (ill.)

Salamander, California tiger, *3:* **582–84,** 583 (ill.)

Salamander, Chinese giant, *3:* **585–87,** 586 (ill.)

Salamander, Texas blind, *3:* **588–91,** 589 (ill.)

Salmon, Danube, *3:* **629–31,** 630 (ill.)

Salvelinus confluentus, 3: **657–60,** 659 (ill.)

Samoa

    coral, branching frogspawn, *3:* **601–4,** 602 (ill.)

San Joaquin leopard lizard, *3:* 779

Sandhill crane, *2:* 325

Sangoritan'i Belalanda, *3:* 757

Santa Catalina Island (Mexico)

    rattlesnake, Santa Catalina Island, *3:* **794–96,** 795 (ill.)

Santa Catalina Island rattlesnake, *3:* **794–96,** 795 (ill.)

São Miguel bullfinch, *2:* 303

Sarracenia oreophila, 3: **713–15,** 714 (ill.)

Saudi Arabia

    dragon tree, Gabal Elba, *3:* **687–89,** 688 (ill.)

    dugong, *1:* **76–79,** 78 (ill.)

    ibis, northern bald, *2:* **372–75,** 373 (ill.)

    wolf, gray, *1:* **251–55,** 253 (ill.), 259, 261

Sawfish, largetooth, *3:* **632–34,** 633 (ill.)

Scimitar-horned oryx, *1:* **185–87,** 186 (ill.)

Sclerocactus mariposensis, 3: 671

Sculpin, mottled, *2:* 545

Sculpin, pygmy, *3:* **635–37,** 636 (ill.)

Sea cat, *1:* 188

Sea cow, *1:* 76, 147

Sea lion, northern, *1:* 228

Sea lion, Steller, *1:* **228–30,** 229 (ill.)

Seahorse, Cape, *3:* 638

Seahorse, Knysna, *3:* **638–41,** 640 (ill.)

Seal, Hawaiian monk, *1:* **231–33,** 232 (ill.)

Senecio, 2: 506–7

Senegal

    chimpanzee, *1:* **56–59,** 57 (ill.), 102, 106

    dog, African wild, *1:* **69–71,** 70 (ill.)

    eagle, martial, *2:* **336–38,** 337 (ill.)

    elephant, African, *1:* **84–87,** 85 (ill.), 88, 89, 90

    gazelle, dama, *1:* **99–101,** 100 (ill.)

    gull, Audouin's, *2:* **360–62,** 361 (ill.)

    oryx, scimitar-horned, *1:* **185–87,** 186 (ill.)

Sequoia, giant, *3:* **727–30,** 728 (ill.)

Sequoiadendron giganteum, 3: **727–30,** 728 (ill.)

Serbia

    salmon, Danube, *3:* **629–31,** 630 (ill.)

    viper, meadow, *3:* **823–26,** 824 (ill.)

    wolf, gray, *1:* **251–55,** 253 (ill.), 259, 261

Setophaga kirtlandii, 2: **470–73,** 471 (ill.)

Seychelles

    dugong, *1:* **76–79,** 78 (ill.)

    magpie-robin, Seychelles, *2:* **389–91,** 390 (ill.)

Seychelles magpie-robin, *2:* **389–91,** 390 (ill.)

Shark, Borneo, *3:* **642–44**

Shark, great hammerhead, *3:* **645–47,** 646 (ill.)

Shiny cowbird, *2:* 299

Short, Charles, *3:* 694

Shortnose sucker, *3:* **651–53,** 652 (ill.)

Short's goldenrod, *3:* **692–94,** 693 (ill.)

Short-tailed albatross, *2:* **293–96,** 295 (ill.)

T

W